Praise for *Blood Diamonds*

"*Blood Diamonds* by Greg Campbell is first-rate journalistic sleuthing, tracing the violence-soaked webs that link the legitimate diamond trade, shady dealers, rebels without a conscience, and organizations such as Hizbollah and al-Qaeda."
—*New Internationalist*

"Campbell punctures the myth that West Africa's descent into hell flows solely from the hands of its warlords and juvenile killers. He locates the sources in London, Amsterdam, and New York, as well as in Freetown and Monrovia. In so doing, he makes the reader fully aware of West Africa's dead-last nations, their hellholes and hecatombs. He also insures that the news from that part of the world will never read quite the same."
—*Commonweal*

"In *Blood Diamonds*, a work of impeccable reportage and meticulous research, veteran journalist Greg Campbell argues that Sierra Leone's diamonds have inflicted terrible suffering on the region and are now financing global terror."
—*World and I*

"The book reads at times like surreal fiction, and Campbell's skill with language comes through in this gruesome, real-life story. He sets the scene masterfully in the diamond region of eastern Sierra Leone and graphically describes the bizarre, horrific methods of intimidation of the population by the Revolutionary United Front."
—*The Post and Courier*

BLOOD DIAMONDS

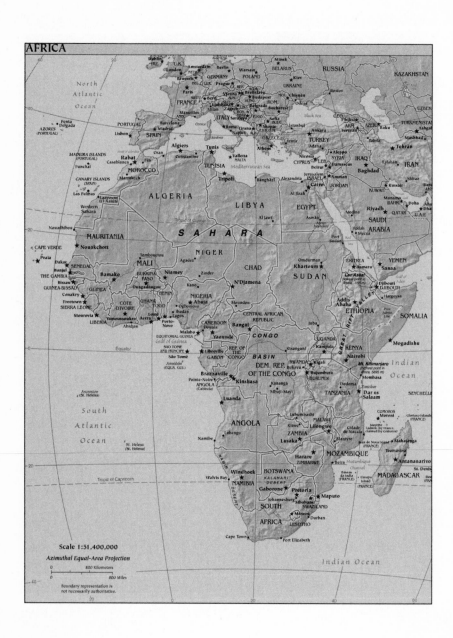

BLOOD DIAMONDS

Tracing the Deadly Path of the

World's Most Precious Stones

GREG CAMPBELL

BASIC BOOKS

A Member of the Perseus Books Group

New York

Author's note: In one instance, anonymity was granted to one person who requested it, and in another a name was changed by the author for the sake of clarity; all others are accurately depicted. Except for minor, conversational dialogue, all quotations were recorded in formal interviews either on cassette tape or with hand-written notes and have not been altered.

Copyright © 2004 by Basic Books, A Member of the Perseus Books Group
Paperback published in 2012 by Basic Books, A Member of the Perseus Books Group

Books published by Basic Books are available at special discounts for bulk purchases in the United States by corporations, institutions, and other organizations. For more information, please contact the Special Markets Department at the Perseus Books Group, 2300 Chestnut Street, Suite 200, Philadelphia, PA 19103, or call (800) 810-4145, ext. 5000, or e-mail special.markets@perseusbooks.com.

Published in 2002 in the United States of America by Westview Press, 5500 Central Avenue, Boulder, Colorado 80301-2877, and in the United Kingdom by Westview Press, 12 Hid's Copse Road, Cumnor Hill, Oxford OX2 9JJ.

Find us on the World Wide Web at www.basicbooks.com

The Library of Congress has cataloged the hardcover edition as follows:
Campbell, Greg.
    Blood diamonds : tracing the deadly path of the world's most precious stones /
Greg Campbell.
        p. cm.
    Includes index.
    ISBN 0-8133-3939-1 (alk. paper)
    1. Diamond industry and trade—Social aspects—Sierra Leone. 2. Diamond miners—Crimes against—Sierra Leone. 3. Sierra Leone—History—Civil War, 1991.
4. Diamond industry and trade—Corrupt practices. I. Title.
HD9677.S52 C36 2002
966.404—dc21

Set in Dante MT by the Perseus Books Group

ISBN: 978-0-465-02991-4 (paperback)
ISBN: 978-0-465-02992-1 (e-book)

10 9 8 7 6 5 4 3

For My Parents

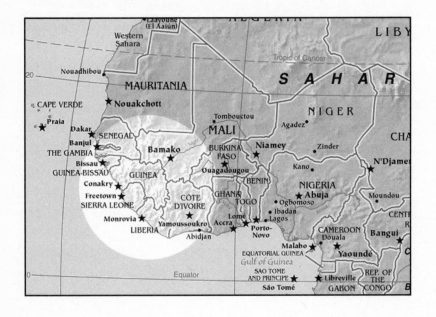

CONTENTS

GLOSSARY

AFRC   The Armed Forces Revolutionary Council, a splinter-group of the Sierra Leone Army that staged a coup in 1997 and aligned with the RUF.

De Beers Group   The largest diamond mining and selling company in the world. Before it was purchased by insiders in 2001, De Beers Group was composed of two entities: De Beers Consolidated Mines Ltd. and De Beers Centenary AG.

DTC   Diamond Trading Company, the London-based marketing arm of De Beers, which sells about 65 percent of the world production of rough diamonds.

ECOMOG   The ECOWAS Cease-Fire Monitoring Group, ECOWAS's military arm.

ECOWAS   The Economic Community of West African States, a regional group of fifteen countries.

EO   Executive Outcomes, a South African private military company, dissolved in 1999.

Kamajor   A warrior sect of the Mende tribe, characterized by animist beliefs and superstition.

LURD   Liberians United for Reconciliation and Democracy, a rebel group composed of an amalgamation of dissident factions fighting to topple the government of Charles Taylor.

MLPA   The Popular Movement for the Liberation of Angola, an Angolan political party representing the majority government.

MSF   Médecins Sans Frontières, a nongovernmental organization that provides medical care to refugees and war victims.

NPFL   The National Patriotic Front of Liberia, the Liberian rebel group led by Charles Taylor, currently the president of Liberia; the NPFL overthrew the government of Samuel K. Doe in 1990.

RUF   The Revolutionary United Front, led by Foday Sankoh, is a Sierra Leone rebel group formed in 1991; trained in Libya with leaders of the NPFL, the two rebel groups have close ties.

RUFP   The Revolutionary United Front Party, the RUF's political arm.

SLA   Sierra Leone Army.

UNAMSIL   The United Nations Mission in Sierra Leone.

UNHCR   United Nations High Commissioner for Refugees.

UNICEF   United Nations Children's Fund.

UNITA   The National Union for the Total Independence of Angola, an Angolan rebel group formed in the early 1990s.

O my mountain in the field,
I will give thy substance and all thy treasures to the spoil,
and thy high places for sin,
throughout all thy borders.

JEREMIAH 17:1

———

CYMBELINE: That diamond upon your finger, say
How came it yours?
IACHIMO: Thou'lt torture me to leave unspoken that
Which to be spoke would torture thee.

WILLIAM SHAKESPEARE, *Cymbeline*

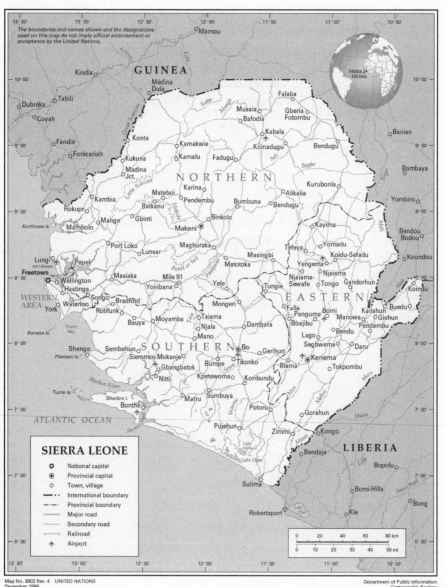

PROLOGUE

Impact:
The Price of Diamonds

*Médecins Sans Frontières Camp for Amputees and
War Wounded, Freetown, Sierra Leone, Summer 2001*

Ismael Dalramy lost his hands in 1996 with two quick blows
of an ax. He didn't—or couldn't—recall the pain of the blows.
But he remembered being ordered at gunpoint to place his wrists
on a wooden stump dripping with the blood of his neighbors who
were writhing on the ground around him trying to stem the flow
of blood from their arms or staggering away.

Dalramy does recall that it was quick and methodical—the victim in line in front of him was swiftly kicked away and suddenly
he faced a bloody wooden block and an impatient gang of heavily
armed teens eager to be done with their day's orders. He didn't
fight his captors or beg for mercy. Instead, he removed a crude
metal ring made by his son from one of the fingers on his left hand

and put it in his pocket, one of the last acts his hands performed for him.

Until that morning, when the rebels of the Revolutionary United Front (RUF) attacked the town with rockets and rifles, speeding through the streets in pickup trucks whose cab roofs had been sawed off to convert them into roofless killing vehicles, it had been easy to think that there would be plenty of time to escape if the need arose. The humid jungle village of Koidu, where Dalramy's family had lived for generations, is an epicenter of raw diamond production in eastern Sierra Leone. In the months leading up to the day that Dalramy's hands were amputated by the RUF, Koidu had been increasingly surrounded by rebel forces who crept through the jungle's dense mesh of palm trees and banana bushes. RUF bandits would enter the town sporadically to steal food and supplies and menace its inhabitants, but an all-out assault seemed unlikely. Though you would never know by looking at it—Koidu is like many bush villages in Sierra Leone, composed of brown shacks and red-dirt streets—the area around the village had long been fiercely coveted in the war that has torn apart this West African nation since 1991. Ever since British geologists first discovered diamonds in Sierra Leone's jungles in the 1930s, miners had been extracting some of the most valuable diamond wealth in the world from small muddy pits scattered throughout the surrounding rain forest. These small chunks and bits of milky-white carbon crystals are transformed into precious jewelry displayed on the hands, wrists, necks, and ears of people around the world, many of whom have probably never heard of Sierra Leone. During the RUF war, people like Dalramy paid for this distant luxury with their own hands.

The RUF wasn't the only armed group around Koidu at the time Dalramy was captured. Both Sierra Leonean government soldiers and West African peacekeepers from a regional security force called the ECOWAS Cease-Fire Monitoring Group (ECOMOG) fought to keep the diamond mines out of the RUF's control. A fourth group—a tribal militia of Mende warriors called Kamajors—added to the confusion and bloodshed, fighting the RUF's assault rifles and rocket launchers with machetes, spears, and ancient mystical battle rituals that they hoped would make them invisible to their enemies and impervious to bullets. Koidu was at the center of these variously disciplined forces, and constant skirmishes and full-out assaults among them were common.

But the RUF had terror on its side. Composed almost entirely of illiterate and drugged teenagers, the rebels respected no boundaries in conducting the war. Mass rape, torture, random executions, looting, and cannibalism were among their strategic resources. But their signature war crime was amputation. In response to Sierra Leone president Ahmad Tejan Kabbah's 1996 plea for his countrymen to "join hands" for peace, the RUF began dismembering their victims and dumping the body parts on the steps of the presidential palace. Although hands were the most common limb severed, the RUF also sliced off civilians' lips, ears, legs, breasts, and tongues to inspire terror. Their battle-group names—General Babykiller, Queen Chop Hands—seem to have been plucked from poorly written and unimaginative comic books, and commanders named their missions to leave little doubt of their intentions. From Operation Pay Yourself, a looting spree, to the chillingly self-explanatory Operation No Living Thing, rebel assaults were as effectively terrorizing in their descriptions as they were in their executions. Though he didn't know it at the time, Dalramy was a victim of Operation Clean Sweep, a plan to exert brutal dominion over the Kono region, a district that included Koidu. RUF soldiers cut a bloody swath through the forest, murdering and mutilating anyone in the way, all so they could control the millions of dollars waiting to be mined from the diamond fields; it was the only thing the RUF has ever wanted—gems to sell for guns and retirement funds.

Like the others who stayed in their cinder block and zinc-roofed homes, Dalramy thought the RUF would be content to occupy the town, using its menacing presence to keep both government soldiers and the Kamajor fighters at bay. The RUF had captured Kono years before, but a private mercenary force hired from South Africa by the Sierra Leone government had won the town back in exchange for the right to mine and sell diamonds. As a result, many families had returned to their homes.

But on that particular morning, instead of awakening to a typical scene of bustling traffic weaving through the crowds growing around the market, Dalramy saw the streets begin to fill with the splayed bodies of his dead neighbors amid a rising chorus of the "pop" of small-arms fire ricocheting off hardened mud walls. He raced out the back of his house and, instead of slipping into the relative safety of the jungle as he'd planned, ran right into the arms of a squad of RUF soldiers dressed in camouflage T-shirts and flip-flops, their crude bayonets aimed at him from under the barrels of battle-worn AK-47s. He was taken to the village police station, which had been commandeered by RUF soldiers, and thrown in with a group of frantic civilians being held at gunpoint. As the sound of gunshots outside slowed, the prisoners—about eight men and women—were taken behind the building and told to form a line facing a man with an ax. The powerful-looking rebel wore no shirt, Dalramy remembers, only black jeans, a black scarf wrapped around his bare skull, and mirrored plastic sunglasses. He twirled the ax in his hands. The first victim was dragged forward and forced to kneel before a stump. As the man screamed, he severed first one limb, then the next.

Those lined up behind him went hysterical, their wails of terror nearly drowning out the wet crunch of the ax's blade meeting flesh and bone. About five young boys guarded the waiting victims, jabbing people with the butts of their rifles or poking them with their bayonets, maintaining the line by giving the captured civilians a quick choice between mutilation or instant death. The RUF commander's sweat-slicked chest became speckled with blood droplets as he moved from one victim to the next.

Dalramy was shoved to his knees in the red dirt, and as one of the young rebels tossed the amputated hands of the previous victim into the thick brush—twirling them in a spray of blood toward a solid wall of green leaves, where they disappeared like food into the mouth of a giant beast—his left wrist was placed palm up in a thick puddle of blood oozing off the stump like wax from a long-burning candle. An AK-47 barrel was pressed to his left temple. Dalramy looked at the indentation around his third finger where he'd just removed his son's ring. There was a quick glint of sunlight on the blade of the homemade ax, and Dalramy squeezed his eyes tight against the blow. The blade slammed through the bones of his arm just above the wrist. The hand came off with one clean chop, a blessing considering many such crude amputations required more than a dozen blows to sever a limb. He saw his hand bounce off the edge of the stump, gleaming white ulna bone seeing the sun for the first time.

The rebels obviously also chopped off his other hand, but Dalramy doesn't remember it. His next recollection is of seeing dirt next to his eyes and hearing the dull arrhythmic sound of ax blows through the screams of the victims who were lined up behind him, a sickening, unsteady metronome of blinding terror.

He staggered to his feet, trying to keep his flowing stumps from collecting too much dirt, and wandered away from the carnage and the growing pile of bleeding limbs. His shirt and pants were soaked in blood. He doesn't remember what was going on around him at this point and he has no idea if anyone tried to stop him. He just knew he should keep his arms raised high over his head, mainly so gravity would slow his blood loss but also to indicate to the dozens of RUF soldiers he passed that he already paid his dues.

He blindly followed the red-dirt road leading away from Koidu. There were no government soldiers, ECOMOG troops, or Kamajor fighters along the way; he didn't know it at the time, but the RUF assault had routed them from the Kono District almost entirely and Koidu's government defenders were either dead or in full retreat. Dalramy estimates that he stumbled perhaps 15 miles before collapsing, a distance that may seem unlikely for someone who just had both hands chopped off, but cleanly amputated limbs don't bleed as much as may be expected. The elasticity of veins and arteries causes them to shrink into the limb and, to a certain degree, self-cauterize.

Someone, perhaps a benevolent villager risking the loss of his or her own arms or legs, dragged Dalramy into a hut and cinched off the blood flow with string tourniquets and torn cloth. With the blood flow stemmed, Dalramy rested for a short while and then continued to stagger down the dirt road. He eventually made his way to a bush hospital, one that was likely all too familiar with treating ax amputations. Within days, he left the diamond-rich Kono District and managed to flee to Freetown, leaving behind not only his 40-year-old hands, but his life as a farmer, his home, and his relatives.

Since the grisly execution of Operation Clean Sweep in 1996, RUF rebels have sold millions of dollars worth of Kono's diamonds into the world's marketing channels, diamonds that are now undoubtedly treasured and adored by husbands and wives who have no idea of their brutal origins.

I MET DALRAMY in Sierra Leone's seaside wasteland of a capital, Freetown, in the summer of 2001.

He and hundreds of others like him live in the Médecins Sans Frontières (MSF) Camp for Amputees and War Wounded, a barren plot of clay dirt and leafless, drooping, Dali-esque trees located on the side of the only road between the city center and the beach district. Formerly a school compound, the MSF camp is now a squalid collection of ten-foot-square shacks made of sea timber and the ubiquitous blue-and-white all-weather plastic sheeting distributed by the United Nations High Commissioner for Refugees (UNHCR), a sort of refugee Saran Wrap that keeps out the rain but intensifies the heat, which reaches well into the nineties and beyond in the summer months. More than two hundred families live there, crammed into the shacks with as many as ten relatives.

Children mob you the moment you walk in the gates, begging for money, to the point where you have to wrestle them off of you before you're dragged down. Little kids, some less than a year old, hobble about on one leg, while others learn to eat with arms that end in smooth stumps. On a crude porch a man smokes a cigarette with a homemade prosthesis—tattered Velcro fastens the twisted remains of a coat hanger to his arm and the cigarette is jammed between the wire twists. Others have fashioned spoon-prostheses so that they can eat unaided. Buttoning a shirt, however, still requires the help of a loved one. Therefore, most amputees wear T-shirts handed out by aid organizations, many bearing out-of-place designs; one man wore a silk-screened shirt advertising the movie *Titanic*, another wore a threadbare shirt touting a St.

Patrick's Day celebration at an Ohio bar. Like Dalramy, all of them have terrible stories, but not all of them are victims of the RUF's mass amputation campaigns. The MSF camp is a living museum to the atrocities Sierra Leoneans have suffered during a decade of fighting between at least four forces who at times were indistinguishable in their tactics of atrocities. Ducking through garbage-choked alleys, I passed a three-year-old whose leg had been blasted off by a Guinean mortar, a man with no ears or arms who had been mutilated by ECOMOG soldiers who had tortured captives as brutally as the RUF, and a limbless mother carefully cradling a newborn to her breasts with her knees and elbows.

Neither on paper nor in person does Sierra Leone look like a country that produces some of the most beautiful and valuable diamonds sold by the $6 billion per year international diamond industry, a luxury market that sells 80 percent of its products to American consumers. Actually, to refer to Sierra Leone as a "country" at all is only a matter of geographical convenience. In fact, it's a vacuum of violence, poverty, warlords, and misery, a tiny corner of West Africa where the wheels have fallen completely off and left no one in charge except whoever happens to be best armed at the moment. The country comes in dead last on the United Nations Human Development Index and life expectancies are among the lowest in the world: Men born in Sierra Leone can expect to live to an average age of 43, women to age 48.[1] The infant mortality rate is one of the worst in Africa, with 146 deaths per 1,000 live births.[2] Nearly 80 percent of the country's 5 million people have been displaced and the government has suffered so many coups, counter-coups, rigged elections, political assassinations, and fractious political fights that it has been rendered almost completely ineffectual. The only thing that seems to have remained constant where everything else has fallen apart is diamond production. In fact, the sale of diamonds to customers around the world is what has kept the war churning.

Prior to the deployment of a United Nations peacekeeping mission in 1999, Sierra Leone had been almost entirely ignored by the powerful nations of the world, even though they were eager buyers of the diamonds that helped drive a decade's worth of death and torture. It's not difficult to see why Sierra Leone is low on most people's list of places in which to intervene. Not only is it hard for most people to find on a map, but like many African countries, Sierra Leone has been consumed by corruption, dictatorial governments, and illiterate and thuggish leaders and victimized by breathtaking displays of otherworldly butchery. The climate is also horrible: Muggy and humid throughout the year, the tropical landscape is an incubator for malarial mosquitoes, polio, yellow fever, river blindness, and dozens of other deadly diseases. During the rainy season, everything—whether indoors or outdoors—remains wet for five months. During the dry season, harmattan winds from the Sahel and Sahara Deserts sandblast the country and the sunlight seems to be focused by a huge magnifying glass. The raw and unrelenting natural environment is reflected in the people and the actions of some of them in times of war.

Unlike the countries of the former Yugoslavia, for example, there is no centuries-old ethnic conflict fueling the bloodshed; the people of Sierra Leone are a mix of indigenous tribes who still practice their animist beliefs and descendants of freed North American slaves. Prior to the RUF war, Sierra Leoneans lived relatively peacefully with one another. When the RUF first invaded the country from neighboring Liberia in 1991, the rebellion was ostensibly a peasants' revolution against the perceived plundering of natural resources for the benefit of the ruling class in Freetown. But then the RUF and its Libyan-trained and Liberian-backed leader Foday

Sankoh developed a taste for diamonds, and the "rebellion" was revealed as nothing more than a savage struggle to control diamond mining. The fact that such violence was occurring in an African country lowered the enthusiasm for international intervention all the more. African wars—thanks to a vacuum of media coverage that almost completely ignores sub-Saharan countries except in times of natural or man-made disasters—seem remote and incomprehensible to most consumers in developed nations. The vast majority of television programming from Africa seen around the world is composed of wildlife shows. In these panoramic and celebratory films actual Africans are largely absent.

What makes Sierra Leone unique among former European colonies that have endured the painful transition to independence is its incredible natural wealth. Not only is the country rich in gem-quality diamonds, but it's also a repository for oil, rubies, gold, rutile, and bauxite. It should be the Saudi Arabia of Africa, but it's not.

Most of those who live in Sierra Leone's dense rain forests are farmers who have never set eyes on a diamond, but they have felt the stone's impacts. Ever since diamonds were first discovered here in the 1930s the government has been unable to control the wealth for the benefit of its citizens, nor has it tried very hard to do so. Instead, the diamond fields have been plundered almost since they were first discovered, first by corporations, then by common thieves, and most recently by the armed thugs of the RUF. Estimates are difficult to come by but it's believed that the RUF profited by between $25 million and $125 million per year by delivering rough gem-quality diamonds into the insatiable maw of the world's diamond market.[3]

The RUF is not alone in this endeavor. Rebels in Angola, whose Portuguese name forms the acronym UNITA, have raided diamond fields and oil operations to fund their decades-old war. The Democratic Republic of Congo (DRC) is in the midst of a baffling civil war between armed forces of several neighboring countries and ideologies; here too, diamonds are the prize for whichever group controls the areas where they're found. Between these three countries, it's estimated that rebel groups have sold enough diamonds to amount to 4 or 5 percent of the global output. Though this figure may seem reassuringly small—after all, 95 percent of diamonds sold around the world come from legitimate sources— it's a testament to the power of their allure and value that such a small percentage is sufficient to cause an estimated 3.7 million deaths and displace 6 million people in these African war zones.[4]

Diamonds are suited all too well for exploitation by organizations with nefarious goals. They are the most portable form of wealth known to man; it's an often-repeated truth that enough diamonds can be carried on a person's naked body to ensure a lifetime of riches, so stealing and smuggling millions of dollars worth from the battlefield to the marketplace is an easy and practically unstoppable practice. As the rebel groups have discovered, there is no lack of buyers for their goods and, until recently, there was little concern about where they originated or the amount of suffering their sellers had inflicted on innocent people.

I MADE A NUMBER OF TRIPS to Sierra Leone in 2001 to document the country's implosion from the trade of what has come to be known as "blood diamonds." I planned to follow the murky trail of the diamonds from the time they're mined to when they enter the mainstream trading channels. I wanted to see for myself the shocking contrast between the insufferable living conditions of the majority of Sierra Leone citizens and the beguiling allure of the diamonds being pulled from the muddy earth of the rain forests. Sierra Leone hosts the world's largest and most expensive deployment of United Nations peacekeepers in history—more than 17,500 soldiers from 31 countries are stationed in a nation the size of South Carolina, and $612 million was spent on the mission in 2001 alone.[5] I wanted to see if the diplomacy, military aid, and money being spent on a country that has been torn apart over diamonds were having any effect on the rampant bloodshed, inhumanity, and corruption.

Before I arrived in Sierra Leone, like most people, I had no idea where the world's most valuable gemstones came from. I knew little more than what I was told by television commercials, that diamonds were apparently forever, that they were rare, and that many of them were priceless. But since 1999, reports had been circulating that some diamonds weren't as pure as their reputation proclaimed. The term "conflict diamonds" was bandied about and it gradually became known that some stones carried the blood of innocent victims, killed or mutilated by rebel groups in Africa who used the profits of diamond sales to continue their campaigns of brutality and inhumanity.

Like almost anyone else who buys diamond rings or necklaces, I didn't realize that the small stones' invaluable reputation was nothing more than a 100-year-old parlor trick born of the greed of one company, De Beers Group, the largest diamond mining company in the world, which has completely manufactured both the worth of diamonds and the demand for them. I had no idea that De Beers's monopolistic policies put in place more than a century ago enabled a band of ruthless killers to wrest diamonds from the heart of an untamed jungle and sell them to willing buyers with connections to respectable diamond centers from London to Antwerp to Bombay.

I didn't know that the proceeds from diamond sales funded not only the RUF's war against its government, but also Hezbollah terrorism against Israel and Al Qaeda attacks against the United States. Nor could I have imagined that I would discover such a complicated and far-reaching network of smugglers, gunrunners, terrorists, corporate manipulaters, and corrupt governments that made such sales possible.

And I certainly had no idea that the jewelry worn by hundreds of thousands of people around the world was bought at the expense of innocent and mutilated Africans who will never be able to wear jewelry of their own. I went to Sierra Leone to see for myself how the trade worked, to speak with the victims, and to discover how it was possible that the world's premiere symbol of love and devotion could have been used to fund one of the most atrocious wars of the 1990s.

1

FROM PITS OF DESPAIR TO ALTARS OF LOVE

Kenema, Sierra Leone

CROUCHED BY THE MINE'S EDGE, I tried to ignore the grilling persistence of the equatorial sun overhead and concentrate on the dirt under my feet. Like everyone around me, I was looking for diamonds.

Unlike the others, though, I squatted and flicked through the gravel on the edge of the water with a stick, trying without much luck to tell the difference between a diamond and a chip of quartz. The others knew what they were doing. I was there to watch.

We were somewhere in the jungle near a town called Bomboma in eastern Sierra Leone, at an open pit mine that had once been culled for diamonds by the Revolutionary United Front. The mine we were in, however, was in a region that had been reclaimed by the government and the men working there were all licensed to find wealth under the jungle floor. No one was really sure of the demarcation, though. The RUF was still nearby and its area of influence and control seemed to change daily, even though UN peacekeepers were also deployed nearby, actively pursuing a disarmament and demobilization agreement intended to end the savagery and displacement of this decade-long war once and for all.

But the war was never more than an economic endeavor, a ten-year-long jewelry heist that continued despite the UN's efforts and the RUF's promises to stop mining. The only difference between an RUF mine and the one we were in is that there were no rifles in sight at ours.

Visiting a diamond mine in Sierra Leone is not easy. Even the operators of those legitimately licensed by the government in Free-town are understandably very nervous about their portrayal in the international media. Therefore, American photojournalist Chris Hondros and I had to pose as government contractors preparing a report on working conditions at government mines, something we weren't aware we had to do until we met our clandestine guide to the Bomboma mine.

Our original plan was to simply wander around the diamond mining and trading town of Kenema until we ran into a miner who, we naively assumed, would be pleased to have two American journalists witness his daily toil in the countryside. But by unfortunate coincidence, the first man we discussed our plans with happened to be an African named Mr. Beh, who was, unbeknown to us at the time, an official with the Sierra Leone Ministry of Mines and Natural Resources, an organization that likes to know who's looking at the mines and why. He seemed jovial and more than willing to take us where we wanted to go, and we had no reason to be suspicious until we left the building where we'd met him after making plans to rendezvous in the morning.

Out on the street, one of our local contacts, a reporter for the state-run radio station, caught up to us and told us to forget our plans with Mr. Beh. The Ministry of Mines and Natural Resources was notoriously paranoid, she said, and it could mean weeks worth of paperwork and intense interrogation before we would be allowed to visit a mine. And even if we were granted permission, it would be to visit a mine vetted entirely of diggers who may be inclined to complain about their working conditions. In fact, she said, if anyone were to ask from that point forward, we should simply say that we were researchers or employees with a nongovernmental organization, anything but journalists. Kenema is a small town and two white reporters stood out noticeably from the rest of the crowd. Being uncooperative with the diamond authorities, even though we were registered with the UN, could lead to arrest, she warned. It was our first introduction to the opaque and clandestine nature of the diamond business. Even legitimate mining operations played it close to the vest.

"My mother was killed here," said our guide, a man who represented a mostly ineffective union for those who toiled in the mines. He pointed to an intersection of two footpaths marked by a knee-high boulder. "Every time I come through here, I think of her."

His mother had been killed while walking from one village to another when the RUF controlled the region. After harassing her, someone stuck a rifle in her gut and blew her into the witchgrass, where she lay until he and other relatives sneaked back to retrieve her body for burial.

We were deep in the jungle, moving along footpaths that seemed to wind along the bottom of a green ocean. Overhead, a cathedral of interlocking branches and an umbrella of dancing leaves 50 feet up hid us from passing helicopters. Dusty shafts of golden sunlight reached like impossibly long crystals through the branches to the ground. Down here, it was easy to imagine how incredibly difficult it must be to fight in the bush. The vegetation was so thick that a regiment of RUF could have been standing two feet off the path and I never would have seen them. Automatic weapons and grenades are good only for a short distance in the jungle; the woody jigsaw of branches and trunks form a natural shield that absorbs and deflects bullets and shrapnel. The RUF perfected fighting in this sort of environment, using the jungle to sneak up close to their enemies and lay ambushes for government troops. They would strike without warning, spewing fire and rockets from the dense forest, then melt back into the trees.

Our journey that morning had started at our guide's hut on the side of a dirt road just outside Kenema, about five miles from the Bomboma mine. He was still rubbing the sleep from his eyes when we nudged into his dark bedroom. "This is going to be slightly dangerous," he said, reaching for a cigarette on the nightstand. "No one can know you're reporters. I want you to see the mines like they really are. And when we come back, don't tell anyone that I took you. I could get arrested."

And we couldn't drive to the mine, either; cars were rare enough in the bush, but a car carrying two white men was bound to draw attention. Therefore, we were going to hike, he said.

We began in Tissor, a small collection of mud huts with thatched roofs assembled in a neat clearing of hard-packed dirt that had been swept clean of leaves and debris. Chickens squawked underfoot and men and women who were so old they seemed to have been carved from wood stared impassively from porches and stools. The village was unremarkable except for its one facet of civic pride: It was here that the first Kamajor militia was formed to fight against the RUF.

In one step, we went from the open clearing into the jungle, like walking from one room into another and having the door slam shut behind you. In the forest, the air was cool and dark and the path ahead of us looked like a giant green tunnel. We walked for miles, emerging from time to time into clearings where men and women burned fields for rice farms. We sidestepped snakes, jumped thick columns of venomous black ants that were more dangerous than snakes, and kicked through the husks of hundreds of mangos, discarded by local diamond-diggers who ate their breakfast during the walk to the mines. And of course, our eyes scanned the ground for milky crystals amid the well-packed gravel. Only a year before some lucky person had found a 25-carat diamond in the middle of Hangha Road in Kenema, a discovery that led to what was probably the town's first-ever civic beautification project as everyone dredged the sewers and sifted mounds of garbage looking for more. "Diamonds," we'd been told the previous evening, "are everywhere."

A few hours later, we emerged from the bush into Bomboma, a village occupied entirely by diamond-diggers and their families. The requisite flock of chickens scattered before us and cook-smoke plumed out from under A-shaped thatch huts. Naked toddlers played with machetes longer than their bodies and, at one house, a group of women dressed in bright scarves attended to a sick woman, covering her skin in a fine white powder.

The first order of business was to convince the village chief that we were from some invented agency of the government, here to independently analyze working conditions at the mine. Any visit to an African village requires the blessing of the local chief, an affair that can involve up to two dozen people and take minutes or days depending on the leader's disposition. We found the old man sitting on the floor, propped up against a wall in an inner courtyard of his house, a simple two-room structure made of packed mud and palm fronds, just like every other building. His face was grizzled with white beard-stubble and he wore a black Adidas T-shirt and soccer shorts. He spoke only the Mende language, so we couldn't follow the specifics of the fabricated story our guide was relating to him, but could see that the chief seemed pleased that someone cared to send two representatives into the bush to check on them. White men in the African outback tend to draw a crowd, and Bomboma was no different. Workers preparing to go to the digging site were happy to be distracted by the sight of two unusual strangers, one of whom carried what looked like a shiny cannon over his shoulder. They stared at Hondros's Nikon and regarded us with friendly curiosity, as if we'd just beamed down from outer space.

After another walk through the forest we soon stepped out onto the banks of the massive Bomboma mine. I immediately understood the paranoia of the Ministry of Mines and Natural Resources. The pit looked more like a slave colony than the first step on the journey of a diamond that would end up in one of the world's largest and most profitable international luxury-commodities markets. On all sides, rib-skinny men stripped to their shorts were covered with mud and slime, the inevitable result of their jobs digging for diamonds. Even though it was barely 10 A.M., they all looked exhausted.

And for good reason: It's hard to imagine a job more difficult or demanding. The workday starts at sunrise and ends at sunset. There are no lunch breaks and no days off. For their efforts at recovering diamonds from the soil, the diggers each receive two cups of rice and the equivalent of 50 cents per day. Bonuses based on the value of their personal production are dependent almost entirely on the trustworthiness of the miner they work for.

The mine was roughly circular and about 300 yards in diameter. Here and there, earthen ledges connected one bank to another across muddy knee-deep pools of groundwater. High up on the banks, surrounding the pit like the jagged teeth of a colossal jungle monster, stood conical mounds of gravel that had been dug from the hole by hand. In such nonindustrialized mines, the process of looking for diamonds is almost exactly the same as it was half a century ago, except that gas-powered water pumps have replaced the bucket brigades of the old days. Essentially, a gigantic hole is dug into the ground until the prospectors hit groundwater, at a depth of usually 30 feet or so. The diamondiferous soil is carefully piled around the edge and covered with palm fronds. Attacking one pile at a time, diggers shovel the dirt into a wooden trough with a mesh sieve at the bottom. Water is pumped through the trough to separate big rocks from the small ones and a boy at the bottom of the trough shovels out the fine gravel, making another pile. In turn, that pile is dumped by the bucketload into circular sieves called "shake-shakes" and shirtless men and boys twirl the muck around and around at the surface of the water, forcing the heavier pebbles—including any diamonds—into the center and the clay and silt slurry to the outer edge.

Teams of about six washers toil under the tropical sun, carefully watched over by one of the miner's foremen, whose job is to keep an eye out for theft. Even the least muscular man washing gravel is rippled with perfectly defined muscles, sculpted from years of prospecting. Their motions are fluid and robotic: twirl, twirl, twirl, scoop, sift, dump, over and over and over. Watching them work, it astounded me how they ever found a single diamond, but their eyes were so attuned to picking out the stones—and there was a never-ending supply of gravel to be washed—that there was no hesitation or concern that diamonds were being overlooked.

When a diamond is actually discovered, there's hardly the celebration one might expect. Instead, one of the washers simply stops all motion, peering intently into his sieve, brushing rocks out of the way. He then plucks a tiny stone from the center of the mesh and gives a low whistle to the foreman, who ambles over to assess the discovery. There in his palm rests the source of all the country's unrest, a puny diamond barely a quarter carat in weight, standing out from his brown hand like an improbably large grain of salt.

It had been formed eons ago, crystallized under extreme pressure and temperature dozens of miles below the surface and carried up through a kimberlite pipe, subsequently shaken loose and eroded out, and then sent on a desultory, waterborne journey that took centuries to carry it here, near the village of Bomboma, where it was embedded in red dirt and gravel under the floor of a wild jungle. People have lost their hands, their lives, and their families for little stones like this one, which looked quite insignificant there on the bank of the pit. The diamond was then wrapped in paper and disappeared into the foreman's shirt pocket. Eventually, after passing from African hands to Lebanese dealers, it will wind up in London and then probably Antwerp, Belgium, or Bombay, India, or New York City, where it will be cut and polished if the quality justifies it. On its own, the little rock that was discovered as I crouched by the mine's edge is too small to make a very impressive engagement ring, but it might end up as part of a $1,000 necklace or bracelet. Our guide guessed that if the quality was decent, the miner might get $5 for it from one of the diamond merchants in Kenema.

The digger who found it gets another bucket filled with gravel to wash.

ABOUT 50 MILES NORTH of the pit in Bomboma, a British geologist named J. D. Pollett made a discovery in 1930 similar to ours. He found diamonds on the bank of the Gbobora River, not realizing at the time that he had stumbled onto one of West Africa's most valuable diamond deposits that would, over the next 40 years, produce more than 50 million carats of diamonds, half of which were of astounding gem quality.[1] Pollett estimated that the diamond field he discovered extended over an area of perhaps 3,000 square miles, bounded on the west by the Sewa River and extending east into Liberia. Towns within that area—Kenema, Yengema, Koidu, Tongo Field, and Bo—would be transformed within two decades from sleepy bush villages in the middle of a rain forest that few people would ever care to visit to centers of violent intrigue and international commerce, both legal and illegal. On that day in 1930, Sierra Leone officially became diamondiferous, a designation that has always been both a blessing and a curse for any nation with a similar geology; the promise of vast wealth invariably invites chaos. The discovery of those diamonds—which, until then, had been deemed to be just another worthless piece of gravel by the locals—placed Sierra Leone on a course that would effectively destroy the entire country by the end of the century.

At the time of the discovery, Sierra Leone had been a British colony for 50 years. Founded by former North American slaves freed for fighting on behalf of England in the Revolutionary War, the country was still 80 percent unexplored when Pollett and other teams of geologists forged into the bush to survey its lands and resources. The vast majority of trade, commerce, and political activity took place in Freetown, home to former slaves and captives from across West Africa and the Americas. Freetown's population was composed of people who became known collectively as Krios, and since very few, if any, originally came from Sierra Leone, they didn't stray far from the capital and enjoyed the modernity that flowed from their British rulers.

The Africans who lived in the bush had no idea of the wealth that they trampled and ignored daily. To them, diamonds held no value whatsoever. It's easy to imagine that the people of the Temne, Mende, and Kru tribes—who lived agrarian lives based on animist beliefs and rituals, much like their ancient ancestors had— were probably amused by the sight of white men digging excitedly for stones that they considered utterly worthless. That attitude was destined to be short-lived.

As far back as the sixteenth century, some societies had viewed diamonds as talismans of strength, fortitude, and courage, attributes undoubtedly derived from the stones' hardness, transparency, and purity. Since diamonds were even more rare then than they are now, it's not surprising that they quickly were ascribed magical qualities. Diamonds were said to reveal the guilt or innocence of accused criminals and adulterers by the colors they reflected. They were said to reanimate the dead and render the virtuous invisible. The stones were also believed to bring the wearer all forms of good fortune, unless it had a blood-red flaw in the middle, in which case it meant certain death.[2]

Theories about the origins of diamonds were no less fantastical. Fourteenth-century alchemists revealed the shortcomings of mineral sciences of the day by suggesting that male and female diamonds reproduce "and bring forth small children that multiply and grow all the year," in the words of the author Sir John Mandeville: "I have oftentimes tried the experiment that if a man keep with them a little of the rock and water them with May dew often, they shall grow every year and the small will grow great," he once wrote.

Several cultures passed along the story of the great Valley of Diamonds, supposedly located on the island of Ceylon. In one version of the tale, Sindbad the Sailor is accidentally deposited there after piggybacking on a huge raptor in an attempt to escape one of the many life-threatening situations he frequently found himself in. But instead of being whisked to freedom, he was dropped in a high-walled gorge, the floor of which was covered in gorgeous diamonds. The trouble was that there was no way out and the diamonds were guarded by gigantic serpents whose gaze caused instant death. Fortunately for Sindbad, ingenuity was an early quality of diamond merchants and the men of Ceylon had invented a crafty system to get the goods. Traders would skin the carcass of a sheep and hurl it into the valley. When it hit bottom, the gemstones would adhere to the flesh and prove to be a tantalizing treat for the oversized eagles that nested on the valley's edge. An eagle would retrieve the sheep—and the diamonds attached to it—and return to its nest, where the traders would converge to scare it into flight and collect the bounty. Sindbad tied himself to a sheep carcass with his unwound turban and was thus lifted to freedom on the talons of an eagle, but not before stuffing his pockets with all the diamonds he could carry.

Diamonds are, in fact, the products of heat and pressure. About 120 miles below the earth's surface, carbon atoms are superheated at 3,600 degrees and compressed under incredible pressures in what's called the diamond-stability field, the level within the earth that possesses the right pressure and temperature to turn carbon into diamonds. Geologists surmise that this superhard carbon material was then driven toward the surface at speeds of up to 25 miles per hour during an explosive geological event, carried along with magma and gas to a much cooler depth that prevented the diamonds from being reheated into a more common carbon form such as graphite. These volcanic eruptions originated far below the diamond-stability field, punching through layer after layer of earth, picking up anything and everything that they intersected, resulting in a bubbling stew of geological debris that, when hardened, is known as kimberlite. Many kimberlites didn't make it to the surface, but for those that got close, the lessening pressure of overhead rock allowed the eruption to pick up speed. Gaseous explosions probably blew through the jungle canopy as the pipes surfaced, showering diamonds and everything else for miles around like so much birdshot.

Kimberlite pipes are found all over the world, but not all of them contain diamonds, as many a would-be millionaire has discovered in places like Pittsburgh, Pennsylvania, and Ithaca, New York, both home to kimberlites that have yielded no diamonds. But the kimberlites that blasted into what would eventually become Sierra Leone—two small chimneys that are about a billion years old and likely stood more than 1,500 feet above the plains—bore beautiful, innumerable diamonds. Millennia of erosion and lavish summer rains on the tropical forests that grip Africa from The Gambia to Somalia have hidden the diamonds under the region's red and yellow dirt like so many undiscovered Easter eggs.[3]

All who have ever coveted this wealth—government regimes, smugglers, lovers, merchants—have historically never cared where they were found or under what conditions they were extracted so long as they could turn a profit or showcase one, or several, on a golden band or necklace. Although diamonds are no longer believed to cure disease or act as crystal balls, they still symbolize wealth, power, love, and honor.

Only in the past two years—as public knowledge has increased about the bloodbaths being waged over the control of Sierra Leone's vast wealth—have people begun to learn that diamonds found in their local jewelry stores may have begun their journey in the hands of those who have tortured and killed to gain them.

"FOR EIGHT MONTHS LAST YEAR, I sat in this office and I didn't buy a single diamond," complained Fawaz S. Fawaz, a heavyset beer-barrel of a man, as he lit a fresh Marlboro off the smoldering butt of his last one. "There are no good diamonds coming in."

He balanced the smoke on top of a pile of crushed filters burying an ashtray on the countertop and continued his clumsy surgery on a tropical bird bought from a little boy on the street. The colorful, scared creature was a gift for Fawaz's young son and once he'd clipped the wings, he untied the twine on its legs and handed it off to a servant, who scurried away to deliver it.

Fawaz is a Lebanese diamond merchant, one of scores whose signs clog the main pothole-ridden road through Kenema, the smoking, popping, wheezing hub of diamond commerce in the heart of the Sierra Leone jungle.

Given its reputation as a diamond capital, it was no surprise when Kenema was attacked by the RUF and its mines captured in 1993. The town was then on the front lines of the diamond war and it was briefly recaptured by government forces in 1994, only to have the RUF win it back a few months later. Kenema stayed under RUF control until 1998, when ECOMOG forces reclaimed it for good. Three years later, in the summer of 2001, it was difficult to imagine that full-scale diamond production had ever been inter-

rupted. Indeed it really hadn't: It was simply conducted by the
rebels and many Lebanese endured the threat of dying in a gun battle or artillery barrage to remain behind to deal with them for their
diamonds. Unlike other liberated towns that are characterized by
the sleepy drudgery of rural life, Kenema is a hectic, overcrowded
anthill of nonstop commercial activity. Guarded by a battalion of
Zambian soldiers serving with the United Nations Mission in
Sierra Leone (UNAMSIL) and a remote base to what seems like
every nongovernmental organization ever incorporated, Kenema
is proof that properly motivated and controlled greed can overcome the threats of warfare.

The main thoroughfare, Hangha Road, is littered with Lebanese
storefronts with large signs announcing "Diamond Merchant" in
hand-painted letters. Every merchant's logo is a jumbo-sized bril-
liant-cut diamond, but the images add little luster to the garbage-
strewn streets filled with beggars and refugees who still hang onto
the old gambler's notion that they are just one lucky find away
from eternal wealth. In the early days, that was certainly the case.
Diamonds turned up in garden patches, latrines, and the middle of
the streets. Like most other places in Sierra Leone, Kenema hid its
dollar-value well: The town smelled like stagnant water and
untreated wounds and clouds of disease-bearing mosquitoes hung
in the air like a cartoon's crowded thought balloons.

Still, Kenema was more pleasant than most places emerging
from the war. On a road parallel to Hangha, a mile-long marketplace seemed to explode with wares: Everything from doorknobs
to underwear was on sale. On the other side of town, a food market was hip-to-elbow with colorfully dressed women selling
mounds of cassava powder by the cupful and endless rows of tables
assembled helter-skelter offering fish meat that had been sitting in
the sun all day, attracting battalions of huge black flies. A stroll

through the food market certainly took care of your appetite; the reeking fish alone were enough to make most visitors swear off eating for the foreseeable future. In an alley, a group of men assembled shake-shakes from freshly cut pine, imported wire mesh, and ten-penny nails, banging them together much as their grandfathers had in the 1930s and 1940s. The finished products were stacked like oversized poker chips next to a towering pile of used shovels and picks for sale. And it wouldn't have been Africa if every other square foot of roadway wasn't occupied by salesmen hawking rare parrots, fish heads, tablecloths, camouflage T-shirts, and black-market cigarettes.

All the Lebanese shops were nearly identical: Each offered racks and racks of cheap Japanese boom boxes for sale, along with shortwave radios, Sony Walkmans, and various other electronic products. But that was just window dressing and giveaways, throwbacks to the time when Lebanese families made their living selling consumer goods in Freetown; the real business happened in the back rooms, usually past a phalanx of slender young men in Tupac Shakur T-shirts guarding the doorway. In these rooms, whose decorations didn't extend beyond the proprietor's state diamond license and maybe a grainy photo of an olive-skinned family on a rare visit to Lebanon, was where the real wheeling and dealing transpired. There was always a desk with a white velvet pad in the center, a low-hanging lamp directly overhead, a full ashtray, seven or eight magnifying lenses of different powers, and an array of jeweler's loupes. From the despairing tone of some of the Lebanese traders we visited, it seemed as though there was probably a thick film of dust on most of those lenses.

"All of the good diamonds are in Kono," Fawaz said, waving his hand to indicate the area 50 miles to the north where the RUF still reigned. He'd invited me and Hondros into his storefront for a cup of Lebanese coffee, which he ordered by simply shouting into the throng on the street, seemingly to no one. Dressed in gray polyester slacks and a tissue-thin 1950s-era button-down short-sleeved shirt—left unbuttoned near the neck to reveal a jet-black carpet of chest hair and a thick gold chain—the 50-plus-year-old Fawaz looked more like a counterman in a Philadelphia deli during the 1960s than a wealthy merchant in the jungles of Sierra Leone, through whose hands countless valuable gemstones have flowed. The Fawaz name was emblazoned on billboards up and down Hangha Road, but he insisted that the network of Fawaz cousins and brothers that operated in Kenema and other diamond villages was small compared to other merchants in town. But at the time of our visit, they were all pretty much muttering the same complaint: No good diamonds have been coming in from the fields.

Whether that was true or whether Fawaz simply didn't want to show us any goods is beside the point. One of Sierra Leone's most important diamond areas—Tongo Field—was a mere 30 miles away from where we sat and under complete control of the RUF. It was universally assumed that rebel couriers sold diamonds in Kenema. We'd seen diamonds everywhere there—including a large, eight-sided rough stone that an old man wandering in the market had popped out of his mouth—and it's likely that many of the stones skirted the legitimate channels. While the official currency is the leone (worth 2,000 to the U.S. dollar), in places like Kenema the currency of choice for anything beyond food and clothing was diamonds. If you needed a new car or motorcycle, you paid in diamonds because they were often easier to come by—and easier to carry—than a mountain of leones. If you owed your friend a favor for watching out for your family during the war, you gave him a nice piece of rough. Even a school for children orphaned by the war, in Freetown's Aberdeen district, sells RUF-mined diamonds to reporters and personnel from nongovernmental organizations and the UN so that they can buy food and books for the students.

Fawaz and those like him are important middlemen in the legitimate diamond trade. Licensed by the Sierra Leone government, they're the first purchasers along a lengthy chain of buyers that ends with consumers in developed countries shopping for tennis bracelets. Out here, amid the sweltering heat and the potential of renewed RUF gunfire, he buys and sells diamonds that will be cherished as keepsakes forever by people whose only experience with such treacherous environments is gleaned from rare three-minute reports on CNN.

Like Fawaz, the majority of such dealers are Lebanese whose parents and grandparents moved to West Africa by the thousands in the wake of World War II to sell consumer goods and general merchandise. Some 120,000 Lebanese are estimated to live throughout West Africa, most of them in the import–export business.[4] When diamonds were discovered in Sierra Leone they were well positioned to enter the gem business, because soon after the war the country was thrown into its first significant bout of internal turmoil over the precious stones.

UNTIL THE EARLY 1950S, diamond production in Sierra Leone was dominated by one company, Sierra Leone Selection Trust (SLST), a branch of the London-based exploration company West African Selection Trust. The company had holdings in gold mines in Ghana and was owned by the South African diamond powerhouse, De Beers Consolidated Mines, Ltd. SLST was founded in Freetown in 1934, after De Beers's vanguard of miners had plucked more than 32,000 carats of stones from the Sierra Leone jungle by hand. The company convinced the government—which was still administered by England—to grant it an exclusive mining concession, meaning that all the diamonds found in the rain forest went to one company.

That was the theory at least. In truth, Sierra Leone provided a horrible mining environment. The deposits were located in the heart of an unexplored jungle, scattered among chieftaincies and villages that weren't used to the sight of white men digging for rocks. The tropical vegetation in the bush grows as thick as anywhere on earth, communications with Freetown were almost nonexistent, and travel into the provinces—often with heavy equipment and supplies—was a days-long endeavor from origin to destination. This harsh reality of jungle mining immediately raised concerns about security. The diamond-bearing region was so extensive and dense with vegetation, wild animals, and villages that few SLST officers were optimistic about being able to control one of diamond mining's inherent costs of business: theft through illicit mining.

In fact, the problem was worse than anyone anticipated. At first, mining went smoothly and SLST built a then-modern processing facility in Yengema, a town in the Kono District. Labor was abundant as the locals took advantage of endless opportunities to mine rivers and wash gravel.

Things changed drastically in the wake of World War II, when Sierra Leoneans serving the British in the Royal West African Frontier Force returned from the battlefields of Burma, having learned the value of the innocuous stones that were being mined out from beneath the feet of villagers. It's not surprising what happened after tales of limitless fortunes began circulating through the bush:

Miners abandoned their jobs and became independent operators. They were also illegal operators, since only SLST had the right to mine for diamonds in Sierra Leone.

But that hardly mattered. In the postwar years, Sierra Leone saw a massive diamond rush as thousands of locals and an equal number of neighboring Liberian and Guinean hopefuls struck out into SLST's private reserve of diamond mines. The boom very nearly sank the country in the mid-1950s as farmers ignored their fields and instead washed gravel day in and day out, usually under the cover of night when they were less likely to be discovered. A food shortage struck the interior and, for the first time, Sierra Leone had to import staples like rice, a grain that was usually so abundant that the country normally exported it. More than an estimated 30,000 illegal miners were operating in 1954, a human tide that was almost impossible to stem.[5] Many of these miners were supported by wealthy Lebanese financiers, most of whom had moved to Freetown in the wake of the war to sell general merchandise. Their business clout and expertise, their possession of import/export licenses, and their ties to supplies in Freetown made them natural partners for the men toiling in the bush.

The Sierra Leone Army, a 1,300-strong force of soldiers whose general duties consisted of little more than guarding their own barracks in Freetown, was dispatched to the Kono District to provide security for SLST, which began to form its own militias, often from the ranks of the local police forces. Violent clashes between miners and these militias became regular events, but even the threat of gun battles didn't slow the illicit trade; the returns provided by illegal mining far outweighed the risks.

The majority of stones were smuggled out of the country. By 1955, it became obvious that there was no way SLST—even with the help of the army and a growing paramilitary police force— could control the smuggling situation. SLST and the government eventually dissolved the single-concession agreement and implemented an aggressive licensing program for indigenous diggers. But even with the dissolution of SLST's private concession and new laws allowing independent operators to sell their goods in Sierra Leone, most miners had already developed contacts outside the country, which also allowed them to avoid export taxes.

With the help of Saika Stevens, the minister of mines for Sierra Leone's government-elect, De Beers instituted the Diamond Corporation of Sierra Leone (DCSL), a company that would buy diamonds from those who were at the time "stealing" them from SLST and selling them in Monrovia, the nearby capital of neighboring Liberia. In turn, DCSL would transport the diamonds to the Diamond Trading Company (DTC) in London, another De Beers concern, which was part of the Central Selling Organization (CSO), the global diamond funnel established by De Beers in the 1930s. At the time, the CSO sold 80 percent of the world's diamonds to the retail marketplace.

For the scheme to work, however, De Beers had to buy the diamonds in the bush in order to compete directly with the illicit traffickers. In real terms, what this meant was that some brave soul— who would have to be an expert in evaluating diamonds—would have to leave the comfort and safety of a downtown office and set off into the heart of an unmapped jungle with a backpack crammed with cash. At the diamond mines and in countless villages he would then compete with savvy local middlemen and smugglers who likely wouldn't be too inclined to share their lucrative turf with the legitimate diamond cartel.

In the beginning, things didn't work out too well. The handful of London buyers who agreed to this risky assignment were up against hundreds of traffickers who outbid them for the diamonds in order to keep a loyal customer base among the diggers. The DCSL buyers were also constrained by rates dictated from London. It took five years and the creation of a new government office before the diamond buyers were able to offer rates similar to those offered in Monrovia. Although illicit sales of diamonds were never halted, by 1960 the estimated loss to the illicit market fell to its lowest point since the diamond rush began.

The job of buying diamonds in the bush fell almost exclusively to the Lebanese traders once the system worked through all of its initial kinks. They were revered in diamond offices in Freetown. "After all, they accomplished the most dangerous part of the buyer's mission, for the idea of walking through the forest carrying large sums of cash appealed to no one," writes Jacques Legrand in *Diamonds: Myth, Magic, and Reality.* "All things considered, the profits made by the Lebanese were commensurate with the work they performed and an equilibrium was established to everyone's satisfaction."[6]

Diamonds only added to the increasing political tension of pre-independence Sierra Leone. Those who would be charged with assuming the mantle of government from the British in 1961 faced both an economic windfall as well as a witch's brew of serious political and economic issues that would challenge any well-seasoned government. Sierra Leoneans, with the oversight of a British administration, had experienced no success in harnessing the country's most valuable natural resource, as the diamond boom of the 1950s had shown. More diamonds were smuggled away than were exported, robbing the country of taxes and contracts that could have been used to build roads, utilities, and medical and educational facilities. Control of the diamond fields would require an incredibly delicate and astute, yet forceful and uncompromising government. The head of state would have to adopt strict border policies with Liberia, modernize export laws, and establish creative trade and labor agreements with diamond exploration companies. The entire monetary system should probably have been over-hauled prior to independence. One of the reasons smugglers went to Monrovia was because Liberia's dollar was fixed to the value of the U.S. dollar until 1997, making it the equivalent of hard currency. The much softer currency of Sierra Leone was good only in Sierra Leone.

None of these measures was taken, however, and the smuggling did not stop once Sierra Leone was granted independence on April 27, 1961. Maintaining the diamond infrastructure was left to the Lebanese traders in towns like Kenema and Bo, and they had organized it in the first place to address the needs of smugglers.

The system employed by people like Fawaz is simple and dates back to the early diamond-rush days of the 1950s. Individual miners obtain a license from the government to dig on a certain plot of land or riverbank. Since the license is extremely expensive to the average would-be miner—who also needs to pay off the inevitable series of bribes—he often needs to find a sponsor, usually a Lebanese merchant. The merchant provides shovels, gasoline-powered water pumps, sieves, food, and pay for the miner's hired diggers. In exchange, the diamonds are sold to the merchant, minus the overhead. Fawaz himself, though he works in one of Africa's most valuable diamondiferous regions and is a conduit for what is eventually hundreds of thousands of dollars worth of gemstones, has never even visited a mine.

When war broke out in 1991, the system was so well established—and the profits so lucrative—that many Lebanese abandoned their businesses only under the most threatening circumstances. Even at the height of the RUF conflict, with the sounds of rocket blasts echoing off Kenema's high hills, many merchants continued to man their offices and buy stones from the rebels. Official diamond exports from Sierra Leone practically ceased in the mid-1990s—whereas 2 million carats per year were exported in the 1960s, a paltry 9,000 carats were exported in 1999—but the old smuggling routes to Monrovia were still open for business.

And there was certainly no lack of buyers. Everyone from legitimate brokers employed by Belgian cutting houses to agents of the Iranian-backed Lebanese terrorist organization Hezbollah crowded the streets and hotels of Monrovia, eager for the chance to buy diamonds from the RUF. Monrovia was a no-man's-land of freewheeling dealing in diamonds that had been soaked in the blood of innocent Sierra Leoneans. For the legitimate brokers, it meant cheap goods and high profits; for the terrorists, it presented a picture-perfect opportunity to launder vast amounts of money undetected, an important development in the role diamonds would come to play in international terrorism in the beginning of the new century.

2

DIAMOND JUNCTION:
A Smuggler's Paradise

Freetown, Sierra Leone

S ITTING ON FREETOWN'S white-sand beaches, it's almost possible to forget where you are, if you can ignore the regular
rotor wash from UN helicopters returning to headquarters at the
Mammy Yoko Hotel. But more tragic reminders are never far away.

A young sand-beggar wandered over to our table and told us that
he was poor and in need of money. He'd escaped the RUF a year
before and couldn't find work. He told us that he was 17 and had
been fighting with the rebels since he was kidnapped at age 9. His
mother and father were killed by RUF in Makeni, in north-central
Sierra Leone, and he was trucked to the rebels' eastern stronghold
in Kailahun and forced to join the rebellion. It was either that or
execution. His weapon had been an AK-58, a more powerful version of the ever-popular AK-47, which can hold up to 75 rounds of

ammunition per magazine. He practiced his aim by shooting coconuts out of palm trees alongside other kidnapped children. After six weeks of training in guerilla warfare, he was ordered into battle.

"You had to go," he said.

"Why? Could you say 'no'?"

"They kill you if you say 'no,'" he said. "Four kids in my unit were killed because they wouldn't fight."

I asked him if he'd ever chopped off anyone's hands and he said he hadn't. But he'd seen it done.

"Why?" I asked.

"We only chop hands by order."

"But why were the orders given?"

"To scare people. To get the diamonds and make them leave the mines."

Less than five minutes after he left, a young child about 7 years old tentatively approached the table pulling an old man in sun-glasses by the sleeves of his sport coat. The sleeves flapped in the breeze below the elbow and it was obvious that he'd had his hands chopped off. The girl wanted money for the man, her grandfather. He said he was once a diamond dealer and banker in Bo, Kenema's sister city 50 miles to its west, and when the rebels attacked, they presumed he was rich. They chopped off both arms and gouged out his eyes with a bayonet. Now, like the young RUF lieutenant, he wandered the beach with his granddaughter leading the way and begged for money.

Other than the Mammy Yoko Hotel, which hosted the offices of UNAMSIL, there was no place to escape the walking, talking evi-dence of how bad and desperate a place Sierra Leone was. Free-town was a city filled with war-ravaged beggars and thieves. There were too many refugees and not enough humanitarian aid to go around. People crippled with polio staked out street corners, and tried to extort money from those passing within reach. Waiters would try to sell you diamonds or offer to rent their sisters to you for weeks at a time. Children with bloated bellies scratched at the windows of downtown restaurants.

Just when you thought you'd found a safe corner to escape to—some dim tent of a streetside restaurant where few people could see into the gloom and you could order yet another beer and let your mind wander to something other than death, disease, and torture—in would stumble a multiple-amputee, a man who'd had his arms, lips, and ears sawn off with a rusted ax. If it was really an unlucky day for you, the guy would also have polio and malaria and be partially retarded. There is no shortage of such people, and when they corner you in a restaurant whose walls are composed of stolen UNHCR rain-plastic, there are only two things to do: Stare stoically through him as if he doesn't exist, or reach for your wallet and hope a limp leone-note worth 50 cents is penance enough.

When giving money to the amputated, you must put it directly into their pockets.

FREETOWN'S VERY NAME is so ironic that no one even bothers to point it out. Its English founders, who had good intentions, however misplaced they might have been at the time, had certainly envisioned a different future. During the Revolutionary War, the British gave American slaves the opportunity to be freed in exchange for fighting for the crown. At the end of the war, more than 15,000 former slaves who had accepted the offer made their way to Great Britain. Although slavery was still legal there, in 1772 a court had ruled that once freed, a slave was free for life. Unaccustomed to making a life of their own, and aided little by the government they had fought for, many of the new residents suffered crushing poverty and unemployment.

In 1787, a group of British philanthropists purchased 32 square miles of land near Bunce Island, a large landmass in the Sierra Leone River just north of the Freetown Peninsula, from local Temne leaders. Their idea was to create a "Province of Freedom" for the ex-slaves. Later that year, 100 European prostitutes and 300 former slaves arrived in what would become Freetown. Many of the freed slaves knew nothing of Africa, having been born in Europe or the Americas. Even if they had, very few of them—perhaps none of them—had ancestors from Sierra Leone. Although Sierra Leone had been plied for slaves prior to that time, Ghana, Ivory Coast, Nigeria, and Cameroon were the main players in the trade. Of the original 400 settlers dropped at the peninsula's deepwater harbor, only 48 survived the next three years, the rest succumbing to a gallery of deadly diseases, warfare with the local inhabitants, or the temptation to leave Sierra Leone in search of their original homelands.[1]

Undaunted, the philanthropists tried again in 1792, this time shipping some 1,200 former slaves from the United States who had fled to Nova Scotia, Canada; they later sent 500 more from Jamaica. It was during this period that the Sierra Leone settlers first started profiting from the country's natural resources: To survive and make a rather handsome living in their new home, many of the settlers got into the slave trade, the irony being either lost on them or deemed inconsequential. Slaving was nothing new to Sierra Leone and the trade resembled that of conflict diamonds in a number of ways. For one, the history of slaving is filled with characters that seem to have been plucked from a lurid pulp novel. Consider the self-proclaimed wretch of a slaving captain John Newton, a man so vile "that even his crew regarded him as little more than an animal," according to historian Lindsey Terry. "Once he fell overboard and his ship's crew refused to drop a boat to him. Instead they threw a harpoon at him, with which they dragged him back into the ship."

Newton, an Englishman, captained a specially designed slave frigate named, simply enough, *A Slave Ship*. She could carry up to 600 people, chained side to side and lined up like timber. The purpose was to pack in as many slaves as the ship could hold since an average of 20 percent died during the two-month-long middle passage to Cuba.

In 1748, Newton loaded slave cargo in Sierra Leone and weighed anchor into a massive storm that lasted eleven days. Convinced that he wouldn't survive, he had a religious conversion on the deck, in the raging storm, bellowing out to God to "save his wretched soul." The experience led to his writing the psalm "Amazing Grace" some 20 years later.

Soon after slavery was abolished in Britain in 1807, the British took over the settlement and declared it a colony of the crown. In their efforts to enforce their antislavery laws—and impose them elsewhere—British warships patrolled the West African coast and intercepted slave vessels bound for the Americas, turning the islands off Sierra Leone into processing centers for "recaptives." After a short time on Bunce Island or the Banana Islands, many of the recaptives were simply put on skiffs to the mainland; some of these lucky Africans came from villages just down the coast.

Even though slavery was illegal, the money to be made kept the trade alive and well up and down the west coast. Tribal chiefs in Sierra Leone would stage slave raids on rival groups and villages and sell prisoners to Portuguese traders, who kept secret forts in the coastal swamps and forests just south of Freetown. Lookouts would scope the horizon for British men-of-war and, when the coast was clear, rush groups of slaves out to vessels anchored just beyond the surf. Convinced that they were destined for death, many captives would try to drown themselves in the surf, but the Europeans and their indigenous Kru partners kept a close eye out for this and thwarted many such attempts. In 1839, hundreds of captives were packed onto the *Tecora,* a Portuguese slaver, and sailed to Havana. They made land under cover of night because importing slaves into the Americas was illegal. But in a parallel to today's diamond controversy, slave traders dodged this by obtaining passports for their prisoners that showed they were Cuban. Fifty-three of these Sierra Leoneans were purchased by Spanish slave owners and put aboard the 60-foot coastal schooner *Amistad* for transport to Puerto Príncipe. But during the voyage, a Mende slave used a nail to pick his locks and freed his fellow captives. They took over the ship and wound up not back in Africa, as they'd planned, but in Mystic, Connecticut. In the resulting landmark trial, the would-be slaves were freed by the U.S. Supreme Court, aided in no small part by one their attorneys, former U.S. president John Quincy Adams.

Back in Sierra Leone, by 1850 more than 100 ethnic groups were living in Freetown, a mixture brought about by Britain's policy of releasing recaptives at Port Kissy. Like an African version of New York City, Freetown's heterogeneous population occupied different parts of town and the different groups lived fairly harmoniously. Collectively, the Freetown settlers became known as Krios and they developed a language of the same name that allowed them to communicate outside their various native tongues. Krio is a hodgepodge of African dialects, its main component being English: The result is a mellifluous babble of pidgin slang, Queen's English, and tribal terms.

For most of its postslavery history, there was nothing remarkable about Sierra Leone, and Freetown likely lived up to its name. For the most part, those living there got along well with their neighbors and their British overseers. It wasn't until diamonds were discovered in the 1930s that Sierra Leone's course toward self-destruction was set.

TODAY, IT'S HARD TO DECIDE if Freetown looks more or less depressing from the air. Flying in from the provinces on one of the choppers that regularly blows sand into the drinks of those trying to relax on the beach, you can look out the port windows to watch the Peninsula Mountains drop away to reveal its jumbled collection of teetering high-rise buildings that seem to be lined up behind one another like a suicide procession, as if waiting their turn to leap to their deaths in Destruction Bay. The bay itself, aptly named, is haunted with the hulls of half-sunken vessels. The city claws its way up the mountains, creeping into the jungle like a disease. At street level the city is a chaos of mud, wrecked cars, zinc roofs, and palm trees, all tied together with all-weather plastic sheeting. It's not surprising that the capital is so decimated and hopeless considering that Sierra Leone effectively ceased functioning during the civil war. The RUF's diamond war has so far killed about 75,000 people and mutilated another 20,000.[2] Eighty percent of its estimated five million citizens have been turned into refugees and most of them seem to have retreated to Freetown. Like everywhere else in the country, Freetown is just another city where people struggle to survive from day to day. The only difference is that their efforts are overshadowed more by high-rise office buildings than palm trees and climbing vines.

Architecturally, the capital is a disorganized landslide of cardboard shacks, cinderblock houses, poured concrete office buildings, and zinc-and-timber Krio formations that look like miniature Southern plantations, minus the beauty, craftsmanship, and inspiration. Downtown is a maelstrom of blaring horns, fish-smoke, money changers, fistfights, immobilized traffic, and 100-degree heat.

Freetown is truly something to behold, a writhing hive of killers, villains, and wretched victims. Refugees and RUF fighters—both former and current—wander the same roadsides. UN officials have beers with con men trying to sell diamonds. Kamajor fighters have taken over a downtown hotel for reasons no one seems sure of, while disarmed RUF fighters stage demonstrations downtown over perceived injustices of the peace agreement. A bar in Aberdeen—Freetown's beach district—is the vortex for this contradictory reality: Every type of human flotsam and do-gooder can be found rubbing elbows at Paddy's on any weekend night. The place is actually a huge bamboo and palm leaf tent, featuring two bars, a TV, and a stage. The parking lot is the domain of beggars and robbers, as former RUF fighters and their amputated victims jostle for the attention of the paying crowd, itself a mix of diamond smugglers, mercenaries, UN personnel, prostitutes, businessmen, journalists, workers from some 120 nongovernmental organizations with headquarters in Freetown, and other assorted riffraff. The strange population of Freetown results in some equally strange encounters.

Among the most disconcerting, especially for those unfamiliar with daily life in Freetown, are those with diamond smugglers, men whose thoughts are not about the ever-present tragedy of Sierra Leone's diamond war visible on every street corner, but only about the profits to be made selling illicit stones. They are as ruthless and barbaric as any drug dealer in South America, a point that was driven home one day by a phone call I got from a Senegalese man named Kahn who had been trying for weeks to sell us diamonds. He was in the car, he said, en route to our room at the Solar Hotel near the beach, and in the passenger seat was an overweight RUF officer I'd met briefly in a downtown café.

"He's got a lot of good, good diamonds," said Kahn, who handed the phone to the man before I could protest.

"Listen, I'm sorry for the mix-up," I began, "but I've told Kahn over and over that we're not interested in buying any diamonds."

The RUF man began to squeal. He told me I was a dead man for backing out on a deal that was never made. "RUF gon' *fuck* you up!" he screeched before the line went dead.

This was not the first run-in Hondros and I had with RUF smugglers in Freetown, but we were determined to do our best to make it our last. As soon as word had gotten out that two white men purporting to be journalists were interested in looking at some rebel goods, our room at the Solar had become something of a magnet for anyone trying to sell anything. We had visitors at all hours of the day and night: If not diamond traffickers, then certainly drug-dealers and prostitutes. The most avid salesmen were a hulking bodybuilder of a man who carried with him a backpack of wares— everything from thick bags of marijuana to carved wooden gim-cracks—and Kahn, a skinny, crooked-standing man with a wandering eye.

A few weeks before, Kahn had picked up me and *New York Times* photographer Tyler Hicks on the side of the road as we were waiting for a cab downtown. One of us made the mistake of thinking out loud that it might be worth the investment to buy a known conflict diamond or two and test how easily we could smuggle it out of the country and try to sell it, with full disclosure of its sources, in New York. No sooner was the thought verbalized than Kahn produced a hand-printed list of the RUF diamonds he had for sale. We made it clear—or so we thought—that we really didn't want to buy anything, especially from a cabbie we'd met only four minutes earlier, but that it might be nice to have some photos of rough goods for the archives. Kahn agreed to bring one of his sellers to meet us later at the Solar.

It was the beginning of the end, in terms of the peace and tranquility of our hideout. Whatever it lacked in ambiance—rooms at the Solar are painted swimming-pool blue and all seem to have sustained massive water damage if the stains on the walls and ceilings were any indication—it more than made up for in personality. The desk manager is descended from former Connecticut slaves and likes Americans, allowing free access to the Internet on the hotel's one functional telephone and looking the other way when we ran up several days' worth of beer tabs at the bar. The bar itself is nothing less than an oasis; hidden in the trees, it's far from the main road and therefore less susceptible to invasion by the tightly wrapped and beglittered hookers who, anywhere else in Aberdeen, will literally assault you for your attention.

The first conflict-gem salesman Kahn ferreted to Room E-2 was a Kamajor, a Mende fighter who relied as much on superstition for protection in battle as shotguns and rocket-propelled grenades. Charmed amulets, ancient tribal prayers, and animist rituals were meant to make Kamajors invisible to enemies, impenetrable to bullets and fragmentation grenades, and unconquerable in battle. To have one of these men standing in your hotel room is unnerving, especially one with thousands of dollars in rough stones stolen from an overtaken RUF mine coming out of his burlap pocket, along with a professional jeweler's loupe.

More unnerving still is the moment when you tell him that you're not interested in buying the stones, just looking at them for journalistic reasons. The smile turns into a blank stare, not understanding because we didn't even make an offer. Then he turns to Kahn, who's smiling at the wall, perhaps thinking that we're being shrewd in our negotiations. Deciding that must be the case, he hustles the baffled Kamajor out of the room with promises to return.

And return he does, time and again, dragging with him one bush fighter after another, whether Kamajor or their RUF enemies. Not one of them believed that we were journalists. Even if they did, they certainly didn't believe that we weren't in the market for goods. It seemed everyone else was, and as far as they were concerned there was no reason we shouldn't have been, too. It got to the point where we dreaded hearing a knock at the door, sure that we'd open it to find Kahn presenting us with a malarial RUF captain clutching a leather bag filled with diamonds, or a Sierra Leone Army soldier eager for the chance to sell diamonds he'd stolen from the RUF during a raid two years ago.

Things climaxed when Kahn called my mobile phone that day, telling me of the RUF colonel sitting in his passenger seat who had millions in diamonds that he wanted to unload quickly. The man was nervous about being in a city filled with his victims, refugees, and amputees who had fled RUF guns and blades from the provinces to hide in camps like the one operated by Médecins Sans Frontières in Freetown.

After the call, we too were on the run and, as a matter of fact, wound up across the street from the MSF camp, at a vagrants' flophouse called the Cockle Bay Guest House and Relaxation Center.

There were no locking fences, guards, or any other filter on the local color, which it featured in abundance. The 10-by-12-foot reception area was dominated by an early 1980s–style boom box, the type that's the size of a footlocker, thundering some sort of religious rap music. Despite the din, four or five people snoozed on the furniture and the woman at the desk eyed us like we would be seeing her later, after she'd knocked on the door wondering if we were interested in a "massage." The rooms were only $7 a night, but that was probably because the locks could be breached simply by leaning on the door.

Outside the main entrance, the city's urban wildlife came right up to the curb.

AGAINST SUCH A BACKDROP, diamond smugglers must feel right at home. Indeed, one of the people I met who was most at peace with himself was an Australian who would have seemed no more at home if we'd met in Sydney.

Jacob Singer is a friendly 50-ish man with a bushy salt-and-pepper mustache and tough, bright little eyes set in a relief-map face of creases and wrinkles. He's a popular figure in Freetown, it's soon apparent, greeted from all street corners and by most passersby at the Solar's open-walled outdoor bar. He returns all waves with a hearty greeting that mixes the indigenous Krio language with his own Australian idioms:

"Ha de body?"

"No bad."

"Well, goodonya then."

Less cheerful and popular, mostly due to his lack of English skills, is Valdy, his Polish companion. Muscular and handsome, Valdy's bald white head is a beacon among Freetown's African citizenry. Except for the fact that they live at the Solar Hotel for months on end, it would be easy to mistake the two for UNAMSIL workers or bosses of a relief group. Both dress smartly and comfortably in shorts and polo shirts and wheel around town in a hired green Mercedes.

In fact, the two men are Mutt-and-Jeff diamond smugglers: Singer has the connections and does the talking; Valdy is the money man. In September 2001, they were struggling to string together a deal for $500,000 worth of rebel diamonds from Kono.

Diamonds are among the easiest—and by far the most valuable by weight—commodities to smuggle. Three hundred grams of diamonds are equal in value to 40,000 pounds of iron ore, but only one of those commodities can be successfully smuggled in one's bowels. Millions of dollars worth of diamonds can be carried almost anywhere in the body or on it and they don't set off airport metal detectors. They can be sold quickly and they are virtually untraceable. This is one of the reasons there is no such thing as "conflict timber"; rebels wishing to smuggle tropical lumber and sell it on the black market have a much harder time transporting and unloading their goods than rebels who deal in diamonds.

The most reliable way for smugglers to get diamonds out of Sierra Leone is to swallow them and hope to time their next bowel movements so that they can be retrieved with some amount of privacy. There is no possible way to detect the stones if they're inside your intestines, but the prospect of recovering them is unappealing and, besides, smuggling out one or two half-carat diamonds is easy enough without having to resort to such digestive measures. They can be carried in your breast pocket or a pack of cigarettes. There is no shortage of incredible tales of intrigue and deception when it comes to diamond smuggling, probably because the tiny size of the contraband encourages ingenuity. In *The Heart of the Matter,* his novel about love and betrayal set in Sierra Leone, Graham Greene described Lebanese smuggling diamonds in the stomachs of live parrots. Ian Fleming, author of the James Bond series of novels, had his hero smuggle goods in Dunlop golf balls in *Diamonds Are Forever.* Over the years, people have carried thousands of dollars of stones inside the knots of their ties, in tins of fruit salad, in the false heels of specially made shoes. One woman who lost an eye in a car accident took the opportunity to hide diamonds in her empty socket, behind a glass eye.

Though it often seems to be so, smuggling isn't reserved to fringe characters covered in scars found sipping cheap gin in tropical airport lounges. It also occurs among the most elite in the diamond world. One prominent British diamond merchant was caught by Scotland Yard and fined back taxes for having illegally smuggled $2 million worth of polished goods from London to Belgium over a three-year period. He was only caught when police accidentally learned that he'd been robbed of $184,000 worth of goods, but hadn't reported the theft because they were smuggled in the first place. What makes this case notable is the fact that the man had served for 11 years on the customs agency's diamond evaluation committee.

In fact, smuggling within respected channels of the diamond industry is, like all else related to it, a well-organized and long-standing system. The largest cutting and polishing centers in the world, in Bombay and Surat, India, were founded on smuggled goods that made their way from DTC customers in Belgium via German courier, with the finished stones then being smuggled back. Courier "companies" made a handsome living employing schoolteachers, laborers, airline pilots, and others who were willing to take a free, all-expense-paid vacation to the Orient in return for carrying home a slightly lumpy tube of toothpaste. All of this was done to avoid the local and value-added taxes for the round-trip journey.[3]

Because of their stable prices and the ease with which they can be moved around the world undetected, diamonds have been the currency of choice for a lot more than weapons that go to African insurgencies. They've been used to buy drugs in South America and they've been used by the Soviet KGB to pay spies. Former FBI agent Robert Hanssen was reportedly paid $1.4 million in cash and diamonds to provide the Russians with intelligence information and classified documents.

The amount of diamonds that are smuggled by individuals, though, is relatively small compared to the wealth of diamonds that can be stolen from the mines themselves by workers. Security at diamond mines the world over makes antiterrorism security efforts at airports look like they're conducted by the Boy Scouts. In Namibia, for instance, at the De Beers–owned Oranjemund claim, the only cars in the town in the 1970s were company cars that could never leave its borders. Private vehicles were banned when an enterprising engineer removed several bolts from the chassis of his car, bored out the middle for holding diamonds, and then screwed them back in tight. The fact that he was actually caught is testament in itself to how high the security was; from then on, De Beers outlawed new cars. All vehicles in the town had to stay there until they rusted away. One worker at the same site stole diamonds by tying a small bag to a homing pigeon, which would fly the diamonds back to his house.[4] One day, he got too ambitious and overloaded his winged courier; the pigeon was so laden with stolen diamonds, it couldn't fly over the fence and was discovered by security guards a short time later. They reclaimed the diamonds and let the bird go, following it to the man's home, where he was arrested after work.

Smuggling one or two small stones out of Freetown is one thing—smuggling a half a million dollars worth is something else entirely. If caught with an attaché case filled with rough at the airport, at best you'll lose your loot; at worst you'll be arrested and prosecuted. Smuggling large parcels out of Freetown requires a bit more cloak-and-dagger than hiding the goods in body cavities.

"The way it will work," Singer explained one night at the Solar over Star beers in the bar, "is that we'll look at the goods here, agree on a price, and then meet in Conakry to complete the deal." Like most nights, the place was almost deserted except for the staff and a few guests who'd gathered under the tin-and-thatch roof to watch CNN. A string of pale yellow lightbulbs gave the scene a jaundiced look and bamboo curtains were partially rolled down around the circumference in anticipation of the nightly rains. Valdy lounged in another booth nearby, smoking and watching TV.

Conakry, the capital of neighboring Guinea, has long been the location of informal conflict-diamond trades. Usually Sierra Leonean combatants will trade small pieces of rough in Guinea for rice or fuel, but there have been allegations of weapons deals being conducted between the RUF and Guinean military officials. One such deal that was said to have gone sour in the summer of 2000 resulted in the RUF attacking Pamelap, the Guinean border town on the road between Freetown and Conakry. The Guinean military retaliated, firing artillery shells into Kambia, on the Sierra Leone side of the border, with the result that more innocent civilians were sent to Freetown's MSF camp.

Guinea's guilt as a diamond conduit is reflected in discrepancies between what it exports to Belgium and what Belgium says is imported from Guinea. For example, from 1993 to 1997, Guinea reported 2.6 million carats of official diamond exports at an average of $96 per carat to Belgium. During the same period, Belgium—through the Diamond High Council, the diamond industry's self-appointed watchdog organization—reported imports from Guinea of 4.8 million carats averaging $167 each. "In other words," reported the UN in December 2000, "Belgium appears to import almost double the volume that is exported from Guinea, and the per-carat-value is almost 75 per cent higher than what leaves Guinea."[5]

People like Singer account for the discrepancy. By doing nothing more than shaking hands in Freetown, Singer doesn't have to carry any cash into the country or carry any diamonds out. Getting the diamonds to Conakry is the RUF's "problem," even though it's not any more difficult than U.S. citizens' traveling across state lines to buy fireworks for their Fourth of July celebrations. If the deal is solidified in Freetown, RUF brokers often take the goods to the Guinean capital via ferry after bribing customs officials to ignore certain items of luggage. Bribery in West Africa is such a part of the culture that it's like tipping a waiter after a meal—I did it myself on arrival in Freetown, paying a customs official a mere $5 to avoid a time-consuming search of my incoming luggage, which, as far as he knew, could have been filled with pistols and $100 bills.

If the deal is made in the bush, the broker takes a backpack filled with diamonds on a motorcycle from Koidu, for instance, through bush trails across the border and on to Conakry. The trip can be made in a day during the dry season. The RUF representative goes to a bank in Conakry and deposits the parcel in a safe deposit box.

Buyers like Singer will then meet them in a café, adjourn to inspect the goods, and the money will be wired from Poland to be converted into cash at the same bank. In some circumstances, Singer said, the RUF rep will prefer to have the money deposited in a numbered account in Copenhagen for use later.

Guinean customs then inspects the diamonds and issues a certificate of authenticity that they originated in Guinea and—voilà—conflict diamonds magically become legitimate. If all goes according to plan, Valdy's company will send a twelve-seat private jet the same day to pick them up and the diamonds will be in Europe by nightfall, squeaky clean as far as the Diamond High Council is concerned.

"But they didn't originate in Guinea," I said.

"So?"

"So how do you get customs to say that they did?"

He looked at me as if I hadn't learned a thing. He rubbed his fingers together, the universal sign language for "bribery."

The certificate accompanying the diamonds is supposed to be the guarantee that the diamonds came from legitimate sources, but obviously such a guarantee is relative, and it's not just an African problem. Perhaps aware that some stones coming into Belgium are from questionable sources, the Diamond High Council in Antwerp until recently recorded the origin of diamond imports as the last country to ship the goods to the city's cutters and polishers. Therefore, a package of rough that began in the forests of Sierra Leone and was smuggled to Liberia before being exported to Belgium was recorded as being filled with Liberian diamonds. This is how Liberia can defy the laws of nature and outproduce South Africa by exporting 6 million carats of gemstones a year, when it can actually produce, at best, 200,000 carats of industrial diamonds from its existing mines.[6] And this is also how the entire issue of conflict diamonds has remained in the dark for so long, allowing the RUF to launder Sierra Leone diamonds under a cover provided by the diamond industry itself.

"I've been doing this in Sierra Leone since 1995," said Singer. "It's not hard. In fact, it's almost impossible to get caught."

If he has any moral qualms about buying diamonds from people who are going to use the money for weapons to kill innocent civilians and kidnap children into their ranks, he doesn't show it. In fact, he's never strayed from Freetown during all of his years doing illicit business in Sierra Leone, so he has no first-hand knowledge of what upcountry conditions are like.

But that's not to say he doesn't know what the rebels are capable of; in fact, he carries a small photo album of corpses that have been mutilated by the rebels to show to anyone unfamiliar with the horrors of the war. He squirreled it out one night, sliding it conspiratorially across the tiled tabletop at me. Four nude female corpses laying in the highway, hands and feet chopped off and laying nearby, genitals mutilated with a tree branch. A disembodied head laying on a table. A corpse minus its head and arms, which were arranged in a macabre pose some feet away.

"Listen here," he said, wagging a finger for emphasis, "if the government made it easier to buy legitimate diamonds, people like me wouldn't have to deal with these savages. But I'm a businessman. What else can I do?"

Unmentioned, but widely understood in these circles, is that rebel diamonds are far less expensive than diamonds that go through official channels. RUF diamonds normally sell in the bush for 10 percent of what the same stones would otherwise cost through a licensed exporter, making them highly liquid and prized by people like Singer who can sell them at a large markup in Europe's diamond centers.[7]

The way it should work is through the Fawaz model. The government issues mining and exporting licenses good for a year to people who apply for them and pass a rudimentary background inspection. The license holder is allowed to employ a certain number of upcountry miners, diggers, and buyers who are also licensed by the government. In theory, the exporter will bring diamonds to Freetown that have been dug up legitimately, and he'll provide proof of that through a series of receipts and invoices detailing the discovery of every gem he wishes to export. The package is valued, taxed, and sealed in a box at the Government Gold and Diamond Office (GGDO) in town with a numbered certificate of origin printed on security paper, the government's official stamp of approval that the package is "clean." The parcel is also photographed with a digital camera and recorded in an electronic database, which is updated when the parcel is delivered to its stated destination. Once leaving the GGDO, the exporter is then free to leave the country without having to open the package again at the airport for inspection.

This is the system that was put in place as a result of UN Security Council Resolution 1306, an embargo on diamond imports from Sierra Leone adopted in July 2000 until such a scheme for certifying official diamond exports was adopted. But it's not likely that this action did much, if anything, to help stem trafficking in conflict diamonds. Clearly, the RUF didn't use official channels to sell its stones. For example, between 1997 and 1999, a mere 36,000 carats were officially exported from Sierra Leone, from a high of 2 million in the late 1960s.[8] Although the war has prevented experts from forecasting Sierra Leone's diamond reserves, it's undisputed that annual output is much higher than the official export numbers indicate. When the embargo was placed on Sierra Leone diamonds, all it truly meant was that the traders who legally exported the 9,320 carats[9] recorded in 1999 would have to smuggle their goods instead to Liberia or Guinea, which had no restrictions or certification requirements. During the period when the embargo was in place, everyone mining diamonds in Sierra Leone became a smuggler.

The problem, even under the new official arrangement, is that the RUF has Kono and Tongo Field, which have the best stones and the best prices. Anyone wishing to buy them in the bush can do so, even requesting a forged "receipt" to show to customs officials. There's no guarantee just because someone has a license that the diamonds presented to the GGDO in Freetown were mined by his employees instead of bought from rebels in Tongo Field. In the end, it's just easier to smuggle them; smugglers don't pay any license fees or the 3 percent export tax.

Most of my meetings with Singer were cut short, usually by someone appearing in the shadows beyond the dim light cast from the bar, motioning for him to follow.

"Right," he'd say with a Father Christmas smile. "Gotta go meet some people. You'll be around right? Goodonya."

He and Valdy would be swallowed by the night.

A FEW DAYS LATER, Singer and I were engaged in our usual sunset activity: smoking, drinking, talking diamonds, and watching the news at the bar. At the time, the news was mostly coverage of America's war on terrorism in the wake of the September 11 Al Qaeda attacks. We were fortunate to watch even that; the bartenders had long tired of the coverage and had begun to play a cartoon videotape featuring Alvin and the Chipmunks in protest. After the initial shock of the attacks had worn off, the locals began to look forward to watching the tape instead of the repetitive reports on CNN; earlier I had asked to watch the news and was resoundingly voted down, twelve Sierra Leoneans to one American. But on this night, the foreigners outnumbered the locals and CNN reigned, even though we were as bored of the coverage as they were.

As usual, Valdy was off to the side by himself. Singer was complaining about the unreliability of most RUF salesmen. "There's no such thing as an office or a phone number you can call to get a hold of them, you know," he said.

On top of that, many "salesmen" were con artists trying to hawk glass to rich fools. The scam was simple, but bold: You'd pay your $100 for what you were told was a 2.5-carat diamond from a mine in Bo and think that you were going to make your girlfriend the happiest woman in town once you had the thing cut, polished, and set in jewelry. And just as you were thinking about how much money you could make doing this for a living, there would be a knock on the door and a phalanx of blue-suited Sierra Leone police would have you on your face on the floor of the guest house. You'd be dragged off as a smuggler captured thanks to a tip from an "informant" and jerked out of the hotel in front of the friendly people at the front desk. As you're half-carried through the lobby you yell at them to please take care of your luggage, your return plane tickets, and your passport, which are all laying in a huge mess in the room, which, of course, hadn't been paid for yet since you planned to spend a few more days there. You'd be shoved into one of their white-yellow-and-blue Range Rovers and taken to a sweat-tank at the station, and there subjected to threatening grilling from customs and the Ministry of Mines and Natural Resources. Your demands to talk to someone at the embassy are ignored and you're given a few good whacks to the face. You're *fucked,* you're told, because you bought a diamond without having a license to do so. And then, amid the panic in your mind, a bubble of desperate lucidity comes to the surface: Can I buy a license now?

Ah, yes . . . postures ease . . . of course you can. It will be a license just to get out of their hands and onto the nearest plane out of Sierra Leone, though. How much money do you have? Six hundred dollars? But a license costs a thousand (unless you have a thousand, in which case it costs two), resulting in more whacks to the head. Okay, today's your lucky day; we'll take the $600, but you'd better leave the country immediately.

Indeed. What a scene: Dumped on the streets without even cab fare back to the room you now can't pay for, where all your possessions are being kept hostage by the innkeeper, reduced to begging to the U.S. ambassador or your friends in the press corps.

People like Singer were invaluable because they'd already screened such riffraff.

"You've got to have good contacts and fortunately I've been doing this long enough that I've got them. That's why he needs me." He pointed to Valdy, whose Polish diamond-cutting company hired Singer to acquire cheap quality stones from the rebels.

"Say, you want to meet one of them? Name's Jango. He can tell you all about RUF mining," he said.

"Why not?"

We headed into the night, the sound of UN helicopters carried to us on the ocean breeze that moved the leaves overhead like bored hand-waving from a local parade. There are few functional streetlights in Freetown and the short walk to Jango's compound took us through an eerie collage of shadowy figures lit by the greasy flames of oil-lamps at sheet-plastic-and-timber roadside kiosks. Glaring headlights from UN Expeditions and Land Rovers speeding their occupants to Paddy's periodically blinded us; when we finally arrived, we were seeing stars and tripping over our own feet.

Jango's neighborhood was typical of most squatter housing in Freetown. Crumbling concrete housing blocks waved colorful laundry like Tibetan prayer flags. Black cauldrons bubbled with rice and cassava, creating a mist of cook-smoke that caught the firelight in a medieval light show. Streams of sewage and rainwater mingled underfoot in the pasty mud. From the shadows, the only thing visible of the people slumped on the porches and tree stumps were the whites of their eyes. Community activity centered around a slapdash kiosk composed of tree branches and UNHCR plastic sheeting. About a half dozen hard-eyed teens lurked inside around a battered boom box that was playing The Spice Girls at deafening volume, sipping tea. Naked children stopped in midstride to stare at the spectacle of two white men arriving unannounced on their doorstep after dark.

"Ha de body?" Singer said cheerfully. "Run get Jango for us."

At the mention of Jango's name, the spell was broken and two of the teens broke off to be absorbed into the night in search of him. Jango apparently carried some weight among his neighbors.

It's not hard to see why. Though physically unremarkable—at 29, he has a typical African physique born of backbreaking labor, a wide friendly face, and a collection of scars from shrapnel and bullet wounds—his history as a longtime prisoner of the RUF has afforded him a certain degree of respect among his peers. And the fact that he now helps the RUF sell their diamonds to people like Singer has only added to his mystique, now seen as a man willing to overlook the atrocities of the war to become a businessman. The only business worth doing in a place like Freetown, as everyone knew, was brokering illegal diamonds. If those diamonds came from people who beat and tortured him for 18 months in the bush, well . . . the money to be earned was well worth putting that aside.

Singer introduced me and soon left to conduct other business. Jango showed me to his room: As narrow as a closet, the door opened against the bed just enough to allow a thin person to squeeze inside. A tattered American flag was hung over the bars on the window as a curtain and a small shelf held a collection of personal belongings: toothbrush, cassette player, ashtray.

In the gloom, he showed me his wounds and told me about his time with the RUF.

WITHIN A FEW DAYS of the commencement of Operation Clean Sweep, the 1996 operation in which Ismael Dalramy lost his hands to an RUF ax, Jango was awakened in the middle of the night by a rocket blast. He was sleeping in the open, huddled under a palm tree and some bushes, near an open pit diamond mine, forced by his RUF captors to sleep far from the rest of the prisoners because he snored so loudly that they feared detection. But on this night, his snoring may have saved his life. The Kamajors had consulted their jungle gods and were told that success in attacking the RUF position was imminent. There's no light in the depth of the jungle at night, not even starlight because of the canopy, and Jango was dead blind when the first detonation rippled through the trees. He sprang to his feet to flee into the night, running instinctively toward the rest of the RUF contingent, simply because they had guns and he didn't and, as their prisoner, he was worth protecting. He hoped.

He never found out. Streaking through the forest suddenly alive with the hammering of automatic weapons fire and the mad designs of tracer bullets ricocheting off coconut trees, he heard a whoosh that was getting louder than all the other sounds. He turned just in time to see a rocket-propelled grenade sailing toward him like a neon football. Only random luck saved his life: His forward momentum carried him behind a tree, which immediately exploded with the rocket's impact, blasting shards of wood into his upper left arm. Jango flew into a hole, a small pit he and his fellow prisoners had just begun excavating for diamond exploration, reeling headfirst into the muddy water, just as the tree toppled behind him with a deafening crunch. He screamed underwater and surfaced to the sound of bullets zipping over the hole like supercharged hummingbirds, rockets pulverizing trees, screams of death from his captors and their enemies, a strobe-light world where there was no up or down.

He passed out from the pain in his arm sometime around dawn, when the shooting slowed, but was replaced with the more menacing sounds of Mende whispers—the language of the Kamajors. Hours later, however, he awoke to find everyone gone and the water in the hole tinged pink from the blood he'd pumped into it. Jango was in big trouble.

The main problem is that he had no idea where he was. He'd been kidnapped in Sefadu, a Kono District diamond-mining village that is Koidu's adjacent sister town, nearly a month before the attack and had been marched through the woods from one mine to another so often that he had no idea how far he'd walked or in which direction. He may have had a better sense of where he was if he'd been selected to be one of the RUF's mules, men who do nothing but walk back and forth to the Liberian border, carrying diamonds one way and returning with shiny new RPG tubes and crates of rifle ammunition. But he was just a digger and he didn't know if he was in RUF territory or Kamajor territory. And he had no idea where to find help for his injured arm. Sitting in his Freetown bedroom, he pointed to the mass of scar tissue on his upper arm and said he spent three weeks staggering lost in the bush, eating nothing but mangos, hiding from voices and approaching footsteps.

Eventually, he made his way to a village. From his vantage point in the trees, it was clear there was no one there but RUF, young men and women lounging on eviscerated pickup trucks and on the crumbling cinderblock walls of front porches, their rifles and machine guns slung on their backs recklessly, the scene highlighted with the soft orange glow of cook-fires in the early evening. Things seemed calm enough, Jango thought, and he'd already decided that he would take his chances with the RUF if he ran across them. His only option was to continue wandering in the forest. The smell of cooking chicken made his decision all the easier.

He nervously left the thick bush and walked into the town. Some people stared at him and his now-infected wound and some didn't pay him any attention at all. He made it to the *barrie,* an open-walled structure in the center of town used for community gatherings in more peaceful times, and lay down on the ground in an attempt to be inconspicuous, evaluating his next move.

The mood was tense; many of the fighters seemed drunk and boisterous, sucking on "gin-blasters," little plastic sleeves of alcohol like thawed freezer popsicles. Diamond smugglers from the Mandingo tribe hung out in the shadows, ready to deal with the RUF for their stones, to negotiate a trade or arrange a shipment. A female RUF fighter was arguing with a young man. Cheap transistor radios played rap music at a volume that completely distorted the tunes.

Jango was considering retreat. He knew that the moment he approached anyone for help he would be the center of the rebels' drunken attention. Before he had time to decide what to do, all of his choices were taken away.

The two arguing RUF fighters escalated their disagreement. The man was mocking the woman because he recognized her as a prostitute from Freetown. He was offering her diamonds to sleep with the entire battalion and everyone in earshot was laughing at her.

Drunk on gin and power, the girl—not older than 16 or 17—whipped her AK-47 off her shoulder and chambered a round. "I'm going to blow your fucking balls off," she announced casually and aimed at his crotch.

What happened next took less than a second, Jango recalls: Laughter cut off immediately, as if everyone in the square realized at the same moment that she was serious. The man standing at the end of the barrel twirled, his right foot lifted. He knocked the barrel aside just as she pulled the trigger. The round flew across the square and blew a hole in Jango's right calf. It was the first time anyone noticed that he was there and he screamed into the night, suddenly surrounded by RUF, all of them screaming right back at him: "Who the fuck are you?" "What the fuck are you doing here?"

Jango opened his eyes to see a smiling Mandingo face next to his. "Hey boy," the man whispered, "they're trying to kill you because they think you have diamonds. Sell them to me right now and it will save your life. I'll give you a good price."

Telling me the story later, Jango said he regretted that he was jerked away so quickly that he couldn't even tell the man to go fuck himself.

SOON AFTER HE WAS SHOT and recaptured by this new band of RUF, Jango was back at work, stripped to his blue brief underwear and standing up to his thighs in muddy water, slinging rocks and dirt around and around in a circular shake-shake. He churned the water with an abandon to task that is all too often found only in young children and prisoners of war. With four or five other prisoners, he was washing away the silt and clay from the stones, eyes trained to look for the gray, opaque ones.

On the banks of the shallow pit where he toiled, men with guns guarded his work, smoking. Other prisoners brought water and food, or just lingered, squatting in the shade of banana trees, staring at a group of soldiers kicking a soccer ball that sometimes caromed off a bare foot and into the water.

When the wind blew from the east, it sometimes carried the sound of small and highly maneuverable Nigerian alpha jets assigned to the ECOMOG force and the flat patter of small-arms fire.

If he heard these things, Jango didn't reveal it. He was there to find the special rocks, not listen to the wind. Even the pain in his leg and arm didn't distract him from the job. He'd given up, determined to do his job well and hope that he would eat that day. He was working on the "two-pile" system, an RUF digging regimen that allowed prisoners to keep any diamonds found in a pile of gravel he was allowed to wash for himself, but he suspected that it was rigged. He'd not found a diamond in weeks in the piles of gravel designated as "his," but he'd been finding quite a few in those designated as RUF piles.

Around and around and around. Finally, he stopped sloshing his sieve, staring down into the soup of mud and gravel it contained. The sudden presence of four AK barrels shoved into his face confirmed what his eyes suspected. A hand reached in and plucked out a stone and dipped it in the water, rubbing away the stubborn clay. In the rebel's hand was a medium-sized rock, gray and white in color, about the size of a small marble. Jango knew from experience that it was probably six or seven carats.

"Boss!" the guard yelled, holding it up between his finger and thumb.

A man on the bank smiled and winked at the boy as the gem was carefully passed to him from hand to hand. The man snatched it up and held it to the sun.

Another diamond began its journey.

REBEL FIELD WORKERS are lucky to end their days exhausted and hungry. Many have ended them in a shallow grave. Workers sleep by the sides of the mine and wake at first light to begin the day's digging. Except for the fact that the labor isn't voluntary and men with rifles guard the prisoners' every move, the process of extracting the jewels from the ground is identical to that in the licensed mines.

Capturing a diamond mine is as easy as showing up with a rifle and ordering everyone in the pit to start handing their discoveries over to the new bosses. The RUF sometimes sweetens the deal by offering to share the loot with the diggers, an arrangement that seems to the workers like a better offer than the rice and pennies they get from their legitimate bosses, as long as they overlook the fact that their bosses won't kill them if they refuse. In addition to the "two-pile" method, which was favored by those who guarded Jango, some units instead allowed prisoners to dig for four days for the RUF, two days for themselves, and have one day off. Even then, however, most diamonds the diggers were allowed to keep were comparatively worthless industrial-grade stones or very small gemstones worth little in the bush. The good stones, it was clear, went to the RUF. Those who refused or argued faced being shot on the spot. Walking away was not an option. Most diggers complied quickly. But given the frequent alcohol- and drug-fueled rages of their captors, thoughts immediately turned to escape.

Running away was a near impossibility, although it had been done. Within days, the RUF captors have broken the men physically by denying them food and water and working them to exhaustion. Few prisoners would have been able to run far and, even if they could, a sprint into the forest would only lead to another RUF unit that might not be as willing to allow them to keep their hands, feet, or lives. But in the bush, diamonds are a currency even more valuable than guns, loyalty to a tribe of warriors, or belief in an ideology. If a digger was clever enough to steal or earn a cache of rough, and lucky enough to offer them to the right person, he may be able to buy himself out of slavery.

Stealing from the RUF is an often fatal practice, however, essentially an African form of Russian roulette. Jango recalled one man who was found with a large diamond tucked into his lip. RUF soldiers slashed open the belly of his pregnant wife and removed the fetus with a bayonet. The fetus died immediately and the wife soon bled to death. The man was tied to the corpses, doused with gasoline, and set ablaze, all on the edge of the mine, in view of the remaining diggers, who were forced to continue their work.

Stealing the good diamonds before they made it into the hands of the RUF overseers was a risky but irresistible undertaking. One technique was particularly ingenious. When learning to wash gravel in the shake-shakes, one of the first tricks a digger learns is to flip a sieve-full of water onto his face without losing all the gravel, a quick way to cool off under the African sun without having to pause work. Seeing the men dousing themselves with mine water was a common enough sight, but RUF prisoners learned to also flip diamonds into the air with the water and catch them in their mouths, whereupon they were instantly swallowed.

Swallowing the diamond is only part of the chore, of course. Retrieving it and keeping it hidden were also difficult.

Over the course of 18 months—after he was recaptured and accidentally shot in the leg—Jango managed to amass six pieces, mostly through the dangerous practice of simply palming the stones once he found them and sliding them into his mouth when the opportunity presented itself. He later hid them in a cigarette pack that he buried in the ground near where he slept.

He'd already begun talking to some of the Mandingo traders who visited Kono, middlemen who organized the transactions between the RUF field commanders and banks, arms dealers, and expatriate rebel bosses in Conakry and Monrovia. Depending on the greed of individual RUF commanders, the needs of the fighting force, and the deals that were cut from day to day, the diamonds were sold in the bush to Mandingos or they were physically walked to Liberia to be traded at the border for weapons. The weapons deals were much more tightly organized—a mule team of twenty-five prisoners guarded by five RUF would hike to the border, load up with weapons, and hike back.

If a commander wanted a retirement fund, fresh clothes, or a new car, however, he dealt with the Mandingos. The system is ridiculously easy. A few good stones are passed in the jungle and a new car—or clothes or electronics—is purchased for cash in Conakry. The merchandise can be delivered to the buyer in the forest or it can be stored in Guinea for later pickup.

The nomadic Mandingos were also largely responsible, according to the UN, for trafficking Sierra Leone diamonds to points on the west coast beyond Conakry and Monrovia, as if they get cleaner the farther they're moved from the scene of the crime. Places like The Gambia are as notorious as Liberia in terms of its reputation as a conflict-diamond laundry. The Gambia has no diamond mines and yet managed to export to Belgium some $100 million worth of diamonds between 1996 and 1999, the height of RUF mining activity. Every one of the Belgian companies that imports stones from The Gambia also imports them from Sierra Leone, Liberia, and Guinea. The explanation is that there are nomadic traders like Mandingos wandering the coast looking for buyers—for some reason, they often find their way to The Gambia, which has been described as a mini-Antwerp by the UN—and the Gambian exporters are simply and legally buying rough on the open market. But the only reason the diamonds would be in The Gambia, one unidentified company admitted to UN investigators, is because they were smuggled there to avoid export taxes in another country or to hide their pedigree as conflict goods. One estimate put 90 percent of all goods exported from The Gambia as likely coming from Sierra Leone.

Farther to the east, the same is true of Ivory Coast: The country is capable of producing about 75,000 carats a year from its modest mines but somehow managed to export thirteen times that amount from 1994 to 1999. The Mandingos represent a subcommunity of illicit traffickers and they didn't care who they dealt with, captor or prisoner, if it meant getting good stones. If you wanted to escape forced labor in an RUF mine, you traded diamonds to the Mandingos for your life.[10]

But before Jango was able to take the final step of offering a few of his stones to one of the dealers in exchange for being ferreted out of the mine, he was presented with another opportunity: a brand new mountain bike, left recklessly in one of the small hamlets near the mining complex by its owner. Seizing the chance, Jango walked as casually as he could over to the bike, calmly mounted it, and rode away on it, six hot rocks in his pocket.

But his escape wasn't to be without some drama. After peddling all day through the green tunnel of the rain forest, he stopped to rest at another village. He still had no idea where he was, but the bristling barrels of AK-47s jutting from over most shoulders told him that he was still deep in RUF territory. Jango managed to blend in and everyone assumed that he was also a rebel. After a meal and some water, he prepared to mount his bike and continue the journey. A soldier asked him for a cigarette and, perhaps lulled into a sense of safety by his good luck, Jango withdrew a battered pack of 555 cigarettes. Three diamonds fell out of a hole in the bottom of the pack as he was reaching in for a smoke.

Instinctively, Jango slid his foot over the stones lying on the ground, but the soldier had seen them too. Like a cheerleader nimbly handling a baton, the rebel whipped his AK off his shoulder and drew the bolt.

"Move your foot," he ordered quietly. No one else was paying attention; the sight of people pointing guns at one another, even those in the same unit, was common enough among the RUF. Jango did as he was told and the stones glittered up, reflecting the equatorial sunlight as only diamonds can.

The soldier bent down and picked them up. "Good stones," he said, rolling them around in the palm of his hand. Jango nodded.

"What do you want for them?"

On the run, fresh from imprisonment, certain he would die before the end of the day, Jango made his first diamond sale. With that one transaction, he became a businessman, arranging sales between the RUF in Kono and smugglers like Singer in Freetown.

3

THE GUN RUNNERS:
From Tongo to Tiffany's

Monrovia, Liberia

O SMAN WAS A MAN whose malignancy ensured him an invisible bubble of personal space. Everywhere he went, people moved out of the way. Children scattered before him like chickens, glancing quickly over their shoulders to see if he was going to follow them into stone doorways or around corners. A small but powerful-looking man with a face like a wrinkled sponge, Osman was a heavy drinker who liked to brandish sharp knives, and there was no telling when he would reach the point of inebriation that would cause him to whip out a blade and scream that he was the baddest former RUF soldier in Freetown. His reputation was so fierce that his battle-group name was General Motherfucker.

The fact that this was not true only increased the berth people give him. Only a lunatic, they figured, would proudly claim to have fought with the RUF when in fact he was their prisoner for nearly two years. In his lucid moments, when he was not menacing neighbors with knives and cutlasses, even Osman himself would admit that he was probably quite insane. He only purported to have been RUF, he said, because admitting to being a victim was too humiliating.

It's easy to see that Osman was once a powerful man; his body has maintained the shape and muscle tone, but now he's stooped and steps gingerly, as if in constant pain. A miner by trade, Osman was popular in Kono before the war because of his beautiful singing voice. Instead of trading diamonds to profess their love, couples preparing for marriage would hire Osman to sing tribal love songs at their ceremonies. Like Jango, Osman was captured by the RUF during Operation Clean Sweep.

When Jango and hundreds like him found diamonds, the stones were placed in leather bags and delivered to units like the one that imprisoned Osman. He was a prisoner of the so-called Bastard Brigade—it was composed of orphans—and his commander was a man who called himself Man Friday. Osman's job was simple: He walked nonstop from the Kono mines to the Liberian border near Kailahun—a 50-mile round-trip—and back again, repeatedly, for two years. He and twenty-four other mules were guarded by five heavily armed RUF soldiers who threatened to chop their Achilles tendons with machetes if they didn't keep up a quick pace through the forest. On the way to Liberia, the prisoners carried only food and water. The RUF carried the diamonds and Osman has still never laid eyes on one. "Prisoners were never allowed to see the stones," he said.

Once at the border, they would meet Liberians with crates of ammunition and weapons in the beds of pickup trucks and larger trucks belonging to timber companies, whose owners had close connections to Liberian president Charles Taylor. They traded the diamonds for the guns, a simple transaction in which the bag of diamonds was given to whomever was in charge of the Liberian group. Once everything was in order, Osman and the other prisoners would be loaded up. They carried brand new rifles and RPG tubes at the head of the line, while the ammo and grenades were carried at the rear so that the prisoners would be less likely to stage a revolt. Then they would cross back into Sierra Leone and return to the mines, the most difficult and dangerous part of the journey. The mules were required to carry up to 100 kilos of equipment each, and a twisted ankle, fatigue, or even a slow pace was enough of an excuse for their RUF captors to shoot them and dump their bodies in the woods. Then the others would have to divide the unfortunate man's load, making it all the more difficult for them to avoid a similar fate.

The life span of a mule was not long. Even if they avoided tripping, managed to keep up with the RUF, and somehow maintained enough health to keep going, it was only a matter of time before their bodies wore down. Osman began having debilitating back pain and severe arthritis in his arms and shoulders. He knew he was drawing closer to earning himself a bullet.

Before he met that fate, however, on another munitions trading trip his mule train was mistaken for an RUF patrol and attacked by Kamajors who exploded from the jungle, belching horizontal fireworks from the carpet of foliage. Osman watched as a Kamajor, barefoot and clad only in camouflage shorts and a wool ski hat decorated with fetishes and shotgun shells, walked from the woods directly up to one of the other prisoners—who was frozen with shock and fear—and shot him in the face with a double-barreled sawed-off shotgun. He said he'd never seen anything as frightening as that attack. The Kamajors seemed unaware that the RUF soldiers were returning fire, as they were wildly killing most of those in the prisoner column and smearing their faces and chests with the blood of the vanquished. As he was about to be killed himself, by a man wielding a sword, he was recognized by one of the Kamajors. Osman explained that half the dead littering the footpath were prisoners and the Kamajors, after dispatching the RUF guards, turned the survivors free. They took a massive cache of diamonds from Man Friday's body and bled back into the bush.

Within a week of being turned loose by the Kamajors, Osman managed to hitch a ride to Freetown, where he embarked on his ongoing relationship with palm wine, gradually losing his mind to the things he'd seen.

THE AK-47 ASSAULT RIFLE is the bread and butter of armed conflicts the world over. Now used by more than fifty armies, the weapon was invented in 1947 by Red Army soldier Mikhail Kalashnikov and adopted for regular use in the Soviet army in 1949. Its distinctive crescent-shaped magazine holds 30 rounds of 7.62×39-millimeter cartridges that can be fired at a rate of 400 rounds per minute, with a muzzle velocity of 2,240 feet per second. Loaded, the AK-47 weighs almost 11 pounds, light enough for a medium-sized child to carry with little difficulty, and because of the simple chamber/action design it is almost impossible to jam. Tooling standards were kept intentionally loose so it could withstand serious abuse on the battlefield; therefore, AKs tend to rattle a lot when fired on full automatic and they don't even need to be properly assembled for them to function or even be reasonably accurate. Made from as much stamped metal and as little milled metal as possible to keep manufacturing costs low, AKs are cheap. Kalashnikov firearms are a guerilla's best friend and Sierra Leone is awash in them.

The United Nations has active arms embargoes on both Sierra Leone and Liberia, while the Economic Community of West African States (ECOWAS) has instituted an arms moratorium over all fifteen of its member states.[1] Arms-producing countries have signed an agreement to voluntarily monitor and control their arms exports to unstable regions. Nevertheless, West Africa is up to its armpits in weapons.

Because of their diamond wealth, throughout most of the war the RUF was better armed than its adversaries. Diamonds bought Kalashnikovs by the hundreds, Browning 12.7-millimeter heavy machine guns by the tens of dozens, and ammunition in million-block orders. Light artillery included rocket-propelled grenades, mortars, and SA-7 shoulder-launched surface-to-air missiles. The RUF bought helicopters for resupply and, whenever they could, they stole trucks, armored fighting vehicles, and armored personnel carriers from the Sierra Leone Army and ECOMOG. The RUF funded all this with proceeds from illegal diamond mining.[2]

In order to trade their diamonds for rifles and ammunition, RUF rebels had to rely on the sympathetic government of President Charles Taylor in Liberia. A Lebanese businessman named Talal El-Ndine, a close aide of Taylor's, provided the vital link for weapons transactions: He not only distributed pay to Liberian and RUF diamond smugglers bringing goods across the border, but he then sold the goods to diamond merchants who in turn exported them to Belgium. El-Ndine paid cash to a small cadre of arms smugglers who flew weapons unimpeded from Eastern Europe to Liberia for use in Sierra Leone.[3]

The process of running guns into West Africa seems to be as easy as smuggling diamonds out, although there are more strategic hurdles. Airspace over Africa's west coast is largely as anonymous as it was before the invention of the airplane. Even some important regional airports lack such basic avionics as radar, allowing all sorts of planes from every imaginable origin to fly completely unde- tected anywhere they like. The only things that can see the entirety of West African airspace are U.S. spy satellites, but they can be avoided simply by flying at night. The precision and high degree of organization of the RUF's gunrunning operations is a powerful tes- tament to the financial might of the diamonds they mine and sell to unsuspecting jewelers and lovers throughout the world. Almost none of it would be possible without the active participation of Liberia and its despotic leader, President Taylor.

For one thing, Liberia provides a safe harbor for anyone wishing to keep their aircraft sheltered from scrutiny, and a Liberian corpo- rate identity can be obtained in one day without the need to list officers, owners, or shareholders. Once an airplane is registered in Liberia, it can be based in another country and used anywhere in the world, often leaving little evidence of its travels.

At least fifteen aircraft identified by the UN as being involved in gunrunning, and purporting to be registered with Liberia's Civil Aviation Regulatory Authority, weren't among the mere seven planes the country claims to have registered. One of the missing planes is an Ilyushin 76, a Liberian "registered" plane based at the Sharjah Airport in the United Arab Emirates that is alleged to have couriered weapons to Angola, Congo, and Sierra Leone via Liberia throughout the 1990s. Owned by a Tajik-born former KGB officer named Victor Bout, the UN is aware of at least four flights this plane has made into Liberia in 2000 to deliver cargo that included military helicopters, spare rotors, antitank and antiair- craft systems, missiles, armored vehicles, machine guns, and ammunition. As a UN report notes: "It is difficult to conceal some- thing the size of an Mi-17 military helicopter, and the supply of such items to Liberia cannot go undetected by customs authorities in originating countries unless there are false flight plans and end-user certificates, or unless customs officials at points of exit are paid to look the other way. The constant involvement of Bout's aircraft in arms shipments from eastern Europe into African war zones suggests the latter."[4]

Liberia and Sierra Leone are two of the poorest countries on earth, and arranging illegal arms shipments from Eastern Europe is no inexpensive endeavor. The diamonds that Osman and hundreds of others helped ferret to the Liberian border are the only currency available to facilitate such a far-reaching scheme to deliver guns into remote jungles. The diamonds are either converted into hard cash—U.S. dollars or euros—through merchants who visit Monrovia regularly to buy diamonds and take them back to Belgium, or the gems themselves are used as payment to pilots like Bout, who finds his own markets for them.

Bout is said to own about fifty aircraft through dozens of small airline companies. Though most of his aircraft stay in the UAE, he's used the Liberian registry to, in a sense, launder their identity and thwart regulators. Prior to using the Liberian flag for his planes, he registered them through Swaziland unbeknown to that country's government. When it discovered the fraud, Swaziland deregistered forty-three aircraft owned by Bout and reported the action to the civil registry of UAE because it suspected that they were used for weapons trafficking, noting that Bout's airplanes "did not operate from Swaziland."[5]

The four known 2000 shipments were coordinated with the help of a Kenyan named Sanjivan Ruprah, who, like most others in the sordid diamonds-for-weapons tapestry, also has a colorful history of intrigue. Ruprah was associated with Branch Energy–Kenya, a company that in the late 1990s owned diamond-mining rights in Sierra Leone, which were acquired from the South African mercenary corporation Executive Outcomes.

Ruprah was tapped by Charles Taylor to act as his "Global Civil Aviation Agent Worldwide" for the Liberian Civil Aviation Regulatory Authority. Ostensibly, his job was to track down illegally registered airplanes like those owned by Bout; according to the UN, his job actually involved helping those aircraft deliver weapons to the RUF. In the summer of 2000, aircraft supposedly carrying attack helicopters bound for Ivory Coast landed in Abidjan under the authorization of a company called Abidjan Freight, a front company set up by Ruprah to disguise the routing of Bout's cargo and its final destination. In truth, the planes were empty. The choppers had been off-loaded in Monrovia.[6]

Bout is hardly alone in this business. Another major player is Israeli businessman Leonid Menin, a Ukrainian-born arms trafficker who uses the RUF-sympathetic government of Burkina Faso to facilitate his deliveries. An extensively documented case study of one delivery demonstrates both the complexity and the far-reaching nature of how AK-47s move from distant manufacturing plants to the bush, transactions that take place solely through the RUF's sale of diamonds into legitimate trading channels.

ON MAY 13, 1999, 68 TONS of weapons arrived in Ouagadougou, the capital of Burkina Faso. The manifest listed 715 crates of small arms and ammunition, antitank weapons, surface-to-air missiles, and RPG tubes and warheads. The shipment was part of a contract between a Gibraltar-based acquisitions company acting on behalf of the Burkina Faso Ministry of Defense and a Ukrainian arms manufacturer. A license for the sale was granted by the

Ukrainian government after it received an end-user certificate for Burkina Faso. Legitimate arms sales must have such certificates, as well as a slew of other paperwork, such as an export license, an airway bill, and a detailed manifest of the cargo. The end-user certificate permitted the Gibraltar company to purchase the weapons on behalf of Burkina Faso and meant that only Burkina Faso could use the weapons. The certificate was signed by Lieutenant Colonel Gilbert Diendéré, head of Burkina Faso's Presidential Guard. A British airline under contract with a Ukrainian freight company delivered the cargo to Ouagadougou.

But it didn't remain there long.

While the shipment was being prepared in Ukraine, a BAC-111 owned by Menin flew from Ibiza, Spain, to Monrovia. The aircraft was a VIP jetliner that had been used in 1998 and 1999 as Taylor's presidential jet. Taylor and Menin were close friends. An alleged art thief, mob boss, gunrunner, and money-launderer, Menin has been arrested dozens of times in several countries, travels under a variety of passports and aliases, and is barred from entering certain countries, including his home country, Ukraine. Menin's plane stayed at Robertsfield Airport in Monrovia until May 15, two days after the weapons shipment had arrived in Burkina Faso. For the remainder of the month, the plane made at least eight runs between Liberia and Burkina Faso, ferrying the weapons from one country to the other. Then it returned to Spain.

This wasn't the first time the plane is believed to have been used for gunrunning. While in use as Taylor's official diplomatic aircraft, it also made at least two flights to Niamey Airport in Niger, where it loaded up with weapons, and returned to Monrovia, where they were off-loaded onto Liberian military vehicles. This occurred only a few days before one of the RUF's bloodiest assaults, the infamous Operation No Living Thing conducted in Freetown on January 6, 1999.

While in Monrovia, the aircraft are stored in hangers at Roberts-field owned by Dutch national Gus Van Kouwenhoven, who had bought them from Emmanuel Shaw, Taylor's former finance minister. Van Kouwenhoven also owns the Hotel Africa in Monrovia, a popular place for gunrunning pilots to bed down on overnight stays.

Once the weapons are in Monrovia, they are driven to the Sierra Leone border in trucks owned by Van Kouwenhoven or Israeli businessman Simon Rosenblum. Both men own interests in timber companies operating within Liberia; Van Kouwenhoven's is Malaysian, Rosenblum's is based in Abidjan. Both companies are involved in building and maintaining roads within Liberia to facilitate timber traffic, and many of those roads are conveniently close to the Sierra Leone border and are used to transport weapons. Another close friend of Taylor, Rosenblum travels on a Liberian diplomatic passport.

At the border, the weapons are either walked into Sierra Leone via human mule-train or loaded onto trucks and armored personnel vehicles the RUF has stolen from ECOMOG or UNAMSIL during ambushes. In the past, helicopters that were delivered by Victor Bout would fly the weapons from their jungle bases in Liberia to the RUF's eastern Sierra Leone strongholds of Beudu or Kailahun.[7]

Such an operation is immensely expensive. A buyer must pay not only for the weapons but also for freight, fuel, transport, labor, and equipment for several arduous legs of a cross-continent journey, and there would have to be substantial kickbacks for participating countries like Burkina Faso, since charges of sanction-busting are serious and could carry heavy international consequences.

Every major player along the route, from the end-user signatory in Burkina Faso to the pilots to timber company representatives to the president of Liberia—as well as an untold number of government officials who provide cover through the issuance of diplomatic passports and aircraft registration—demands substantial compensation for their illegal work. And there was no lack of Sierra Leone's wealth to be found in Liberia for just that purpose. Liberia has its own diamond fields, but according to a report issued by Partnership Africa Canada, "While the estimates of Liberian diamond mining output are between 100,000 and 150,000 carats, the [Diamond High Council, based in Antwerp] records Liberian imports into Belgium of over 31 million carats between 1994 and 1998—an average of over six million carats a year."[8]

Most of the cash transactions take place in El-Ndine's office on Old Road in Monrovia. Pilots, arms traffickers, diamond smugglers, diamond buyers, and wheel-greasers of all shades meet there to get their cut of Sierra Leone's smuggled wealth.

ON THE OTHER SIDE of the front line, the Sierra Leone government was broke. It could barely afford to pay and feed its soldiers, much less equip them with top-notch military hardware.

The war in Sierra Leone reached one of its many murky lows in 1995. Ignored by every country in the world, including its neighbors, which either had their own problems to contend with or were actively helping the rebels, Sierra Leone was bankrupt and in danger of being overrun by the RUF. Refugee movement was cyclonic; they roamed everywhere—even into Liberia and back as, indeed, many Liberians were doing—looking for a safe haven, then picked up and moved again when they found none. The army was a shambles and most battles in the bush involved different factions blindly firing magazines of ammo toward the other and then running for cover. The recently formed Kamajor militia was armed with axes, spears, and the odd shotgun or two, hardly the arsenal needed to deal with the RUF's constantly resupplied stock of Kalashnikovs, FN rifles, and rocket launchers.

Equally problematic was the fact that, since the RUF launched its first attack in 1991, the Sierra Leone government has been a revolving door for one inept military leader after another. When the RUF first struck, the government was headed by a man named Joseph Momoh, the head of the Sierra Leone armed forces since 1971 who, in 1989, inherited a one-party government, a nonexistent economy, and a highly agitated and disenfranchised citizenry from his dictatorial predecessor, Saika Stevens.

By 1991, Sierra Leone was ripe for a revolution. Decades of government corruption and one-party rule under Stevens's iron fist had ruined the national economy to the point where Sierra Leone was one of the poorest countries on earth. In the early 1990s, while Freetown enjoyed modern amenities such as paved streets, fairly reliable electricity, and regular imports of foreign goods, the remaining 95 percent of the country was still living in the dark ages. Only one 50-mile stretch of road in the bush (out of 7,000 miles of roads) is reasonably enough paved to allow vehicles to travel the speed limit. Electricity in the larger towns like Bo and Makeni was generally unreliable, and farther east it was nonexistent except through Honda generators. Medical facilities and schools were woefully inadequate, if they existed at all. Slash-and-burn agriculture struggled to sustain a population that was multiplying with each passing year. Diseases like polio, malaria, and river blindness plagued those living in the bush and many felt that they'd been completely forgotten by their government in Freetown. And looming over all this unrest was the indignation of foreign-controlled diamond mines and the presence of wealthy Lebanese merchants. If these rocks were as valuable as everyone says they are, the sentiment was, then why aren't the rural villagers benefiting from them?

Along with three other Sierra Leoneans schooled in the "art of revolution" by Libyan president Colonel Muammar Qaddafi, former Sierra Leone Army (SLA) corporal Foday Sankoh trained about 100 men in northwestern Liberian camps run by Taylor's rebellion, the National Patriotic Front of Liberia (NPFL). In 1991, Sankoh's soldiers of the newly formed Revolutionary United Front marched into Sierra Leone and captured Kailahun District.

At first, the RUF was greeted as a heroic army that would return the country to a multiparty government that could achieve better equity in wealth distribution. The best way to get the current government's attention, it seemed, was to capture some of their diamond mines, holding them for ransom for a more democratic system and a brighter future for the majority of the country's citizens, who lived much like their ancestors had in the provinces.

But instead of rolling into the diamond areas and seeking the support of the locals, the RUF killed and mutilated them. Composed of mostly uneducated youths with no other outlet for their sense of disenfranchisement, the RUF was quickly revealed as an army of murderous thugs rather than justice-seeking rebels. RUF fighters fueled this impression at every opportunity. Field commanders adopted nicknames that both inspired terror and revealed their ruthlessness. Soldiers were named Rambo, Blood Master, Blood Center, What Trouble, and Wicked to Women. Their "tactics" of warfare were unbelievably brutal. Sometimes, after capturing a village, RUF fighters would gather civilian prisoners in the town square and make them choose small strips of paper from the ground that described different forms of torture and death, such as "chop off hands," "chop off head," or simply "be killed." Soldiers would bet with one another about the sex of pregnant women's unborn children. Winners were determined after the baby had been removed from the womb with a bayonet. In one instance, a young boy was beaten and roasted nearly to death on a spit in front of his mother for refusing to kill her. The RUF's depravity served a military strategy: It induced tectonic population shifts away from the diamond areas.

Ibrahim Abdullah and Patrick Muana, writing in a compendium of articles about African guerilla movements, describe the RUF's goals, or lack thereof, as succinctly as anyone:

> The RUF has defied all available typologies on guerilla movements. It is neither a separatist uprising rooted in a specific demand, as in the case of Eritrea, nor a reformist movement with a radical agenda superior to the regime it sought to overthrow. Nor does it possess the kind of leadership that would be necessary to designate it as [a] warlord insurgency. The RUF has made history; it is a peculiar guerilla movement without any significant national following or ethnic support. Perhaps because of its lumpen social base and its lack of an emancipatory programme to garner support from other social groups, it has remained a bandit organization solely driven by the survivalist needs of its predominantly uneducated and alienated battle front and battle group commanders. Neither the peasantry, the natural ally of most revolutionary movements, nor the students, amongst whose ranks the RUF-to-be originated, lent any support to the organization during its [first] six years of fighting.[9]

The RUF's almost instant alienation of the people they were purportedly fighting on behalf of allowed Momoh to rally a defense by dispatching the Sierra Leone Army to quell the uprising, a force that was bolstered with a formidable—but totally undisciplined—"volunteer brigade" of bums and criminals from Freetown.

Momoh acted as any head of state would have by dispatching the army to deal with the insurgency, but unlike most other heads of state, he neglected to pay his soldiers. And those soldiers got stomped. Sierra Leone has never been at war with anything other than itself and the army was poorly prepared to fight in the bush against the comparatively more astute and better-armed RUF, whose leaders had been trained in guerilla warfare by Libyan leader Qaddafi. In fact, other than participating in the odd coup once or twice a decade, Sierra Leone Army soldiers were mostly called upon to carry the national flag during federal holidays and march at arms at Lungi Airport when important foreign diplomats paid a visit. And now they were getting slaughtered in their own jungles and not getting paid for it.

In 1992, 27-year-old SLA Captain Valentine Strasser decided that enough was enough and marched a band of soldiers from the battlefield in the Kailahun District back to Freetown to demand their pay. When that failed within hours of arriving, he persuaded his followers to join him in overthrowing the government. The coup was popular in Freetown: Momoh had been promising a return to multiparty politics under mounting pressure from citizens who'd had enough ineffective one-party leadership, but he'd used the war with the RUF as an excuse to postpone elections. Strasser set up the National Provisional Ruling Council, the NPRC, and was sworn in as the youngest head of state in Sierra Leone's history. Despite the fact that later in 1992 he executed twenty-five people suspected of plotting a countercoup, he was a popular leader. He instituted a monthly program called National Cleaning Day, during which the country virtually shuts down while residents clean their yards and roadways, successfully campaigned for residents to pay their income taxes, and promised elections and a return to civilian rule by 1995.

But these efforts paled in comparison to the ongoing slaughter taking place in the provinces. The RUF cranked up its efforts to capture diamond fields and, by 1994, the northern and eastern portions of the country had descended into complete anarchy, a murderous black hole where only the AK-47 held authority. Diamond fields fell one after the other and the RUF was on course to roll straight into Freetown before the end of the year. In 1995, Strasser made a bold and controversial decision that delayed the inevitable fall of Freetown: He hired a private army to fight the RUF.

The use of mercenaries in warfare is as old as human conflict itself. In the words of P. J. O'Rourke, war is a great asshole magnet, attracting all types of human flotsam to the battlefield for reasons of their own. American mercenaries fought with the Croatian Army in the Balkans while Russian soldiers of fortune fought for their enemies, the Serbs, on the other side of the front lines. In any conflict involving Muslim forces, mujahideen fighters trekked from Iran, Saudia Arabia, and Afghanistan to help the cause. Some do it for the money, some for the thrill of killing, some for ideology. In Africa, the man who symbolized the international diamond industry, De Beers founder Cecil Rhodes, used an army of mercenaries in 1893 to beat down the Matabele people in what is now Zimbabwe; each soldier who volunteered was given nine square miles of land and two gold claims, an amount that equaled roughly

10,000 pounds sterling. Rhodes conquered the territory for the sake of his British South Africa Company, a gold-mining venture, and he named the country Rhodesia, after himself.

But while mercenaries of old still exist—that is, men who will fight for any cause so long as the price is right—they tend to be both unreliable and unprofessional. Within the past few decades, some former soldiers have changed the face of "mercenaries" into legitimate private armies, run by companies with articles of incorporation, profits and losses, and strict codes of conduct. The first company Strasser hired was Gurkha Security Guards, under the leadership of American Vietnam veteran Robert MacKenzie. Ironically, prior to going to Sierra Leone, MacKenzie had served in the Rhodesian Army.

MacKenzie's efforts in Sierra Leone didn't bear much fruit. After two weeks of training SLA and Kamajor fighters in the bush, he was killed in an RUF ambush near Port Loko, near the coast. Rumor has it that his remains were eaten by the RUF. The remainder of the Gurkha force refused to mount a counteroffensive and their contract was quickly canceled.

Strasser turned next to Executive Outcomes, a South African security company that is to private armies what De Beers is to diamonds. Founded in 1989 by Eeben Barlow, a former South African special forces officer, EO is either the embodiment of all the worst things about mercenaries or a source of stability and security in a continent that has been effectively abandoned by Europe and America to fend for itself. It depends on whom you ask.

EO's operations are necessarily shady. It's known that the company has worked extensively in Angola against the UNITA rebels, who also illegally mine and sell diamonds, and in Papua New Guinea and perhaps Colombia. The company is capable of rapidly deploying a battalion-strength force almost anywhere in the world with impressive asset support. EO owns a slew of armored fighting vehicles: two Boeing 727s and a C-47, attack aircraft such as Mi-24 gunships and two MiG-23/27 fighter planes, and all manner of light and medium artillery. According to its glossy brochures, EO provides its clients (either directly or through affiliated companies) military training and VIP protection; gold, diamond, and oil exploration and mining; airline transport; civil engineering; and even a chartered accountancy and offshore financial management services. Finally, EO also provides its own Russian technicians, medical support, intelligence, and infrared photo reconnaissance, and, before the company dissolved in 1999, was reportedly contracting with private firms to provide satellite imagery. With fourteen permanent staff at the time of its intervention in Sierra Leone, EO maintained a database of possible recruits numbering around 2,000.[10]

Hiring Executive Outcomes was not cheap, but if Strasser's government lacked money, it surely had diamond mines and exploration concessions to give away. A contract was signed with EO that in effect legalized war bounty. If the company could rout the rebels from the diamond areas, the government would grant it rights to those mines. EO has done this before—most notably in Angola—and was familiar with handling the complexities of the arrangement. Sierra Leone quickly saw its only decisive military victory against the rebels. A mercenary force of about 200 men, supported by an Mi-24 gunship, retrained the SLA and in a matter of weeks drove the RUF back from the capital and recaptured the country's diamond mines, including the most valuable ones in Kono. EO's presence provided Freetown's only period of stability and security—however brief—throughout the 1990s. The company established an effective intelligence service in Sierra Leone, which still operates; rebuilt supply and communications networks; and trained and equipped the Kamajors.

The government paid EO in diamond-mining concessions and EO promptly sold the rights to a close "friend," Branch Energy Limited. Branch Energy is incorporated through South Africa and the Isle of Man and is a wholly owned subsidiary of Diamond-Works, a Canadian exploration company. Not surprisingly, the company has a checkered past in African war zones. In Angola in 1997, Branch hired a security company called Teleservices that was owned by Executive Outcomes. Its responsibility was to secure future mining regions so that Branch could begin operations. Tele-service's security apparatus was headed by South African J. C. Erasmus, a man the South African *Weekly Mail & Guardian* called a "former member of apartheid South Africa's notorious Civil Co-operation Bureau death squad." Erasmus told a reporter for the newspaper that Branch and EO were "good friends."[11]

Combined with Branch's new EO-gained holdings in Sierra Leone, the company owned two kimberlite complexes, four alluvial fields, two minor development projects, and one exploration project in two African war zones. The holdings were said to potentially yield 20 million carats, with production peaking at over a million carats per year.[12] DiamondWorks later took over Branch's Sierra Leone operations, but the company still maintains a presence. (British press reports that EO owned 40 percent of Branch Energy have been repeatedly and vociferously denied by DiamondWorks representatives, who claim that there is no connection at all between the mercenary company and their diamond companies.)

IN SPITE OF THE IMPRESSIVE RESULTS of the EO operation, many world leaders balked at the morality of hiring private soldiers to conduct war for governments. Never mind that for years

Europe and America had been promising funds to train and equip a pan-African peacekeeping force that never materialized and that Executive Outcomes had prevented a coup against Strasser and an untold number of civilian deaths at the hands of the RUF, and had also effectively ended illegal diamond mining. The message from the world community was clear: Get rid of EO or else. That was more or less the directive from the International Monetary Fund, which was withholding financial aid on those very grounds.

Strasser capitulated and canceled the EO contract. The company's helicopters were barely out of sight when chaos erupted again. In January 1996 he was overthrown in a coup led by Julius Bio and the RUF once again captured the diamond areas, including those in Kono. Nevertheless, previously scheduled elections were held two months later and Ahmad Tejan Kabbah was elected president, but he didn't get a chance to lead for long. Another coup followed soon after he asked his citizens to "join hands for the future of Sierra Leone," and bag after bag of amputated human hands began to appear on the steps of the presidential palace. This time the coup was led by Johnny Paul Koroma, who headed a new rebel group, the Armed Forces Revolutionary Council (AFRC), a band of former army soldiers who were aligned with the RUF.

Less than a year and a half after EO's departure, the capital fell to combined AFRC/RUF forces on May 25, 1997, in an unprecedented assault on Freetown's civilian population and ECOMOG observers.

4

DEATH BY DIAMONDS:
Operation No Living Thing

Freetown, Sierra Leone

Much of our wealth has come from things most people have
little knowledge of. They should have been a blessing;
instead they are a curse. They have torn Sierra Leone apart
in a bloody civil war, because who controls them controls
the country. They are diamonds.

SORIOUS SAMURA,
director of *Cry Freetown*

IF THINGS IN SIERRA LEONE were bad before 1997, they were
destined to only get worse. By the time Johnny Paul Koroma's
AFRC junta had taken control of the government with the help of
600 criminals released from a Freetown prison by mutinous army
soldiers, it seemed that everyone wanted to get their hands on
Sierra Leone's diamonds and would stop at nothing to do it. While
the RUF quickly regained control of the diamond mines they'd lost
to Executive Outcomes in the east, joint AFRC/RUF forces con-

ed on securing the capital in a bid to take over the entire country. Still, the United Nations and the Western world did nothing; only a small force of ECOMOG soldiers and observers prevented complete anarchy.

Before the end of the decade, however, repercussions of the RUF diamond war would ripple across the world, creating turmoil in the UN Security Council, involving the fighting forces of some thirty countries that would contribute soldiers to a UN-led peacekeeping mission, and sparking political controversy in Great Britain. Countless diamonds were being openly stolen from the country's eastern mines and sold unimpeded to the world market, and the chaos they sparked in Sierra Leone would eventually attract the world's attention and start sucking the resources of developed nations into the morass.

On May 25, 1997, RUF and AFRC soldiers marched through Freetown's downtown streets shooting at anything that moved, the opening assault of a bloody coup that would send President Kabbah into exile and leave the killers in control. The judiciary building at the center of town is still pockmarked from small-arms fire and the landmark City Hotel, where novelist Graham Greene wrote his celebrated book *The Heart of the Matter*, was flattened. The streets were filled with the sound of gunfire and the silhouettes of people scuttling into fire-blackened doorways while bullets and rockets ripped through the air around them. The ammunition and weapons were provided by sales of diamonds, which were giving the RUF millions of dollars of spending money a year. Fighters looted downtown stores and, drunk on a sense of invincibility, they donned women's wigs to add further terror to their assault. They smoked marijuana between volleys of gunfire with ECOMOG troops, who were busily retreating west toward Aberdeen and the capital's edge.

Once-vibrant markets were deserted, their tables overturned and their wares spilled into the street along with the sprawled bodies of the dead. Pandemonium broke out among Freetown's population and people fled into the wooded hills surrounding the city or stole canoes to row out to the safety of the sea. U.S. Marines stationed in Monrovia flew helicopters to the Hotel Bintumani in Aberdeen to evacuate diplomats and U.S. citizens ahead of the wave of RUF advancing from the city center ten miles to the east. At the time, this was the extent of the West's involvement in a country that provided it with millions of dollars worth of diamonds every year.

Meanwhile, ECOMOG, the country's only hope, was cornered in the basement of the Mammy Yoko Hotel, surrounded on all sides by AFRC and RUF forces. The hotel was rocked with rocket-propelled grenades and chipped away by AK-47 rounds. Staff were forced to walk into the storm of bullets carrying bed sheets on which they'd written "We are RUF!" with black electrical tape in the hopes of escaping alive. Dozens of them made it, but most of the Nigerian ECOMOG soldiers trapped inside did not.

Further down the beach, the AFRC took over the Freetown Golf Club and installed an antiaircraft gun on the roof of the clubhouse to shoot at the Nigerian alpha jets that streaked in from the sea to bomb targets in the city.

Days into the coup, hundreds of bodies rotted in the street and in the surf and Freetown's postcard-perfect beaches were littered with bones and skulls.

The bloodshed didn't raise much publicity outside of West Africa. Most international media organizations wisely pulled their journalists out of the country and Sierra Leone's descent into anarchy was given little more than perfunctory treatment in the U.S. press. Humbled by a disastrous African intervention in Somalia four years earlier—in which eighteen U.S. soldiers were killed in Mogadishu—there were no calls for humanitarian or military intervention from the United States. Another factor that probably lowered enthusiasm for involvement was that it was difficult to understand a motive for the bloodletting from afar; only those in the international diamond industry who understood that the war was simply an economic activity could place the warfare into an understandable context. Most of the world knew nothing of the connection between Sierra Leone's diamonds and its war, however, and dismissed the conflict as a confusing and tragic waste.

Kabbah fled to neighboring Guinea and immediately began desperate negotiations with arms dealers to equip an army that had been left gutted by EO's withdrawal. Finding little support from developed countries, Kabbah was forced to look to the fringe of the military supply industry, and one of the men he dealt with was Rakesh Saxena, a man memorably described by UK foreign secretary Robin Cook as "an Indian businessman, traveling on the passport of a dead Serb, awaiting extradition from Canada for alleged embezzlement from a bank in Thailand." The weapons were to be delivered to Kabbah's soldiers—the remnants of the effectively disbanded SLA who fought alongside ECOMOG—through a private British arms dealer, Sandline International, a company with close ties to Executive Outcomes. Again, the guns were going to be paid for with diamond-mining concessions, the only thing of value in Sierra Leone and the one thing that kept the warfare at a high pitch.[1]

There was, however, a problem. In the wake of the coup ousting Kabbah, the UN drafted a poorly worded resolution that was mostly composed by British lawmakers imposing an arms embargo on Sierra Leone. But according to the wording of the resolution, the embargo applied not only to the occupying junta, but also to the legitimate government that the British supported and wanted to see returned to power. British lawmakers interpreted the resolution as a blanket ban on weapons to Sierra Leone, regardless of whom they were destined for.

But Kabbah had a foreign friend who was willing to do all he could to restore Kabbah's government to power: the British Foreign Office's representative in Freetown, Peter Penfold, who interpreted the UN resolution differently than the lawmakers in his home country. Exiled by the coup to a hotel in Conakry, Guinea, Penfold was more or less cut off from his bosses in London: His satellite telephone didn't work, crucial documents were either lost or destroyed by the German embassy in Guinea, which allowed Penfold to send and receive coded faxes, and high-tech communications gear delivered to him was left at the airport because it was too big to fit through the door of his hotel room. So chances are that he may not have been entirely aware that Britain had outlawed all arms deliveries to Sierra Leone, and he helped coordinate Kabbah's contract with Sandline to provide Sierra Leone weapons in exchange for diamond-mining rights.

When it became known that the British High Commissioner to Sierra Leone was helping coordinate a gunrunning plan in contravention of British law and UN sanctions, a gigantic political scandal erupted in London. Foreign Office secretary Cook had built his reputation on mercilessly prosecuting the Conservative government's secret delivery of arms to Iraq in the late 1980s, and he returned to his residence one night in April 1998 to find a fax from solicitors acting on behalf of Sandline, saying that it was under investigation by Customs and Excise for sanctions busting. The diamond war in Sierra Leone was capable not only of causing the deaths of thousands of innocent victims, but of jeopardizing the political careers of foreign politicians as well.[2]

Sandline sent 35 tons of Bulgarian AK-47s to Sierra Leone for use by the Sierra Leone Army and the Kamajors, but the brewing political scandal in London put deeper involvement on permanent hold. Meanwhile ECOWAS reinforced ECOMOG and its Nigerian soldiers in Freetown in an all-out military bid to restore Kabbah's government. Interestingly, this force was considered "legitimate" despite the fact that Nigeria had been expelled from the Commonwealth of Nations for the army's gross violations of human rights within its own country, which culminated in the military murder—under the dictatorship of the Nigerian General Sani Abacha—of environmental activists in 1996. Worse still for the prospects of brokering peace was that, at the same time it was deployed to Sierra Leone, portions of the ECOMOG command stationed in Liberia had more or less gone into business with Charles Taylor, whose support of the RUF was well known. Taylor was a close friend and political ally of Sani Abacha, and some of Abacha's soldiers assigned to ECOMOG in Liberia saw the opportunity to enrich themselves by stripping the country of railroad stock, mining equipment, and public utilities and selling them abroad.[3] Sandline and EO may have gotten results, but the fact that they were private armies apparently made them more unpalatable than ECOMOG to world tastes. It appeared that the developed countries were willing to put Sierra Leone's rescue in the hands of a less effective security force—one that was prone to flagrant corruption, bribery, savagery, and a disdain for human rights—just because it was quasi-governmental and not run by profiteers—at least not so openly.

ECOMOG'S ATTEMPT TO WREST control of Freetown from the RUF/AFRC was a human rights disaster. Its first order of business was to free the capital from AFRC and RUF occupiers and reinstate Kabbah to power, an operation that nearly involved destroying the city in order to liberate it. In fierce street-to-street fighting, ECOMOG lost hundreds of soldiers and the RUF/AFRC forces looted and burned everything they could in retreat. Drugged RUF child-soldiers wearing clothes donated by aid organizations dashed into Freetown's burning streets, blindly firing deafening volleys of gunfire in the general direction of their enemies, hitting anything that happened to be in the way. ECOMOG was largely doing the same thing, its soldiers modifying their uniforms by fighting shirtless or with bandanas flapping around their heads. It was often hard to tell who was who, and RUF fighters began tying white bandanas around their heads in order to be recognized by their comrades.

While ECOMOG attempted to liberate Freetown, the Kamajors ran roughshod throughout the bush, storming RUF defenses and engaging in some of their hardest-fought battles, now armed more substantially by both the Nigerians and Sandline than they'd ever been before. The Kamajors proved to be a force unto themselves; although they were ostensibly fighting on behalf of the government, they soon proved to be beyond the government's control. They fought the RUF, but they also looted villages, stole food, and killed civilians suspected of aiding the rebels. Their vigilante tactics would later be a stumbling block to peace once UNAMSIL deployed in 1999.

ECOMOG's own scorched-earth tactics reduced Freetown to a smoking, corpse-filled hull of a city, but they did chase the RUF back to the bush to defend their diamond mines. Then field-commander Issa Sessay and Major General Sam "Mosquito" Bokarie helped Johnny Paul Koroma, the AFRC leader, flee to the eastern RUF stronghold of Kailahun and into Liberia, discovering in the process that he had hidden a large cache of rebel diamonds in his clothing to facilitate his escape.[4] According to the United Nations, Koroma had enough goods to ensure quite a comfortable life in Europe. Mosquito and Sessay took the diamonds from him and sent him into Liberia at gunpoint.

Kabbah was restored to power in March of 1998. RUF leader Foday Sankoh was captured in Abuja, Nigeria, ensnared in a gun-running plot. He was arrested and shipped back to Freetown, where he was sentenced to die for his role in supporting the AFRC junta. If ever the sordid tale of Sierra Leone should have ended, it should have ended there.

But the RUF's insatiable lust for money and power is not easily extinguished. The RUF quickly regrouped in the wake of its defeat at the hands of ECOMOG and planned its worst assault yet: an all-out bid to take over the country and its wealth of diamonds. Although nearly a quarter of Nigeria's entire military was based in Sierra Leone at the beginning of 1999 and the rebel leader was on death row in Freetown, the RUF rearmed with the help of Charles Taylor's presidential plane, trading diamonds for weapons from Niger. It staged a bold assault on Freetown on January 6, 1999, code-named Operation No Living Thing. The date is burned into the mind of anyone living in the capital at the time. In the words of journalist Sebastian Junger, war does not get much worse than it did on that day.

JOSEPH KAMARA REMEMBERS the humid, overcast day well—it was the day he lost both his hands and his family in the space of about twenty minutes. He was in his home near Kissy Harbor in eastern Freetown when he heard a rocket sizzle down the boule-vard in front of his house, exploding in the street several hundred yards away. He ran out the front door to see what was happening and saw two "technicals" careening down the street stuffed with RUF fighters. Technicals are pickup trucks that have been modified into combat vehicles; many have had their windshields and roofs taken off with a chainsaw and all of them have a heavy machine gun or antiaircraft gun bolted into the bed, weapons too heavy to fire without being stabilized. One of the trucks broke off from its high-speed run and skidded to a stop in front of him, spilling fighters bristling with gun barrels.

"You! Today you'll die!" yelled one man, whom Kamara assumed was the commander. He tried to plead with them to spare his family, but the other soldiers ran into the house and dragged out his wife, 6-year-old son, two teenage daughters, and his brother. The brother was shot immediately, one bullet through the head with a nickel-plated revolver. Kamara remembers his body falling straight down, as if all the bones had suddenly been removed. Then a Molotov cocktail was pitched through the doorway of the house, a modest concrete cube, but one that was comfortable by Freetown's standards.

Kamara shouted to his family to run while he tried to distract the soldiers. Everyone fled but the 6-year-old, who hid behind the carcass of a car about twenty yards away. He didn't want to leave his father.

Kamara pled with the soldiers for his life, but they forced him to his knees and placed the hot barrel of the revolver to his head.

"Why are you doing this to me?" he screamed. "I don't know you. I've never done anything to you."

"We must cut off your hands," the commander told him, matter-of-factly. "Those are our orders."

He was then forced to lie on his back in the street with his arms outstretched. He wanted to yell to his son to leave so that he wouldn't have to witness his mutilation, but did not want to reveal his hiding place to the soldiers. An ax was raised into the smoke-filled sky while the surrounding soldiers pinned him down and stood on his hands. It took more than a dozen blows to sever each arm, just below the elbow. The strangest sensation, he said, was that one minute he could feel his knuckles being ground into the asphalt by the soldier's boot and in the next he watched as the man kicked his arm away as he felt nothing.

Once the amputation was complete, the soldiers fired a chain of machine-gun ammunition into the flaming remains of his house and then sped off looking for more victims. Delirious with pain, eyes stinging with tears, Kamara looked for his son, but he was gone. He staggered to the nearby Connaught Hospital in the hope that the doctors could keep him from bleeding to death. He never saw any of his family members again.

Scenes like this took place throughout Freetown for the next four days as the capital continued its now familiar plunge into chaos and anarchy. Recalling the horror of the May 1997 coup just two years before, international aid groups wasted no time evacuating their people, as did the media organizations and the diplomatic corps. Once again, Freetown's population was left to fend for itself in the face of battalions of crazed RUF soldiers, with only ECO-MOG to hide behind.

ECOMOG soldiers, caught off guard by the assault, went haywire and embarked on their own version of Operation No Living Thing, executing suspected RUF on the Aberdeen bridge and dumping their bodies into the river below. Roadside justice was the order of the day. Anyone remotely suspected of being involved with the RUF was tortured, raped, and summarily executed by the Nigerian soldiers, including an unknown number of perfectly innocent civilians whose elbows were tied behind them before they were shot at point-blank range. One retarded 9-year-old boy, whose plight was highlighted in the documentary film *Cry Freetown*, was stripped naked, beaten, and tortured by Nigerians who suspected him of being an RUF sniper. It's hard to tell which is worse; that ECOMOG beat and tortured children, or that the RUF had enlisted young kids so extensively that ECOMOG was put into a position where it had no choice but to suspect even the least suspicious of being an RUF killer. Alpha jets and artillery emplacements fired on civilian targets and some soldiers in the Sierra Leone Army imitated the rebels they were ostensibly fighting, taking the arms or legs off anyone they suspected of being a rebel.[5] ECOMOG's wanton targeting of civilians and their property led Sierra Leoneans to quip wryly that the force's acronym actually stood for "Every Car or Moving Object Gone."

ECOMOG eventually routed the RUF from the city once again, but this time the death toll was nearly 6,000.

Still, no one outside the orbit of West Africa seemed to pay much attention to the matter. Operation No Living Thing was given brief and perfunctory treatment in Western media, which was busy with other matters that dominated the news. At the time thousands of Africans were dying over control of diamonds sold in shopping malls around the world, U.S. president Bill Clinton was impeached for perjury, NATO began bombing Yugoslavia, and everyone else was preparing for digital disaster from Y2K.

Nevertheless, the horror was too graphic to ignore completely. With little thought to the causes of the conflict, the U.S. Department of State dispatched negotiators—including envoy Jesse Jackson—to the region with one goal: End the war and secure a peace agreement. The agreement that was reached in Lomé, the capital of the small West African nation of Togo, was nothing less than a hands-down victory for those who started the war in the first place, for no better reason than to control and sell diamonds, a fact that seemed to escape all scrutiny from the diplomats and negotiators in Lomé.

With a single frenzy of bloodletting, one that was openly named after its intention to kill everything in the RUF's path, the rebels effectively won their diamond war, at least for a time.

THE 1999 LOMÉ PEACE ACCORDS, signed by the RUF, AFRC, the Sierra Leone government, and the United Nations, is a diplomatic work of art. According to the agreement, the RUF would end their hostilities in exchange for amnesty for war crimes committed since the beginning of the conflict and its leaders would be appointed to government posts. RUF leader Foday Sankoh—still in jail awaiting execution for his role in the 1997 coup—was to be released from prison and installed as the vice president under Kabbah, the man he and Johnny Paul Koroma had ousted two years earlier. Sankoh was also to be appointed as the chairman of the country's Commission for the Management of Strategic Resources, National Reconstruction and Development. In other words, the internationally brokered peace accord gave the RUF total control of everything it had fought and killed for from the very beginning—the diamond mines. In exchange, the RUF agreed to demobilize and disarm to a UN peacekeeping force, dubbed UNAMSIL. After disarming, the RUF was to be given legal status as a political party. It's hard to imagine that the band of killers who'd murdered thousands and sold the country's most valuable natural resource out from under it for the past decade could have been happier with the agreement.

Western countries that helped negotiate the Lomé Accords enthusiastically supported the agreement, not because they were fair—but because it was a swift solution to what they perceived to be a nagging problem. Responding to criticism that the Lomé Accords were too favorable to the RUF, the U.S. assistant secretary of state at the time, Susan Rice, practically put it in those words when she said: "There will never be peace and security and an opportunity for development and recovery in Sierra Leone unless there is a solution to the source of the conflict. And that entails, by necessity—whether we like it or not—a peace agreement with the rebels."⁶

Not everyone was convinced that for peace to succeed the RUF should be granted such a conciliatory arrangement. The UN secretary general, Kofi Annan, in a bold but ill-advised move, signed an amendment to the peace agreement stating that he didn't agree with giving combatants amnesty for war crimes, one of the document's most important concessions to the RUF. By making such a statement, he essentially nullified the agreement in the eyes of the RUF before it was implemented and then sent 6,000 UN soldiers to Sierra Leone to try and enforce it.

Meanwhile, peace deal or not, the diamond channels were wide open. Hundreds of thousands of carats of diamonds flowed from the blood-soaked jungle of Sierra Leone to brides everywhere, and 7.62-mm Kalashnikov rounds flowed back. Rebels still controlled the diamonds and thus the country.

ENTER UNAMSIL. Created through UN Security Council Resolution 1270, and deployed to Sierra Leone in October of 1999, UNAMSIL originally consisted of 6,000 military personnel and 260 observers. The majority of them were again Nigerians, the UN's first mistake among many. Given the atrocities committed by Nigeria's last foray into Sierra Leonean "peacekeeping" through ECO-

MOG, it was natural that most Sierra Leoneans looked on them warily. And as far as the RUF was concerned, the Nigerians were nothing less than a hated enemy, one to which they were now expected to turn over their arms.

Compounding this lack of respect and authority were consistent rumors that some ECOMOG units—which were to be absorbed into UNAMSIL—had made arrangements with the RUF to share the spoils of their diamond plundering, in much the same way as they had with resources in Liberia. That the Nigerians may have been interested in agendas other than peace was clear to UN force commanders from the early days of the UNAMSIL mission. By the time the mission was deployed, Nigeria's dictator, Sani Abacha, had died unexpectedly of a heart attack—some say it was brought on by an overdose of Viagra—and that nation's dictatorial dynasty, which always relied on equal amounts of corruption and military screw-turning, was in question. Given the growing uncertainty over Nigeria's leadership, top military officers commanding troops under the UNAMSIL banner were presented with a tempting opportunity to amass war chests and hedge funds in Abuja, the capital of Nigeria.

But the biggest problem with the Nigerians was in their perception as aggressors and war criminals.

John Bolton, at the time the senior vice president of the American Enterprise Institute, complained to the U.S. Congress about this seemingly obvious obstacle. "Why should Nigerians have been embraced by UNAMSIL?" he questioned the House International Relations Committee in October 2000. "Given that the RUF effectively considered them the enemy, this was virtually a guarantee of a repetition of the Somalia problem, when [local warlord] Mohammed Farah Aideed saw the UN forces allying themselves with local clans and subclans that he considered his enemies. . . . Inexplicably, the lessons of Somalia do not seem to have been applied in Sierra Leone."[7]

UNAMSIL fell apart almost before its acronym was christened. The original force consisted of a hodgepodge of member-states' militaries, and they didn't exactly represent the cream of the crop, seeming to have been culled from those smaller states that could be pressured into troop commitments by the more influential UN members who didn't want anything to do with a morass like Sierra Leone. While effective, experienced, and well-equipped soldiers from countries like the United States, Great Britain, Canada, Germany, and France stayed home, soldiers from Nepal, Croatia, India, Bangladesh, Nigeria, Zambia, and Ghana were dispatched to Freetown. The idea, perhaps, was that countries in the common continent should be deployed to handle an African problem, but the result was that variously disciplined forces that had never operated in concert were thrust into what was at the time the hottest military zone on earth next to Kosovo. And the disastrous results of this strategy were almost instantaneous.

The first problem was that UNAMSIL unwisely attempted to deploy everywhere at once—with 6,000 soldiers into a country-wide battlefield with some 40,000 to 50,000 combatants. When the RUF was suddenly faced with a heavily armed force of Nigerians demanding their disarmament—many of whom had served with ECOMOG before joining the UN's mission—they naturally went on the defensive. In May 2000, the RUF killed seven UN peacekeepers and took fifty more hostage, stealing their weapons and vehicles. The number of captured soon rose to over 500, many surrendering their rifles and ammunition without a fight, further humiliating the UN. Many of those captured happened to be Zambians, and the Zambian president sharply criticized UNAMSIL and its Sierra Leone force commander, Major General Vijay Jetly of India. Only months into the mission the UN was having an embarrassingly public debate about command-and-control issues while a twelfth of its force was held prisoner. The Security Council's decision in February 2000 to increase force strength to 11,000 troops did little to help the situation. Within weeks of the UNAMSIL deployment, Victor Bout made a series of arms shipments to Liberia for the RUF. The cargo, including several attack helicopters, demonstrated that the RUF had little intention of complying with the disarmament agreement.

UNAMSIL was so inept in its early days that the British sent in paratroopers independent of the UN mission to help stabilize the country, a move that was interpreted—mostly correctly—as an attempt to rescue the UN mission behind the scenes. Though they were to have pulled out by mid-June 2000, the British paratroopers were still there as of November 2001, operating beyond the UN's channels and mandates.

Because of the troubled UN mission, the Lomé Accords were rendered useless. The RUF had yet to disarm and they continued to mine and smuggle diamonds under the noses of the UN. The Secretary General proposed increasing UNAMSIL's size yet again to 20,500 troops, including eighteen infantry battalions, and changing the scope of the mission from neutral peacekeeper to ally of the government. But the Security Council refused to change the parameters of the mission and the UN couldn't find any member-states willing to contribute the increased number of troops. While this debate ensued, a Sierra Leone Army splinter-group calling themselves The West Side Boys captured eleven British soldiers east of Freetown. The soldiers were soon freed, but it required a daring commando mission into the West Side Boys' headquarters and cost one paratrooper his life. The British found $38 million worth of rebel diamonds in the hideout.

Meanwhile, in the midst of what was more or less unchecked warfare between UNAMSIL and the RUF, Jetly, the UNAMSIL commander, was busily preparing a secret report on the shortcomings of the mission's Nigerian contingent, accusing them of undermining the UN's mandate and pursuing their own agendas. The unfinished report was leaked and the Nigerian commander demanded Jetly's dismissal as force commander. India eventually withdrew all 3,000 of its soldiers from Sierra Leone, including Jetly.

In testimony to the U.S. Congress, John Bolton aptly described the mission as a "meltdown." He placed major blame on the Lomé Accords themselves and the UN's hesitancy to fully endorse the amnesty clause:

> There was never any serious review by the Security Council or the Secretariat whether the Lomé Agreement represented a true meeting of the minds of the parties, and whether it provided any real basis to believe that the peacekeepers could undertake the missions contemplated for them. This failure is a damning indictment of the Council's entire approach to Sierra Leone and the decision to deploy substantial UN peacekeeping forces reflects a simplistic, knee-jerk to conflict resolution. Subsequent events demonstrate beyond question that there was never any real peace to keep and that the peacekeepers' mission was almost certainly doomed from the start.[8]

For at least one person, things couldn't have been much better. Sankoh, just released from prison and settling into his new cabinet position, resumed earnestly plundering the diamond fields with bureaucracy, political connections, and old-fashioned corruption rather than with machetes and machine guns. Though he was now a government official, he still had the RUF doing his dirty work by mining diamonds on his behalf. In the book *Fire*, journalist Sebastian Junger presents evidence of organized diamond-gathering activities by RUF on Sankoh's behalf while he was ostensibly in a position of responsibility over the diamond fields. A notebook discovered at Sankoh's residence detailed an RUF agent's diamond collections from October 1998 to July 1999—"a nine-month haul of about 786 carats of white diamonds and 887 carats of industrials. The RUF is thought to be exporting about half a million carats a year, which would suggest there were about 300 guys . . . gathering diamonds for Sankoh," Junger wrote.[9]

And Sankoh wasted no time trying to find buyers for the gems. Even though the governmental commission he chaired had yet to be activated—a commission that oversaw Sierra Leone's diamond exports—he was busy negotiating with British and Belgian diamond brokers and American hustlers disguised as businessmen. Junger detailed one particularly bold scam that was orchestrated by the president of the U.S. Trading & Investment Company, John Caldwell, who was also the former vice president of the U.S. Chamber of Commerce. Shortly before the commission he chaired was activated, Sankoh wrote up a contract between the RUF and Caldwell and his business partner, Belgian Michel Desaedeleer, giving the men monopoly mining rights—through a Virgin Islands–chartered company of which they were directors—to all the gold and diamond claims in Kono District. "The RUF was to provide security and labor for the mining operations and facilitate the transportation of diamonds out of the country," Junger wrote. Caldwell and Desaedeleer's company would split the profits with the RUF.

According to Junger, Desaedeleer then immediately tried to sell the contract to anyone he could think of for $10 million, including De Beers, DiamondWorks, and—unbelievably—to the Sierra Leone government itself. The government's ambassador to the United States, John Leigh, was naturally aghast at the audacity of a hated rebel group's asking him to pay for the country's sovereign natural resources. And being asked by a partner of the former vice president of the U.S. Chamber of Commerce added incredible insult to the offer.[10]

There's no evidence that Sankoh got very far with his plans because, like nearly everyone else involved in the tragic tale of Sierra Leone's diamonds, he also seems to suffer from congenital incompetence and terminal greed. Not content with his potentially influential position in Kabbah's government, many believe that Sankoh was planning a coup for the summer of 2000, smuggling in fixers like Brigadier General Issa Sessay—who went by the code name General Emperor—to coordinate the plot.

Before it could be executed, though, RUF commanders in Makeni spoiled the plan by surrounding a base filled with Kenyan peacekeepers and demanding the release of ten fighters who'd surrendered days earlier. A gunfight ensued and seven peacekeepers were taken hostage. The UN raided Sankoh's Freetown compound in retaliation and unwittingly averted the coup plot. Sankoh was again arrested and, as of November 2001, was being held on Bunce Island in the Sierra Leone River under heavy guard.

General Emperor took over as acting leader of the RUF.

WHILE PEACEKEEPERS, rebels, and mercenaries were busily slaughtering one another in a mostly forgotten jungle battle in West Africa, London residents Charmian Gooch and Alex Yearsley were busily working on the heart of the matter and preparing to knock the wind out of the $6 billion-per-year, century-old diamond industry by revealing its deepest and darkest secret. Their non-governmental organization, Global Witness, released a detailed report in December 1998 that tied illicitly mined and sold diamonds from the UNITA rebels in Angola directly to De Beers. By inference, Global Witness explained that all the death and destruction in that country, as well as other diamond-producing nations enduring brutal civil wars, result from the international diamond industry's willingness to pay the rebels for their ill-gotten goods.[11]

Angola is Sierra Leone's mirror hellhole. Its body count—half a million over ten years of civil war—has outpaced that of the smaller country only because it has a larger population. A former Portuguese colony, Angola launched into nearly nonstop warfare from the moment the colonialists pulled out in 1975. On one side was the Marxist MPLA government supported by Russia and Cuba; on the other was the Maoist UNITA, backed strangely enough by the United States and China. This Cold War chess game was funded on the government's side by oil revenues and on the rebels' side by the country's impressive diamond mines. Global Witness estimated that between 1992 and 1997, UNITA reaped $3.7 billion from the diamond mines, which led to a UN Security Council resolution in July 1998 aimed at stemming their sales. In spite of that, there has been no significant reduction in UNITA's diamond earnings.[12]

The reason for this goes all the way back to the 1870s and a greedy megalomaniac named Cecil Rhodes. At 18 years old, he strode across the moonscape of diamond mines near Kimberley, South Africa, with one goal in mind: world domination of the diamond market.

5

THE SYNDICATE:
A Diamond Is Forever

London

No diamonds in this box have been purchased in breach of
UN Resolution 1173. The intake of diamonds being purchased by De Beers and its associated companies and
being sold into the market through the Sight system does
not include any diamonds which have come from any area
in Africa controlled by forces rebelling against the legitimate and internationally recognized government of the
relevant country.

—NOTICE TO SIGHTHOLDERS
placed in parcels sold by De Beers's Diamond
Trading Company as of March 2000

THERE IS NO QUESTION that De Beers abhors conflict diamonds. Perhaps more to the point, the company abhors what
public outcry over conflict diamonds could do to its empire, a point
that was being made to me at teatime in London on September 11,
2001. Neither I nor the men to whom I was speaking was aware
that at that very minute thousands of people were dying at the

hands of Osama bin Laden across the Atlantic Ocean in New York City, Washington, D.C., and rural Pennsylvania. Even further from our imaginations was that bin Laden's African operatives had been buying millions of dollars worth of Sierra Leone diamonds for the past three years in preparation for that day. In our ignorance of real-time events, we were perfectly comfortable discussing in frank terms why diamonds sold by ruthless killers were bad from De Beers's perspective: Like all else in the hermetic world of diamonds, it came down to economics.

"No one in this industry is going to hide behind wringing hands, or a hearts-on-your-sleeves kind of thing," said Andy Bone, chief media officer of De Beers's Diamond Trading Company. "There is a big moral dimension to this, but we're very happy to talk about the enormous commercial loss and gain potential of this as well. And the enormous long-term benefit for West Africa if the industry remains unharmed. . . . Yes, let's get rid of conflict diamonds. We've got more to gain than anyone else on this, apart from the victims. The next big prize is for the industry if we can get rid of this."

Like most of that week in London, September 11 was chilly and fogbound. We were in a conference room on the second floor of the Diamond Trading Company (DTC) on Charterhouse Street in east London, a building through which 65 percent of the world production of rough diamonds flows, some $500 million worth of rough sold every five weeks to the same cadre of handpicked buyers. Located next to a fresh food market that smells like fish and attracts seagulls, the DTC operates out of an austere building, a huge cement block that looks like it could have been designed by the U.S. Department of Corrections. Indeed, it is probably more secure than most prisons. Visitors are greeted by a man sealed in a bulletproof cabinet who will, assuming your name is on a list, buzz you through ballistic glass doors that are so thick they seem like they'd be impossible to see through. Only then are you allowed to speak face to face with a receptionist, who then ushers you into another room. Sitting there, amid mismatched furniture and oddly arranged desks, I wondered if this was the same room the prospective buyers—called "sightholders"—are required to wait in.

The second-floor conference room, though, was comfortable and was clearly designed to impress first-time visitors. Giant maps of De Beers's diamond holdings were built into the walls, and behind more bulletproof glass were models of famous diamonds, including the 986.6-carat Star of Sierra Leone, the third largest ever found. It was the size of a small brick and even the model is considered priceless. Samples of rough diamonds were displayed at lighted kiosks along the walls, as if in a museum. Tea and cucumber sandwiches were served on a silver tray, and a slickly produced video about conflict diamonds was eternally poised inside the VCR to explain the official stance. I was assigned two handlers, Bone and Tim Weekes, perfectly attired gentlemen whose first duty was to impress upon me the gravity of what I was there to talk about. Conflict diamonds are terrible, they agreed, but they represent a very small portion of rough stones found around the world and sloppy or sensationalistic reportage about them—dwelling on amputated civilians, for instance—could have dire consequences on their industry. There was no threat in their disclaimer—not even a hint of one—but it was clear that their jobs were to juggle acknowledgment of the horrors caused by conflict diamonds within the context of all the good that diamond mining does for some countries and more than a million employees worldwide.

None of us could have known that, at the very moment Bone was downplaying the spin-off horrors of the policies pursued by his industry, policies that have been exploited by rebels and terrorists from Sierra Leone to Lebanon to Afghanistan and that have generated vast profits for De Beers and others throughout the industry, horrors worse than our collective nightmares were happening in America.

THE INCORPORATION of what was to become the undisputed world behemoth of diamond buying, selling, and marketing came only twenty-two years after the first discovery of the jeweled wealth in South Africa; the time frame alone is testament to the exploding nature of the boom in that country. In 1866, a 15-year-old boy named Erasmus Jacobs found a pretty-looking rock on the banks of South Africa's Orange River, and he pocketed it to give to his little sister, who collected interesting stones. A short time later, while the children were playing with the pebbles in the street, the glittering one caught the eye of a passerby, a local politician. Suspecting that it may be a diamond, he liberated it from the children and passed it on to a local peddler, who in turn mailed it to the government mineralogist. The stone turned out to be a 21.25-carat diamond, and it was sold to the governor of Cape Colony for 500 pounds sterling. The following year, it was displayed at the Paris Exhibition, mainly as an oddity. At the time, no one knew of the wealth to be had in South Africa.

Until diamond mining took permanent hold in South Africa in the 1870s, most diamonds were found in India and Brazil; in fact, the discovery of Jacobs's stone did little to change anyone's opinion that those two countries were the only places to find diamonds. The find in Africa was written off as a fluke initially—at least until more were plucked from the riverbank: The second find was a magnificent 85-carat white diamond. The discovery was so awe-inspiring that Cape Town's colonial secretary, Sir Richard Southey, laid it on the table at the South African Parliament and proclaimed proudly, "Gentlemen, this is the rock on which the future of South Africa will be built." The diamond was named the Star of South Africa.

Similar in many ways to the California Gold Rush, the South African diamond rush lured hundreds, then thousands of prospectors to South Africa's scrappy farmland, usually men and families with few other viable opportunities who were enticed by the dream of instant wealth that, for many, turned out not to be dreams at all.

Southey's comment to legislators would have been equally accurate if he'd said the stone would also be the foundation for the world diamond industry. But he couldn't possibly have guessed that the serendipitous discovery would lead, over the course of the next century, to the creation of one of the most successful commodities monopolies in world history and, as a result, to brutal warfare over natural resources that would plunge at least three African states into chaos, poverty, and destruction at the end of the twentieth century.

The harbinger of that course of history came marching across the South African scrub flats that were quickly vanishing beneath the swiss-cheese landscape of diamond pits in 1871 in the form of an 18-year-old boy in cricket flannels carrying a bucket and a shovel. When Cecil Rhodes arrived in Africa from England, the rush was already on, not only along the Orange River but also in the Vaal River valley farther north, at the end of a torturous 700-mile overland journey from Cape Town. He found a chaotic, disorganized chain of tent communities populated by vagabond diggers, many of whom didn't even know what a diamond looked like, but who had been lured to the fields by tales of vast riches. They scratched away the land with the fervent hope that eternal wealth lay just below the next crust of earth. Indeed, sometimes it did. In his book *The World of Diamonds: The Inside Story of the Miners, Cutters, Smugglers, Lovers and Investors,* Timothy Green writes: "'An English gentleman,' reported one visitor to the diggings, 'having worked a claim for six months and found nothing, went home disgusted, giving away his claim. The man who got it found on the same day a fine diamond of 29½ carats before he had gone six inches deeper than his predecessor. I believe he was offered 2,500 [pounds] for it.'"

Rhodes pitched his tent at a site called New Rush, a diamondiferous hillock near a farm that was purchased by diggers for 6,000 pounds from local farmers Johannes and Diedrich De Beer. The brothers were disgusted by the mining activity that was wrecking the farmland and wanted to move to more peaceful environs. This little knot of land would achieve everlasting fame over the course of the next century as Kimberley Mine, also called the Big Hole— the deepest open pit mine ever dug by human hands. The mine eventually reached into the earth over 1,300 feet, following a snaking kimberlite pipe that has yielded some of the best and most valuable diamonds ever discovered. The mine was named after the British colonial secretary of the day—not for the kimberlite that produced the diamond wealth—because he couldn't pronounce either Colesburg Kopje, the name of the hill, or Vooruitzigt, the name of the estate where it was located. And he refused to call it De Beers New Rush, as it was known locally among the diggers, because he deemed the name wholly undignified for a community under the dominion of Queen Victoria.

By 1880, South Africa had far surpassed the annual diamond production of Brazil, churning out over 3 million carats per year. Diamond production, whether it's done legally or illicitly, seems to always have global ripple effects, and at the close of the nineteenth century most of them were positive. The surge of diamonds on the world market spurred industrial growth in the United States and Germany, who were huge customers for industrial-quality diamonds. The European cutting and polishing industry was pulled out of a slump caused by declining Brazilian production, and Antwerp, Belgium, became as much of a boomtown as Kimberley, quickly boasting of forty businesses that specialized in cutting and polishing stones. The price of diamonds during the early years of the rush remained surprisingly stable.

But Rhodes knew that this economic stability wouldn't last forever. He was clearly different from the majority of other prospectors, whose definitions of "wealth" often didn't extend beyond the scopes of their own lifetimes. Rhodes wanted an empire.

He quickly realized that there was a lot of wealth in the South African soil to go around, too much in fact. He was smart enough to know that if all the claims that were producing good finds continued to do so, it wouldn't be long before there were too many diamonds in circulation, hurting everyone by dragging down prices. Therefore, his goal became not to just find as many high-quality rocks as possible in his lifetime—which was essentially the goal of 90 percent of those digging in South Africa at the time—but to buy as many claims as possible that may contain those diamonds. By controlling the land, he could control the production. And by controlling the production, he could ensure that there were just enough diamonds on the market to meet demand, thereby keeping prices high and stable.

Over the course of the next decade, he did just that, trading and consolidating his holdings through dozens, then hundreds of arrangements with miners who didn't have his patience or forethought. By the early 1880s, he was a majority stakeholder in the De Beers Mine, one of the area's most prolific.

Keeping pace with the growing number of acres under Rhodes's control was his obsession with power and market dominance. "When I am in Kimberley, I often go and sit on the edge of the [nearby] De Beers Mine and I reckon up the value of the diamonds in the blue and the power conferred by them," he once wrote of the blue kimberlite that seemed to be under every acre of dirt in Kimberley. "Every foot of the blue ground means so much power."

It's hardly surprising, given his admission that he often communed with the pit in the way many people commune with their lovers, that he named his empire De Beers after the mine in which he owned a majority stake.

Unfortunately for Rhodes, the De Beers Mine wasn't the only treasure trove in the region. Nor was Rhodes the only prospector staring into the gravel with visions of titanic fortunes. Once South Africa began producing its superb diamonds, gem houses all across Europe dispatched their best men to the country to claim a bit of it for themselves. Among the competitors was a treacherous man known as The Buccaneer, who often tried to sabotage Rhodes; Alfred Beit, a quirky financial wizard who soon joined Rhodes's burgeoning company; and Francis Gould, a majority stakeholder in the Kimberley Mine with excellent financial contacts in London. And there was Barney Barnato, a Cockney odd-jobber who rushed to South Africa to sell cigars once word of the good times reached him in London.

There are few historical clues regarding the fate of Barnato's cigar business, other than that it obviously didn't last long. He soon began buying and selling diamonds, aided immensely by his working-man image and his generally good demeanor. He and his brother used the proceeds from their sales to buy up small kimberlite claims and began digging like crazy, under the auspices of the Barnato Diamond Mining Co. The blue ground was good to them and they wisely kept investing their returns in more and more claims, finally buying into Francis Gould's Kimberley Central Mining Co., a purchase that instantly gave them as much clout as Rhodes. Barnato owned as much of the Kimberley Mine as Rhodes did of the De Beers Mine. In ten years, Barnato had morphed from a hustler hawking smokes to one of the richest diamond entrepreneurs in Africa.

Rhodes took this development as any fanatical businessman bent on market domination would—as an act of economic war. His goal became to own the Kimberley shares of Barnato's company and Kimberley's other major stakeholder, Compaigne Francaise des Mines de Diamant de Cap de Bon Esperance (otherwise shortened locally to a far simpler moniker: The French Company). What followed was one of the most astute and far-reaching corporate takeovers in the history of business. In the mid-1880s Rhodes made an offer to buy The French Company's stake in the Kimberley Mine that Barnato quickly countered. A compromise was worked out; Rhodes would buy The French Company's claims and immediately sell them to Barnato in exchange for a one-fifth stake in the Kimberley Mine. With a foot in the door at the region's best mine, Rhodes then furiously began buying every other Kimberley Central share that he could find, a buying frenzy that spurred Barnato to follow suit, ratcheting up prices to obscene levels. But Rhodes was more astute than Barnato: He was offering Barnato's own shareholders lucrative holdings in a new company that he promised would control the world's diamond supply—and by extension, the world's diamond prices.

Like African rains that eventually pounded powerful volcanoes down to mere scrub flats, Rhodes systematically hammered away at Barnato's resolve until he saw that surrender was imminent. Barnato, now the largest shareholder, put Kimberley Central into voluntary liquidation and Rhodes bought all the company's assets with one check, the largest ever written at that time: $12.8 million. In exchange, Barnato was given the largest shareholding and a lifetime governorship in Rhodes's new company, De Beers Consolidated Mines, Ltd., incorporated on March 13, 1888.

At age 35, Rhodes now controlled 90 percent of the world's diamond production.[1]

OVER THE COURSE of the twentieth century, De Beers pursued a plan that was as simple as it was ruthless: Buy as much of the world production as possible and tightly control global distribution through its London offices. Since diamonds suddenly became far less rare as a result of the South Africa boom, price controls were needed to maintain their value. The trick, in other words, was to turn something that should have been relatively cheap into something verging on priceless. Doing that meant controlling the supply and creating a demand. The company could control the prices of the stones during economic downturns—such as in the wake of both world wars—by curtailing either production or distribution, carefully keeping the supply of stones on the market in line with demand.

De Beers had a hand in nearly every diamond mine in the world and agreements with all the major producers and brokers to sell their stones only to them. What developed was a cartel of diamond producers, buyers, and sellers overseen by De Beers, which took on the role of "market custodian" for rough goods bought and sold throughout the world. That way, De Beers could sell the stones to a small clique of hand-selected "sightholders," or preferred customers, at regular "sights" held ten times a year. Amazingly, the sightholders agreed to buy the gems at a price set by De Beers without ever laying eyes on the stones. Sometimes, sightholders got a real gem of a package, so to speak; other times they got diamond chips not worth the price they paid. Of course, they could refuse to pay, but they'd never be invited back to another sight.

This business plan meant that the company had to keep up with where diamonds were being discovered. If diamonds were making their way to the retail market outside their channels, it would play havoc with the price controls. A few times, De Beers narrowly averted economic disaster; in 1902, tales began to circulate about a rich find near Kimberley being mined, but the early reports were dismissed as inaccurate or outright lies. Scam artists often "salted" their claims with real diamonds in the hopes that someone like De Beers would swoop in and pay a huge sum for what would turn out to be a worthless field. But the talk persisted about this particular mine and finally De Beers's governor Alfred Beit went to investigate. When he arrived at Premier Mine, he is reported to have been so shocked by the quality of the diamonds being pulled out of the ground in front of his eyes that he suffered a stroke on the spot.[2]

Naturally, De Beers ended up owning the mine.

Over the decades, it ended up owning a lot of mines, so many in fact that their combined production would have toppled the gems' price years ago. De Beers solved that problem by simply limiting the amount of stones sold to its sightholders, amassing over the course of the past 100 years a stockpile of diamonds in a vault at the DTC worth $4 billion. At the artificial price, of course.[3]

The other economic sleight of hand the corporation had to simultaneously perform was to manufacture a need and desire for its products. After all, owning the vast majority of a commodity is only good if that commodity is worth something, and aside from their limited manufacturing applications, diamonds are good for next to nothing. Their only intrinsic value is that they're very hard and well suited to cutting other very hard things, a characteristic that translates into a mere $30 per carat. Therefore, another pillar of De Beers's price-control system was manufacturing a demand for a product that is essentially worthless to retail consumers. Part of that strategy was to generate and maintain the myth that diamonds are both rare and necessary for people who fall in love.

Diamonds themselves do a good amount of the work in this regard: The gems are beautiful. What make them so precious are the hardness, clarity, and ability to absorb and recast light in sparkling tones. But diamonds aren't born beautiful. Most rough is less attractive than dime-store marbles. It takes the talent of the world's cutters and polishers to produce stones worthy of the empire they represent. Once walked out of the DTC's Charterhouse Street doors, the diamonds are dispersed around the world to have their values exponentially increased during each remaining step leading to the final consumer.

Before any diamond is worthy of any bride—to say nothing of the price the groom will pay for it—it must first be cut, and the first and most important cut is called the cleave. Diamonds are composed of layers, which make up a stone's grain. Although they are indeed the hardest known substance in nature, it's a mistake to think that they can't be broken because they can be cleaved along their planes. In the 1500s, French King François, a sponsor of navigator Jacques Cartier, devised a disastrous method of testing stones sent back by the explorer and thought to be diamonds: He smashed them against an anvil to see if they could withstand the blow, and it's not unlikely that many good stones were shattered and kicked away as quartz. Cleavers now use lasers and high-speed diamond-dusted saws to create the "cleavage cut," but before the advent of modern technology, cleavers would rub one diamond against another to produce a groove on the diamond to be cut wide enough to fit the blade of a cleaving knife. The person performing the surgery would give the knife a good rap and the stone would either break in two or be destroyed.

"The tale is told of Joseph Asscher, the greatest cleaver of his day," wrote Michael Hart in his book *Diamond: A Journey to the Heart of an Obsession*, "that when he prepared to cleave the largest diamond ever known, the 3,160-carat Cullinan, he had a doctor and nurse standing by and when he finally struck the diamond and it broke perfectly in two, he fainted dead away."

Cutters may take weeks to decide on a strategy for cutting diamonds, and the largest ones can take years to polish. Their internal flaws and fractures often determine not only their eventual weight, but their design as well. In general, it's up to the diamond whether or not it will eventually be emerald-, brilliant-, or heart-cut. Cutters aren't just producing a pretty geometric shape; they're also manipulating it so that light will enter where the cutter wants it to, bounce around inside properly, and emerge from the top, creating brilliance. Also, cutting diamonds isn't like sawing wood; only diamonds can cut diamonds and it can take hours for a saw to create a fissure in a stone. Diamonds can lose a lot of weight during the process and it's not unusual for a cutter to grind off up to 50 percent of a diamond's weight to achieve a higher degree of brilliance.

The skill, hard work, and stress of the cutting and polishing side of the industry reveal clearly enough why diamonds shoot up in price as they travel from being rough to finished. It's demanding and exacting work and it's not cheap. The diamonds are eventually sold to customers at up to ten times the price paid for them from De Beers, which, of course, can be up to a hundred times the price paid for them at the source.

Like practically every other facet of the industry, the cutters and those who employ them rely on De Beers to ensure that diamonds keep their value, and De Beers has more than kept up its end of the bargain.

One of the most successful advertising campaigns in history can be recounted in four words: "A diamond is forever." Generations of future diamond buyers have grown up believing that love equals diamonds; this simple declaration is drilled into our heads thanks to De Beers's relentless marketing and advertising campaigns. Much less expensive cubic zirconias don't have the same chemical properties as diamonds, but they can be just as beautiful—but try giving one to your girlfriend when you ask for her hand in marriage. When shopping for a ring for future brides, grooms throughout the United States—who, along with male spouses preparing for an anniversary, buy 80 percent of all diamonds sold in the world—are told very gravely that the standard price to pay for a diamond engagement ring is two months' salary. Anyone who stops to think about it for even a minute realizes the peculiarity of such a thing—after all, who could have started that "tradition" other than people selling diamonds? But we're a nation built on traditions and giving your bride a diamond ring has become one of them. Another De Beers's slogan helps fuel this need: "Show her that you'll love her for another thousand years." This ad illustrates the market perfectly: Men buy diamonds for women. Period. Little do those future grooms know that they're falling into a trap laid more than 100 years ago. De Beers's founder Cecil Rhodes said that the future of his fledgling empire was guaranteed as long as "men and women continued to fall in love."[4]

If every diamond ever found had been sold on the open market instead of hoarded in London, they'd probably be less expensive than emeralds, rubies, and sapphires. And the fact that some of the world's best diamonds come from killing fields and hellholes unbeknownst to anyone outside the hallowed halls of the diamond world for so long, well . . . so much the better in the thinking of the De Beers's marketers. There's nothing that can ruin a carefully crafted mystique better than the stink of reality.

And the reality is that if the century-old price controls and policies were to be honored for the sake of keeping diamonds valuable and avoiding a glut on the market, they would be bought from whomever was selling them. That included the RUF, UNITA, and any one of the dozens of factions fighting in the Democratic Republic of Congo, another war-torn diamond-rich African country. Those in the international diamond industry—revered throughout the world as merchants of love, honor, and faith—did not want it known that they actively and knowingly funded some of the world's most vicious wars simply for the sake of ensuring that jewelry stayed expensive. A close-knit, cloistered business, the diamond world felt so insulated from criticism that De Beers even boasted of its buying practices in its 1996 annual report, the year in which the RUF began its amputation campaign.

"The CSO [De Beers's Central Selling Organization] buys diamonds in substantial volumes on the open market, both in Africa and in the diamond centres, through its extensive network of buying offices, staffed by young diamond buyers often working in difficult conditions," the report reads, in a statement penned by then chairman Julian Thompson. "Purchases in 1996 reached record levels largely owing to the increased Angolan production. Angolan diamonds tend to be in the categories that are in demand, although in the main these buying activities are a mechanism to support the market."[5]

Those record levels were achieved during the height of rebel/government fighting in Angola, when UNITA controlled 70 percent of the country's diamond production.

AT THE SAME TIME that Al Qaeda–piloted airplanes were crashing into the Twin Towers of the World Trade Center—and I was being told of the huge economic impact that bad publicity about conflict diamonds could have on sales—representatives from thirty-five countries were meeting privately about 45 miles outside of London, in the suburb of Twickenham. It was their fourth meeting that year, held September 11 in a rugby stadium to figure out the best way to handle the same blooming public relations nightmare that Bone described.

They were an odd mix, representing the United States, Russia, Canada, England, South Africa, Botswana, Egypt, Australia, and Bangladesh, among others, and diamond industry leaders, all members of the so-called Kimberley Process. I intended to go there later in the week to witness the rare and historic public discussion by diamond countries and industry representatives about rebel groups in Africa and the unwanted publicity that had been generated by buying diamonds from them. But the events of the day threw everyone's schedule into turmoil. I missed the opportunity to see the dirty laundry of the diamond world publicly aired. The practice of selling rough stones outside the boundaries of established taxing and exporting structures for the sake of funding insurgencies against legitimate African governments was well established and accepted by the diamond-producing and -importing countries of the world, but it was never, ever discussed in public. It was tolerated for one simple, economic reason: Taking the moral high ground was bad business. After more than a century in the making, the industry had its price controls, and in the diamond business price is everything, more important and valuable even than the life and death of entire countries.

But suddenly, within the last two years, diamonds were becoming synonymous in some circles with death and mayhem, the precise opposite of the stones' carefully marketed image as symbols of love, peace, and devotion. Most consumers have no idea where diamonds come from, either physically or geologically, and for the most part that was fine with the people who sold and marketed their jewelry to them. But now the lines between the rebel groups in Sierra Leone, Angola, and the Democratic Republic of Congo; their barbarous tactics; and how they manage to fund their long-running insurgencies were being drawn with a good deal of precision. Without quick action and a skillful public-relations response, diamonds would be facing the same consumer backlash that fur suffered in the 1980s.

Civil wars are nothing new in Africa, but in Sierra Leone in particular the carnage was numbing and the direct involvement of diamonds was a serious threat to the business of romance. Images of civilians whose arms have been crudely hacked off with rusty blades didn't mesh well with television commercials featuring hand-shadows proudly displaying expensive jewelry. One diamond industry leader is said to have had nightmares in which the tag line at the end of such commercials reads: "Amputation is forever."

Therefore, the international representatives embarked on a roundtable discussion that floated from country to country throughout the year, discussing how they could certify that diamonds offered to retailers and consumers come from "clean" sources. The procedure was dubbed the Kimberley Process, after the famous De Beers mine in South Africa, and was designed to hammer out a united front, a game plan for cutting off the flow from the rebel groups that, even if most of them knew it was practically impossible, would at least give the impression of a positive, pro-active response to the mounting criticism of the industry.

Bone himself had left the meeting to talk with me about conflict diamonds and summarize the concerns of its participants. As he noted, the potential financial impacts were "enormous" and therefore everyone involved was sincere about ending the trade.

As cold as the company's response to publicity about conflict diamonds sounds—the potential commercial loss is "enormous," but the moral dimension is merely "big," as if it were an afterthought—De Beers is at least consistent in its thinking. Very little, if anything, has been done in the company's lifetime that didn't further its commercial potential, even if it meant funding warfare to do it. Before the conflict-diamond issue gathered steam, it made economic sense to continue to trade with killers since no one was paying attention and it didn't threaten the demand for the goods; after the issue began attracting the attention of human-rights organizations and people started whispering the dreaded "B" word (boycott), it made economic sense for the industry to condemn the trade and to wash its hands for good. Since De Beers is the world's largest dealer in rough diamonds, not only was a great deal of responsibility placed at its feet in early 2000, but so were many expectations that the company would act swiftly to end the practice.

The De Beers reaction to the mounting crisis could have come from a handbook on corporate disaster management, but to understand the reaction, it's first necessary to understand the structure of what some diamond insiders still call "the syndicate."

If the name evokes images of the Mafia, it's not surprising. The world of diamond brokers, traders, smugglers, and sellers is unique unto itself, operating by rules that it sets and accountable to very few but its shareholders. There are rarely any lawyers involved, no contracts, and multimillion-dollar deals hinge on a handshake. De Beers itself is treated almost as an organized crime operation in the United States; it's barred from doing any business in America because it's considered to be in violation of U.S. antitrust laws, which seek to prevent price-fixing. In fact, the U.S. Department of Justice leveled charges against De Beers of conspiring to set prices in 1994, but the company didn't respond to them, leaving the charges in limbo until executives can be subpoenaed. As a result, De Beers executives usually don't travel to the United States, the diamond industry's largest market, because they may face a subpoena if they're tracked down. It's actually illegal for the company to have more than three executives in the United States at a time.

Because of a loophole in U.S. antitrust laws, De Beers executives can only be detained in the United States if they're in the country on "ongoing business," which is defined in the statutes as requiring three or more officers to conduct. Therefore, De Beers bosses wishing to take a vacation to Aspen, for example, must phone Johannesburg for clearance and a head count is taken of employees in the States at the time.

Most diamond houses are family-run or concentrated in the hands of a few tightly knit business associates who pass the firm down through the generations. Vast amounts of wealth flow through the 2,600 small diamond shops on 47th Street in New York, Charterhouse Street in London, and the claustrophobic cutting and polishing bazaar on Antwerp's Hoveniersstraat. Rough sales averaged $6 billion per year, and in 1999 the world's retailers sold it back to the public for $11 billion.[6] In New York City, casually dressed Russian and Hasidic men stand their posts near garbage cans keeping an eye out for window shoppers. What are you looking for? they ask quietly. Gold, diamonds? Right this way. And you're hustled into a turn-of-the-century stairwell and escorted into the narrow veins of a merchant's office, plunked in a vinyl chair and told to wait for the boss, who's either a slickly dressed Russian, a Jew with half-moon glasses, or a Lebanese chomping the stub of a cigar like he's trying to open a beer bottle with his teeth.

Like the Mafia, once you're inside the diamond syndicate, you're part of a family, one that values its privacy and jealously—even insidiously—protects the family business. De Beers has used agents to spy on competitors in Canada and in the 1950s hired a man named Sir Percy Sillitoe to run antismuggling interdiction in Sierra Leone. Sillitoe was the former head of MI-5, the British intelligence agency.

As the world's largest diamond buyer and seller, De Beers also enjoys the monopolistic perk of both buying a commodity and placing a value on it, a fact of business life that members of the cartel simply have to accept. That doesn't mean that there haven't been dissenters, however. One famous tale involves Sierra Leone and the miner who ran Selection Trust's West African operations for De Beers. In the 1950s, Edward Wharton-Tigar had his suspicions that De Beers could fairly value the diamonds he was shipping to the Central Selling Organization in London since it was the stones' sole buyer. As a test, he had 1,000 carats of his best Sierra Leone products valued by the CSO and then sent the same package to the Accra, Ghana, market for valuation. As he suspected, in Accra the parcel was valued at twice what De Beers offered.

Wharton-Tigar flew into a rage and wrote a sharp letter to Philip Oppenheimer, the nephew of Sir Ernest Oppenheimer, who had been running De Beers since 1929 and was the most powerful mining tycoon in the world. Philip told Wharton-Tigar to mind his own business, and even his friends at Selection Trust began to turn on him, warning him not to complain about the functions of the cartel.

But he was unswayed and ordered De Beers to release his Sierra Leone master sample, the cache of rough that acted as a marker for price setting. He had the diamonds independently evaluated and was told that the prices were outdated and should be raised. De Beers agreed to this, but when no increase in price was forthcoming, Wharton-Tigar stopped sending diamonds to London from Sierra Leone altogether, the equivalent of an act of mutiny.

De Beers did all it could to jerk the rug out from under the upstart miner, including threatening to remove him from his position and ban him forever from the world of diamonds, but Wharton-Tigar held his ground and was eventually invited to South Africa to discuss the problem with Harry Oppenheimer, Sir Ernest's son. The men battled it out for days, but in the end De Beers agreed on a higher price for West African goods and when Wharton-Tigar returned to Sierra Leone, the shipments to London resumed.

But De Beers isn't easily bullied and it still had one trick up its sleeve. Suddenly, Wharton-Tigar's shipments seemed to consistently contain more and more industrial-quality diamonds, according to the CSO valuators. The supposed decline of valuable gemstones in the packages neutralized the price increases. Again, Wharton-Tigar tested the system, ordering that 1,000 carats of the best gemstones be removed from the packages sent to London. The percentage of gems reported back to him barely changed, remaining stable at about 18 percent of the package. He then ordered that *all* of the gems be removed from one package and paid a visit to the official who sorted and valuated his stones. He told the man to pay particularly close attention to the gem-count in his specially prepared package and, again, it was duly reported that it contained 18.4 percent cuttable diamonds. Wharton-Tigar then plucked a bottle of gems from his pocket that had been removed from the package and denounced the scam.

Harry Oppenheimer agreed to reevaluate all of Wharton-Tigar's shipments from the previous two years and sheepishly paid him 250,000 pounds sterling in adjustments.[7]

DE BEERS EVEN KEEPS close tabs on the doings of its customers, the 120 sightholders who buy its rough once every five weeks.

Being a De Beers sightholder is a strange thing—it's a pedigree that all diamond dealers want, but at the same time it can be quite humiliating. As mentioned, the sightholders buy their goods at sights in London held every five weeks, the most important sales in the diamond world. Because different sightholders have different needs for their clients, they're required to deal with intermediary brokers—there are only six, and all have close ties to the company as their livelihood depends on staying in its favor—to try and get more of what they want in their parcels and less of what they don't. This works about as well as can be imagined. Obviously, De Beers is interested in selling its goods whether or not the sightholder wants certain types of stones, and sightholders have to rely on a combination of their broker's skill, the mood of the person preparing the parcels on their behalf, and the whims of the overall De Beers structure.

On week five of the sight cycle, brokers from all over the world fly to London and march through the same Charterhouse Street doors that I did on September 11. They're herded through mazes of guards and bulletproof glass and into a viewing room, where they're given attaché cases containing their goods. There, they inspect the diamonds and see how well they made out. De Beers calls this "feeding the ducks," a cute term for the only situation in the world where a person will pay up to $20 million—in advance—for something he hasn't even seen and be thankful for the opportunity.

To balk or refuse the parcel is to risk being kicked out of the club, forced to tramp for rough in Antwerp, Bombay, or Tel Aviv or, worse, buy resold DTC rough from another sightholder. Five of the largest of the 120 sightholders are owned by De Beers itself, making the company one of its own biggest customers. This is a means of tracking what sightholders make off their sights, allowing the company to measure their complaints about quality against their in-house earnings. The company also owns a London cutting and polishing business, which receives the same type of parcel as the sightholders so that De Beers can test-market the goods and set sight prices. Sightholders who toe the line are rewarded. Richard Wake-Walker, a former De Beers employee whose jobs included preparing selling mixtures, client selection, and "deselection," said, "We didn't hand out envelopes stuffed with cash, but there was a Christmas allocation of specials and they went to valued clients. We might charge them $20,000 for a stone worth, say, $200,000."[8]

To fall out of favor with De Beers means finding another line of work for many diamond merchants.

All of this ruthlessness, espionage, and secrecy serves two purposes: protecting value and wielding control, which are more or less the same thing in the diamond business. It's a curious symbiosis—diamonds wouldn't be what they are today without De Beers and De Beers would be nothing without diamonds. And over the century, De Beers's policies have become critical to governments, nearly a million employees the world over, and thousands of retailers, all dependent on the continued marketability of diamonds.

It's ironic that men who give themselves names like Rambo, Superman, and Mosquito—and whose greatest achievements are measured in body counts—can pull the rug out from under such an organization. By chopping off civilian arms and legs, they've managed to do the one thing that all the syndicate's policies, henchmen, and founding fathers have worked so hard to avoid over the past 120 years: crack the carefully polished façade of the hardest substance known to man.

THE DIAMOND INDUSTRY knew all along where some of its stones were coming from, but that's not to say that midstream processors like cutters, importers, and resellers actually bought the gems from someone with a pistol in one hand and a bag of rough in the other. In this close-knit world, the vast majority of diamond deals are based on trust and a person's word. In a world as small as that of the diamond industry, that's usually enough to foster long-term relationships. A long-time buyer of polish from a shop in Antwerp, for example, wouldn't dream of asking to see the paper trail for the diamonds he's buying. If a dealer says they're clean, they take their word for it. Once cut, it's almost impossible for anyone to tell where a diamond originated.

"It is a known fact that if you take a diamond out of the blue and you give it to any expert, they cannot tell where the goddamned thing came from," said Tom Shane, the owner of jewelry retailer The Shane Company, one of the largest U. S. importers of polish. "You take a diamond that's been cut and polished and there's no human being on earth who can tell with certainty where that stone came from."

Like most jewelry companies, The Shane Company doesn't deal in rough at all. Such businesses are the final link between the sightholder stage, the manufacturing stage, and the consumer. To get the diamonds that his company sets in jewelry, Shane employs full-time diamond buyers in Antwerp and Tel Aviv and often visits shops in Bombay. He pays cash on the spot to a network of thirty or forty long-time suppliers who produce the type of stones that Shane's U.S. customers buy: under 5 carats in weight with high quality and high color.

Like everyone else in the diamond industry, Shane is worried about what conflict diamonds could do to his livelihood and he therefore requires the polish houses to provide an affidavit that the stones he's buying haven't come from war zones. Needless to say, this gives him little control on his pipeline. Outside of taking the dealer's word, Shane has no way of independently knowing where exactly the diamonds originated. The rough that his suppliers work with likely passed through dozens of hands and perhaps as many countries before ending up on the cutting wheel. Even the polisher may not know for sure where they come from.

But Shane considers the affidavit good enough for two reasons. One, he has specific needs from the suppliers, stones of a particular size and quality, and if they're unable to produce a consistent yield to meet his weekly—and sometimes daily—orders, he'll find another supplier. Conflict diamonds, he said, are about as reliable in their supply as stolen diamonds. The Shane Company doesn't need one or two good diamonds once in a while, it needs a lot of the same type of diamond regularly.

And the second reason is that, given the intimacy of the industry and the amount of money circulating through it, Shane doesn't believe any of his suppliers would risk getting caught with an RUF or UNITA diamond.

"We have affidavits from the owners of these firms, and if they ever were caught dealing in one single conflict diamond, they would be thrown out of the entire community," Shane said. "They wouldn't jeopardize themselves. They're not going to fraudulently sign an affidavit and risk what would be their destruction. There's no way they're going to knowingly violate that trust, they've got nowhere to run and hide.

"The industry as a whole is truthfully outraged, and you can also say scared to death," he continued. "We're outraged that these wars are being funded in Africa and possibly some ties to terrorism. You're dealing with basically several hundred multimillionaires and none of us are so stupid as to risk what we've got for what is only two or three or four percent of the business. We have much more to lose and we have so much at stake if the public were to turn against purchases of diamonds because of this three or four percent. No one is that greedy or that dumb."[9]

Although it's obvious that no one wants to be associated with diamonds from people named Colonel Backblast or Queen Chop Hands, it's inevitable that many are indeed unwittingly selling such stones to an equally unsuspecting public. A mere glance at the glaring anomalies between Belgium's import statistics compared to the records of the exporting countries shows that there is a very high volume of questionable stones floating throughout Antwerp. The Gambia, Guinea, Liberia, and Ivory Coast sent volumes of diamonds well beyond their production capacity into Belgium throughout the 1990s, while legal exports from Sierra Leone—the only country that could account for the crush of diamonds coming out of West Africa—were only a fraction of its suspected reserves. And none of them were thrown away because they were suspicious. It's apparently no big deal to show up in Antwerp with a box of rough and proclaim that it's from anywhere you can think of because it will be duly recorded as an import, even if it exceeds the known annual output of the originating country.

Such obvious anomalies are the result of the Diamond High Council's lenient import requirements that importers list only the diamonds' country of "province," that is, where they were last located before entering Belgium. That's why the Swiss can claim that 97 percent of their imported stones are "British," and the British can claim, if those same stones are shipped back to them, that 97 percent of theirs are "Swiss." This brazenly dishonest shell game is simply a way to launder illicit diamonds and render them acceptable to the industry.

At the end of the 1990s, the Diamond High Council took steps to correct this weakness and provide some transparency to the process by requiring that importers list both a diamond's province as well as its origin, the place where it was mined. This turned out to be a laughable failure, however. When a UN panel of experts reviewed import licenses for one company shuttling goods between Liberia and Belgium, they discovered that "diamonds *far in excess of the quality or quantity available in Liberia* had been imported as Liberian in province *and in origin*" (original emphasis).[10]

ALTHOUGH THERE'S NO EVIDENCE that De Beers was directly involved in schemes such as these, the company had an obligation to move quickly to distance the industry from such practices for the sake of its reputation and that of its goods, especially after the conflict-diamond issue broke. That's the problem with having a big name in an industry known to have a disreputable side; the sins of the few are multiplied to encompass the many. Economics dictated that De Beers react and that it do so precisely, quickly, and according to a disaster-management plan that could have been scripted by a politician caught in a sex scandal.

The first order of business was to vacate the scene of the crime, and within a year of the Global Witness report, the company shut down its Conakry, Guinea, buying office because diamonds from Sierra Leone were almost certainly trading hands there. Tim Weekes of the Diamond Trading Company admitted as much to me. The company had cleared out of Freetown and Monrovia in 1985, a fact that's quickly stated in any conversation about conflict diamonds with a De Beers representative. The hope is that anyone who hears that will assume that the company receives no diamonds from Sierra Leone.

But Partnership Africa Canada, an organization that has been particularly vocal about the blood-diamonds issue, has said that it's "virtually inconceivable" that this is true. The De Beers shop in Guinea was kept open because it had been relatively quiet on that front, because RUF-smuggled diamonds had to travel farther to reach Conakry. With the breakdown in diplomatic relations between the governments of Sierra Leone and Liberia—which led to the border being closed in 2001—Conakry stepped into the vacuum and has begun filling Monrovia's laundering role. Yet the border closing didn't exactly create a new phenomenon, as Kamajor fighters had been trading their own ill-gotten diamonds in Conakry since the mid-1990s, and it's a much shorter trip to the Guinean capital from Freetown for fringe buyers like Jacob Singer. Once Monrovia became off-limits for everyone but the top RUF traders, however, the trip to Conakry looked more appealing.

The next step for De Beers was to wheel 180 degrees from its chairman's 1996 statements to shareholders and vituperate madly about conflict diamonds, but in the same breath defend the diamond industry and its profits by qualifying that the trade accounted for only four or five percent of world diamond output. True or not, and it likely is true, this self-serving defense seemed more like spin control and did little to redeem the tarnishing reputation of diamonds. Four or five percent still killed a lot of Africans and made the industry hundreds of millions in profits. The same is true of De Beers's lame excuse of hiding behind their definition of conflict diamonds, which sounds accurate enough, but provided the company with linguistic wiggle room. According to De Beers, conflict diamonds are "mined or stolen by rebels who are in opposition to the legitimate government of a country."

According to that definition, De Beers didn't buy rebel diamonds from Angola at all from 1990 to 1998 since a UN-brokered peace process was in effect and UNITA was technically part of the government as a recognized political party under the agreement, even though it engaged in diamond-funded combat with its MLPA "colleagues" almost the entire time.

Aside from self-preservation, De Beers's desire to cushion the industry from a fatal blow from blood-diamond publicity has a number of legitimate arguments. The industry, after all, is bigger than the company alone and in fact is critical to the economies of at least four nations. Botswana, the largest gem-diamond producer in the world, exported $1.7 billion worth of diamonds in 1999 and had an economic growth rate of 9 percent that year, making it the fastest-growing economy in the world. Botswana has a stable, democratic government and diamond exports account for 75 percent of the country's annual foreign exchange earnings, 65 percent of the government's revenue, and 35 percent of its gross domestic product. Likewise, the diamond industry in Namibia is the country's largest employer and its annual $400 million in diamond exports accounts for 40 percent of its foreign exchange earnings. South Africa would not be the economic powerhouse that it is today without the diamond industry: Fifty percent of De Beers's mining profits in South Africa go to the government in the form of taxes and more than 11,000 people are employed in the diamond industry there. South Africa also has a large cutting and polishing industry, a rarity among diamond-producing countries. Farther afield, in India, home to the largest diamond-cutting and -polishing sector in the world, nearly a million people are employed in the industry.[11]

The fact that De Beers's profits are tied directly to the production of all three African countries—it has a 50 percent stake in the production of both Namibia and Botswana—doesn't dilute the fact that a diamond boycott would have disastrous economic and geopolitical effects in these countries.

But arguments on the merits of the diamond industry's contribution to economic development in African countries wasn't enough to stem criticism. The potential for mounting outcry demanded tangible action, so the company vowed to expel any diamond bourser—a diamond house that deals in rough and polished stones—caught dealing with rebels, a threat that's on par with excommunication from the Catholic Church or having a hit put on you by the mob. De Beers took the first step in that direction by ending all trade on the open market, a move that included refusing to buy diamonds at all from Angola even if they are purportedly from clean channels. This action delivered a resounding blow, instantly wiping out $15 million a week from the market, demonstrating that when it comes to abolishing war goods, De Beers holds the most sway. In early 2000, De Beers began placing notices in each of its sightholders' parcels promising that the rough they were sold was squeaky clean.

Few people believed that. As mentioned, De Beers is what it is because of its aggressive buying policy, a corporate strategy meant to keep the diamond market in tune with its wishes. Since diamond prices would have crashed a long time ago if every stone ever discovered had been allowed to make it to market, the strategy resulted in a massive stockpile of stones in London, gathered over decades from sources around the world, and valued by the company at $4 billion (the actual value is probably much less because if De Beers attempted to sell the stockpile, the price of rough would plummet). Open-market buying didn't end until 2000, so it is impossible that De Beers can certify that 100 percent of its diamonds in the stockpile are from clean trading streams. Furthermore, the certification is only good for the sightholder. Many De Beers clients buy rough from sources other than the DTC, most of which are unsheltered by such guarantees, and so the De Beers warranty can be used to mask the presence of conflict goods if the unwarrantied stones are mixed with the De Beers goods.

SO IN THE WAKE of the campaign by Global Witness, it was widely agreed that conflict diamonds are bad, both for the countries in which the conflicts are occurring and for the future health of the industry, as well as, by extension, the health of some of the few successful and peaceful countries in Africa.

Now the question was what to do about it.

Underlying any talk of further actions is a slew of legislation: In 1998, the Security Council passed Resolution 1173, a sanction against diamonds from Angolan rebels, and 1176, one against diamonds from the RUF. In 2000, it passed Resolution 1306, which banned all countries from importing any rough from Sierra Leone until a certification process could be designed with the help of the

Diamond High Council in Antwerp. In the United States, Congressman Tony Hall and Senator Judd Gregg introduced the Clean Diamond Act in 2001, a law that seeks to ensure that all diamonds imported into the United States are verifiably from clean sources.

None of those laws did much in a real-world sense to stop the flow from Sierra Leone; the RUF and those who helped them were smugglers, after all, and not deterred by legal restrictions. Even the Diamond High Council's introduction of the Sierra Leone authenticity certificate didn't seem to do a whole lot of good. Men like Jacob Singer barely noticed that there was a new system in place for the exportation of legitimate goods. After all, he was in the business of smuggling illicit goods. More drastic measures were also implemented, including the formation of the World Diamond Council in Belgium in 2001, an organization meant to speak for the industry as a whole, from mine to retail, and to liaise with the UN on the issue of conflict diamonds. The World Diamond Council's only purpose is to handle PR and spin control for the conflict-diamond issue.

And of course, there's the Kimberley Process, which was organized by the South African government and held its first meeting in Kimberley in May 2000. The issue the group tackled seemed simple but in fact was frustratingly complicated: How to ensure that diamonds sold around the world by legitimate houses, retail stores, and producers are not from African rebel groups. Coming up with a solution would prove nearly impossible.

Suggestions have ranged from the impossible to the simply unworkable, and there's no magic bullet in sight. Some groups have proposed branding the rough with a laser at its on-site origin so that it can be monitored and verified as it makes its way to the cutting houses and eventually the consumers, who could rely on the mark as proof that their gem was clean. In written testimony before Congress in 2000, De Beers torpedoed this idea as "completely impractical." Diamonds can lose up to half of their weight during cutting and would almost certainly lose their identifying marks. In addition, the cost of branding small stones wouldn't be worth what the producers could recoup on their sale.

Another idea was to create an international database of chemical and physical characteristics of diamonds from all the locations where they are found in the world. Diamonds could then be identified by source through mass spectrometry. With this system, a laser would vaporize a tiny portion of a sample diamond and the vapor would be analyzed for impurities. The ratio of these impurities—which can contain up to fifty different elements—varies from mine to mine, because the kimberlite they erupted from ages ago was composed differently from pipe to pipe. Analysts would, in theory, be able to identify which pipe a rough diamond had come from (although that may not necessarily help figure out the source country; erosion can carry diamonds for miles and what started in one country might get picked up in another after being washed downriver).

The difficulty with this plan lies in data collection. There are hundreds of diamond-producing kimberlite pipes in the world and those being worked are highly guarded. Why would a company want to share with the world the chemical makeup of its claim? Such information is treated as trade secrets and competing geologists could use the information to sniff out unclaimed diamond fields in the region.

The solution that seems to have the most support within the Kimberley Process is also the easiest to implement, although it may never work. It's simply an extension of the certification process of the type used by the Sierra Leone government. The idea is that anyone wishing to sell diamonds on the international market would be required to provide a uniform, unforgeable paper trail for all the goods being sold. What that means is that anywhere diamonds are sold legitimately—whether in Kenema or Freetown or Tel Aviv or London—a potential buyer or customs investigator can ask to see the documentation and from it ascertain exactly where the diamonds were discovered and whose hands they've flowed through. Customs inspectors can follow the trail if there are questions and levy proposed sanctions against the diamond house selling the goods if they prove to be fraudulent. De Beers suggested that anyone caught dealing in conflict diamonds be banned forever from all professional diamond organizations worldwide, which would be the financial equivalent of the guillotine, a fitting metaphor considering the actions of the RUF gem-producers.

The problem is that diamonds are not timber or ore. They're so easily mobile that there's very little that this plan can do to address the mixing of legitimately purchased diamonds with those bought from rebel groups. For example, representatives of the Diamond High Council, as a final step in developing Sierra Leone's certification program, visited upcountry mining towns to inspect goods and ensure that they were from state-licensed mines. But since they weren't there when the diamonds were actually mined, how can they say for sure?

This approach would also require an as-yet-unseen level of both organization and honesty on the part of customs officials and government overseers in developing nations. In a place like Sierra Leone, where the average monthly income for a customs official is less than the daily earnings of a minimum-wage employee in the United States, why not take a cut of the action in exchange for a certificate? And lastly, diamonds are passed from hand to hand dozens if not hundreds of times before wending their way into the mainstream, often in jungles and deserts where it might not be convenient to produce a certificate. Complete uniformity in a $6 billion-a-year industry involving pebbles—where transactions take place in some of the world's most desolate areas—seems a remote possibility.

Diamonds are so portable—and their value so enticing—that no system of certificates will ever be able to answer, for certain, whether or not the diamonds in an engagement ring came from perfectly legitimate sources in South Africa or from under the tongue of an RUF rebel called Colonel Poison.

IN SPITE OF THE BAD PRESS and evasive solutions, public awareness about conflict diamonds couldn't have come at a better time for De Beers. Even though it still dominated the diamond industry, its once iron grip was slipping, thanks in no small part to new Canadian fields in the Barren Lands that were turning out stunning gems and selling them largely outside De Beers's channels. The company's control over rough had slipped from 90 percent in the time of Rhodes to 65 percent at the end of the twentieth century. The company's manipulation of diamond prices was actually benefiting its competitors as well as itself.

Earlier in the same year that Global Witness delivered its roundhouse punch to the industry, De Beers hired an outside analyst to review its finances, the first time in its history this had been done. The Boston consulting firm that did the review suggested that De Beers abandon its self-appointed role as "market custodian" and let diamond prices take care of themselves in true market fashion. Again, timing was critical. The suggestion came at a time when demand from American consumers was at an all-time high.

According to author Matthew Hart, "In response to strong demand, De Beers shoveled its stockpile out of Charterhouse Street as if it were clearing the driveway of snow. In the first half of 2000, compared to the same period the year before, De Beers profits rose by 226 percent, to $887 million."[12]

With the stockpile reduced by a fourth, De Beers planned to make up any potential profit losses from deflating global prices by getting into the downstream business for the first time: the retail market. In early 2001, the company announced a joint business venture with French luxury retailer LVMH, the company that sells TAG Hauer watches and Moet & Chandon champagne.

Thus, in an industry already largely identified with its name, for the first time the company began selling cut and polished De Beers *brand* diamonds. It is now the only company that sells both rough and finished stones, stones that—once the stockpile is depleted—have been in its possession from the time they're found in its private mines in Africa to the time they walk out the door on the finger of a customer. The conflict-diamond PR "disaster" will actually do nothing but benefit De Beers. Now that it has officially ended its policy of buying on the open market, it will be the only company in the world that can guarantee that its finished jewelry comes from clean sources.

In the words of Israeli diamond writer Chaim Even-Zohar, "The brave man would write that the whole issue of war diamonds can only benefit De Beers."[13]

DE BEERS'S OVERHAUL of its business plan included another massive change that effectively draws the curtain around the diamond giant's operations once and for all. The entire De Beers Group—which is composed of both the original De Beers Consolidated Mines, Ltd. and De Beers Centenary AG, which operates all the company's mining interests outside South Africa—was purchased off the London and South African stock exchanges by insiders in 2001, rendering the company's operations invisible to the public. Events in Canada made such a move necessary.

In 1999, a diamond rush in Canada made history not only by locating a fresh field of superb gem-quality diamonds—a yield that will amount to 15 percent by value of the world market once fully on line—but by thwarting De Beers's attempts to corral the find. If any place in the world represented Sierra Leone's spectral opposite in terms of hellish mining environments, it's clearly the Barren Lands in the extreme northern reaches of Canada. In November, three-quarters of the day is darkness and temperatures average 30 degrees below zero without wind. And there's always wind.

This was the situation in 1991 when miners Chris Jennings and Gren Thomas boarded a Twin Otter airplane in one of Canada's hinterland cities, Yellowknife in the Northwest Territories, and flew 200 miles farther north, in a desperate race to stake claims before De Beers. When the men arrived in Yellowknife, they learned that De Beers was already there, chartering helicopters for a big push into the north.

In such an environment, locating diamonds is rather different from in places like Sierra Leone. Frozen tundra, nine months of nonstop snowfall, and glacial movements require astute geological surveys, not just blind luck. Therefore, in the early days the Barren Lands explorers were hunched over in the land of caribou and bears, digging holes and lugging around sacks of dirt and rocks, the only humans for hundreds of miles amid the eskers and frozen lakes. Their samples would be flown to laboratories and examined for kimberlite indicators, traces of minerals that can be expected to

be found in diamond-rich kimberlite. If you find red pyrope gar-
nets, green chrome diopsides, or black ilmenites, you might be
sniffing in the right place. From that point, it's just a matter of
detective work, intuition, and good luck.

What made Canada such a threat to De Beers wasn't its harsh
mining environment or the high quality of goods being discovered,
but the fact that Canada is home to most of the diamond industry's
pilot-fish—small, publicly traded exploration companies known in
the business as the "juniors." Usually comprising little more than a
few close friends and exploration experts, the juniors had the ability
to track down rumors and move quickly to stake claims. De Beers's
mode of operation has usually been to allow these companies to find
diamonds and then buy out their claims once the hard exploratory
work has been done and the discovery has proven its worth.

And that might have been the scenario again if the major find
hadn't been discovered by BHP Minerals, a subsidiary of Broken
Hill Proprietary Company, an Australian mining company. BHP's
North American headquarters was in San Francisco and the company owned several coalfields in the U.S. Southwest, a fact that
scuttled any possibility of a De Beers partnership: The conglomerate's antitrust troubles in the United States would likely jeopardize
any arrangement. The fact that BHP already had a solid presence
in the United States was equally worrisome. The belief was that
arctic diamonds would flow almost exclusively south, into the maw
of the world's hungriest diamond consumer, America. Therefore,
one of the most valuable diamond discoveries of the twentieth
century seemed likely to be out of reach of the company that had
made diamonds what they are in the first place.

De Beers was facing similar challenges on other fronts. Once
his work in Canada was finished, Chris Jennings boldly began

looking for diamonds on De Beers's doorstep, in Kimberley—and he found them.

Not 200 miles from the conglomerate's stomping ground in Kimberley, Jennings used old cartographical information, gumshoe footwork, and modern exploration methods to discover a 25-mile-long kimberlite fissure and a micropipe on a farm called Marsfrontien. Although De Beers eventually was awarded the claim in court, after the heirs to the farm sold it the mineral rights, Jennings wasn't finished pounding on the giant. He moved to Angola, where his company won the right to explore one of the largest diamond-producing kimberlites in the world, in Camafuca. Under the deal, Jennings's company paid the MPFL mineral and exploration fees and shared the profits with the government.[14]

This trio of blows, all delivered within a few short years in the 1990s, knocked De Beers off balance. In 1999, it took the advice of its financial consultant and agreed to quit its role as "market custodian" of the global diamond market, selling a quarter of its London stockpile. The timing couldn't have been better; in 2000, economic prosperity in the United States was at an all-time high. The company ended the year selling a record $5.7 billion worth of diamonds. Profits exceeded $1.2 billion.[15]

The new business strategy for the company was retail selling. It's such an obvious move that it's a wonder it hadn't been pursued earlier. The De Beers name is synonymous with diamonds, luxury, romance, and commitment. Every other retailer in the world will now have to compete with "A Diamond Is Forever," one of the most recognized advertising slogans in the history of marketing. As these companies attempt to stir up demand for their product, they will fill that demand—where else?—from De Beers, the only diamond retailer in the world that will also sell millions of carats of rough a year to its competitors. It's estimated that retail sales could account for $500 million a year to De Beers.[16]

On June 8, 2001, De Beers officially disappeared from the radar. All publicly owned shares of the company and its subsidiaries were purchased by a consortium of buyers collectively called DB Investments. The buyers were the Oppenheimer family, which has controlled the company since the 1920s; Anglo-American Corporation of South Africa, De Beers's sister corporation that focuses on gold exploration; and Debswana, the diamond exploration company owned jointly by De Beers and the government of Botswana.

The absorption of the company from the South African and London stock exchanges into private hands means that De Beers no longer has to make detailed public financial reports to securities organizations or shareholders. According to the script drafted by Cecil Rhodes more than 100 years ago, De Beers is officially accountable to no one.

6

WAGING PEACE:
Taking the Conflict out of "Conflict Diamonds"

Makeni, Sierra Leone

WE FOUND RUF MAJOR Gabril Kallon hungover from a night of indulgent marijuana and gin intake; there was apparently little else to do in Makeni, the RUF's northern stronghold, except get blinded on drugs and wait to see what would happen with the UNAMSIL peace agreement. Even in his exhausted state, Kallon was a fierce person. In his mid-twenties, he had the eyes of an experienced killer, a look I'd seen almost everywhere in Sierra Leone, a look that said life can be taken without a second thought. He was an important cog in the RUF diamond machinery, a man whose brutality inspired enough terror in his countrymen that they would abandon any place the RUF wanted for itself.

I was sitting on the front porch of Kallon's compound, a pink concrete house that, according to the sign still standing in the front yard, was once the Makeni headquarters for Concern, an aid organization that had fled the city like most other groups. Makeni was the RUF's political and military base in the summer of 2001 and most peacekeepers were unwelcome there. I'd hitched a ride with three employees of the UN's World Food Program to meet some RUF leaders, an endeavor that, until I ran into Kallon, proved almost utterly fruitless. I'd had a five-minute conversation with Eldrid Collins, one of the RUF's military leaders turned political bosses, but he wasn't happy that I'd arrived unannounced in the middle of a strategy meeting. I told him the name of my guest house in Freetown and he promised that his men would look me up in a few days for a formal interview, something that never happened.

So I wandered the pulverized town of Makeni with Aya Schneerson, one of WFP's directors, as she scouted the market for aid food being resold on the black market. Hundreds of RUF supporters and refugees were jammed into the market, a four- or five-block maze of kiosks, rough timber food stands, upturned buckets, and gaunt faces, all centered around a dump truck that reeked of fish. Shirtless men stood on top with shovels, yelling down into the crowd, selling the skinny fish by the spadeful. Movement was practically impossible without resorting to shoving and jostling and the cacophony was deafening: hundreds of people yelling, screaming, mumbling, laughing, and crying, a sardine tin of humanity that emanated body heat like sun-baked asphalt.

We made our way to a quiet corner of the teeming market and bought Cokes, wondering about our next move. We hadn't found any illegally sold aid food and we hadn't found any RUF leaders who had time to talk with us. Just as we were contemplating leaving for Freetown, a tall black woman in an ankle-length dress recognized Aya. She was one of Kallon's wives and she offered to take us to him.

"Is it far?" Aya asked.

"No, no," the woman answered. "Small-small walk."

Based on that description, we decided to leave the WFP Land Cruiser and walk, none of us thinking that a "small-small" walk might be different for us than for someone used to walking everywhere. We were soon out of the city center and meandering down one of the access roads, the street lined with widely spaced houses that had been destroyed during the recent years of fighting. Most were now occupied by RUF fighters who'd claimed one for themselves. Several sat on their porches, polishing rifles and looking with suspicion on two white-skinned people trying to act calm during a stroll through RUF territory, heading deeper and deeper into the jungle. We were nervously discussing the intelligence of leaving the truck behind when we came upon a UNAMSIL checkpoint manned by Nigerians, one of the few times in my life when the sight of a peacekeeper only made me more uneasy.

"The Nigerians won't lift a finger for us if something happens," Aya said, reading my thoughts.

But we glided through the checkpoint and after another hour of walking, when we were ready to give up and go back, our guide pointed to the former Concern building. "There," she said.

The compound looked like an African version of a fraternity house. The porch was clogged with armed fighters lounging with a tense boredom and gangs of chickens fought in the courtyard. Two black pickup trucks were parked in the dirt, tricked out in suburban ghetto-style, festooned with antennas, decorated with peeling and sun-faded stickers depicting Bob Marley, marijuana leaves, and geometric designs. We were regarded warily by Kallon's squad and were eventually invited to sit with them.

Aya was the center of attention. White people tend to draw stares in the African outback, but attractive white women with long blonde hair are rare enough that their presence can stop the economy, if there were one. I was pointed to a chair on the corner of the porch and ignored as she did most of the talking.

Kallon emerged from the gloom of the house, shirtless and wearing tight-fitting black jeans. Even though he was only a midranking officer, he was the commander of Lunsar District, centered on the town of the same name about 55 miles west of Makeni. We'd been through Lunsar earlier in the day. The site of ferocious battles the year before, the town was deserted except for RUF patrols. Almost all the buildings in Lunsar are flattened and the jungle has moved in like a hungry scavenger plundering a corpse. We hadn't stayed long there; Lunsar's distance from Makeni made it a tense and boring outpost and those we encountered seemed to be weighing the opportunity to terrorize unexpected visitors. One young RUF soldier who reeked of ganja followed me throughout the town, staring nonstop from behind thick wraparound sunglasses, saying nothing, but obviously waiting for me to fall behind like a wounded fawn being tracked by an inexperienced hyena.

My relative anonymity on the Concern porch was shattered when I introduced myself to Kallon.

"Greg *Campbell*?" came a booming voice from the other end of the porch. A huge RUF soldier leaned toward me with sudden interest. "From Colorado?"

What? How could he know that? I thought quickly back to everything I'd done in Sierra Leone up to that point that could have caused my reputation to precede me, way out *here,* in the middle of the jungle, to a commandeered headquarters deep in RUF territory. I could think of nothing.

"Yes?"

The man laughed. "We talked on the phone!"

It took a few minutes for it to sink in. Before embarking for Africa, I'd gotten one of the RUF's satellite phone numbers from a colleague who worked for the *Washington Post* and I'd placed several late-night calls from the comfort of my Colorado home to the jungles of Sierra Leone trying to talk to Gabril Massaquoi, the RUF military spokesman. I never managed to connect with Massaquoi, but had several long conversations with the people who'd answered the phone. By the most random of coincidences, this man happened to be one of them.

It was just the icebreaker we needed. The soldiers softened up and Kallon finally turned his attention from Aya to me for a time. I was of course interested in knowing from the RUF's perspective if the peace process touted so earnestly in UNAMSIL headquarters in Freetown was really going to work and how. And especially how RUF commanders would adjust to living without their diamonds-for-weapons economy, the only one they've ever known.

The civil war over diamonds in Sierra Leone is unique in that everyone involved in the fighting is so equally culpable in the violence and human rights violations—accusations of civilian amputations are leveled not only at the RUF, but also at the SLA, Kamajors, and ECOMOG—that peacekeepers are in the unenviable position of having to deal directly with killers and torturers and entrust them to varying degrees within an uncertain peace process. The Lomé Accords are a stark illustration of this, in which RUF leaders were given high positions in government without the benefit of elections, but it was evident elsewhere at lower levels.

Kallon, for instance, was the commander of a force that looted, terrorized, and besieged Lunsar, and on the day that I met him, he was preparing to transition into a new job as Kono District coordinator for child disarmament with UNICEF. It's not unusual that the advocacy organization would rely on local fighters to negotiate with their colleagues to release child soldiers, but Kallon seemed far from the best choice for such a delicate job. The World Food Program had to negotiate with Kallon to coordinate aid-food deliveries to schools in Lunsar and other areas under his control, and during our long walk to meet him, Aya had warned me to be very careful in my interaction with him. Educated in little more than terrorist-style guerilla warfare, he knew nothing of compromise, preferring to settle disputes with a MAC-10 machine-pistol. "These are very bad guys," Aya said more than once.

But he seemed to be warming to his new job. As we were leaving, he invited me to accompany his men on a mission to Kono the following week, on behalf of UNICEF. He planned to load up one of the pickup trucks with guards, rifles, and rockets to barnstorm the Kamajor front near Koidu to see about evacuating young RUF fighters there. "We'll get in a big fight and save some little children," he grinned.

I declined.

ONE OF THE BEST WAYS to end the trade in conflict diamonds is to end conflict where diamonds are found. If you have no war, you have no problem. Even though smuggling will likely never stop completely, it's easier to live with the possibility that your diamond paid a common thief rather than an uncommon band of savage murderers. If there ever seemed a time in the past ten years when peace may have a lasting chance in Sierra Leone, it was the latter half of 2001, even though every previous peace attempt had been a dramatic and bloody disaster.

From the perspective of Margaret Novicki, the civilian spokesperson for the UN mission, things couldn't be going better, despite the fact that in the summer of 2001 the RUF still mined and sold diamonds uncontested in areas where the UN had only a marginal presence. A disarmament deal signed in Freetown by UNAMSIL, RUF, and the government in May 2001 was no different than any of the dozens of peace prospects that had failed miserably in the past few years, but you'd never know it talking to UNAMSIL representatives, who rarely acknowledged the hurdles yet to be overcome. The RUF was to morph into a political party and all of its soldiers and those of the Kamajors were to have laid down their arms by November 30, 2001. Although some 37,000 fighters—out of an estimated 50,000 combatants—had in fact turned in weapons to UNAMSIL by then, the most important RUF posts in Kono and Kailahun had yet to begin the process of demobilizing.[1] Although the RUF was still firmly in charge of the diamond areas and continuing to mine and sell gems across the border in Liberia, RUF leaders continued to promise compliance with the agreement.

"They agreed at the highest levels," Novicki had assured me. Novicki is a large American woman with a fondness for billowy African dresses and Marlboro Lights. "The commanders are playing a very big role in terms of sensitizing the soldiers on the ground about what the disarmament means. The only real problems we face now are logistical problems with having the facilities on the ground to receive a large number of combatants."

Well, that didn't seem to be the only problem, which I discovered traveling to Makeni with the WFP that day. Our overland trip had begun in Freetown and included a stop along the way at a disarmament camp in Port Loko, about 50 miles from the capital. Strategically, the village is in a treasured location at the end of Port Loko Creek, a freshwater tributary that feeds into the Sierra Leone River and leads directly to Freetown, providing perfect access for seaborne government assaults and the movement of heavy equipment to an interior staging area. It's also a key source of bauxite, with an estimated 46 million tons of reserve waiting to be mined. But the government has rarely been able to control the area and the RUF fought bitterly for Port Loko all the way up to the summer of 2000, when two journalists and several Nigerian soldiers were killed in an RUF ambush on the road leading from nearby Rogberi Junction to Lunsar.

The fact that more RUF and Kamajor fighters turned up at the gates of the Port Loko disarmament center than UNAMSIL expected perhaps has more to do with miscommunication than with a true desire to end the war, something I learned simply by showing up there.

The camp itself looks more like a POW compound than the first stage in a reintegration process. Located in a former school complex, the camp is a square of high fences and barbed wire guarded by Nigerians with heavy machine guns in fortified sandbag bunkers. Even though UNAMSIL provides security, WFP provides the food and UNHCR provided the tents, the camp is administered by the government's National Committee for Demobilization, Disarmament and Reintegration, called the DDR. And it seemed to operate about as well as anything else run by the government.

More than 3,000 former fighters—both RUF and Kamajors— roamed the dirt courtyard or lounged in hot plastic tents that accommodated up to twenty people. According to the agreement, anyone who arrived at the gates with an unloaded AK-47, FN rifle, or other long-barreled rifle would be given flip-flops, a rattan mat, food, and the opportunity to enroll in carpentry or masonry classes. The combatants are encouraged to spend up to six weeks at the camp phasing from combat mode to civilian mode, at which time they're given an ID card and the equivalent of $15 for transportation anywhere in the country.

But the combatants I met weren't clear on some of these details. They were under the impression that they'd be given the Sierra Leone equivalent of $300 once they were discharged, a fortune in bush terms. This had been the case for a short while, but then UNAMSIL discovered that for every rifle turned in to the UN, $300 would buy two or three more on the arms market. So UNAMSIL's private sponsors that provided the cash—including the Soros Foundation and other philanthropy organizations—pulled their funding of the program. So the $300 was whittled down to $15, something few combatants discovered until they'd already turned in their arms. And they weren't pleased with it.

"I have sent a letter to my field commander in Kambia telling him to stop the disarmament," announced a young RUF commander, Lieutenant Mohammed Fofanah. Like many of the others, he was decked out in a Tupac Shakur T-shirt, Hawaiian shorts, and sunglasses. Also like the others, he was highly agitated at the decommissioning process. "I told my men to put down their weapons and trust that the DDR will do the right thing. This camp is fucking bullshit."

Indeed, there was a long list of "bullshit," which was shouted to me by an increasingly large and unruly crowd of ex-combatants. There were no medical facilities, not enough food, no video entertainment, no soccer balls for the younger kids, poor-quality flip-flops, and—most importantly—not enough money waiting at the end of the process. One kid was mostly agitated because he was promised a bicycle if he disarmed and he hadn't seen one yet.

"What makes you think you're getting a bike?" I asked him.

"It's in Lomé!"

Of course, the peace accords mention no such thing, but the fact that this boy and others were so out of touch with the reality of what was happening did not seem to bode well for the peace process; where UNAMSIL was trying to end a brutal war that has killed and mutilated thousands of people, many RUF were acting like they were enrolling in summer camp. It was simultaneously frightening, amusing, and depressing to hear ruthless killers complaining that they didn't have movies to watch or balls to play with. Frightening because it spoke to how tenuous the peace process was and illuminated the mentality of the fighters; amusing because the camp had almost everything they said it didn't (including soccer balls, which were being booted about within sight of our gathering; medical facilities; and food delivered almost daily from the WFP); and depressing because you were reminded of how young most of the RUF's soldiers were and how fundamentally they'd missed out on childhoods that most people take for granted. The kid who complained to me was probably no older than 13. He had likely killed people and could fire an automatic rifle in combat, but he'd probably never ridden a bike.

But there was little time to reflect on this at the moment. The crowd had lathered itself into a righteous froth about the perceived injustices of the camp and attacked a food-aid truck while we were talking. The hapless driver had just delivered sacks of rice and grain and was leaving for more when some former fighters surrounded the truck and began rocking it back and forth, threatening to topple it. Across the compound, the Nigerians looked on with amusement; seeing that he was in his predicament alone, the driver gunned the truck and plowed through the crowd, scattering women and children from its path.

"Ah! You see?!" shouted Fofanah, arms outstretched, his face incredulous. "He tried to run them over! We will never disarm if these are the conditions we must suffer under."

We decided to leave; our very presence was inciting unrest that lacked only the spark to transform it into a riot.

A FEW DAYS LATER, I was typing in the lounge at the Mammy Yoko in Freetown when I was interrupted by a bedraggled Irish radio reporter. He'd just been held hostage for three hours, he said, at the Port Loko DDR camp. The camp residents had barricaded the gate and refused to allow anyone to leave until living conditions improved. The Nigerian UNAMSIL soldiers barely changed their postures during the whole ordeal, he said, and their captors finally grew bored and opened the gate for them. The camp has been the scene of unrest ever since, hosting riots, beatings, and often-repeated threats of further trouble. The source of the trouble is always the same: The RUF's contention that the DDR and UNAM-SIL have duped them into surrendering by making false promises.

Port Loko isn't the only trouble spot and the RUF isn't the only group complaining of underhandedness by the peacekeepers. A few days after visiting Port Loko, I took a helicopter to Daru with *New York Times* photographer Tyler Hicks and French freelance photographer Patrick Robert and ended up accidentally spending the day at the DDR camp there. Tyler and I had planned to fly to Tongo Field, a strictly controlled RUF diamond district about 30 miles northwest of Kenema, but at the last minute the RUF changed their minds about allowing the UN to land. We diverted to Daru, where we found ourselves trying to hire a car to take us to nearby Kenema. We quickly learned that the only vehicles in Daru that hadn't been rendered skeletal by looters were those owned by the UN and none were going to Kenema. Our plans foiled, we tagged along with Patrick to the camp, where he was hoping to photograph a group of Kamajor fighters who'd been picked up and disarmed a week earlier.

Patrick had more than just a passing interest in this group of Kamajors: He'd met them months before while working on a photo story about Sierra Leone refugees escaping to Guinea and quickly developed a friendship with the commanders. The Kamajors were in Guinea, he learned, to rest and rearm in preparation for an assault on the RUF in Kono, entirely disregarding the peace process and the efforts to disarm those fighting in the bush, Kamajors included. They invited Patrick to join them in the bush, and for the previous month, he'd been hiking with them through the jungle to the battleground. He endured shootouts with the RUF, sleeping in the open on the jungle floor, and mysterious magical rituals that the Kamajors performed before battle. Once, a sacred totem that they carried before them into battle blew over in a high wind and their advance was delayed for days while they prayed to the god it represented for forgiveness for allowing it to touch the ground. During one ceremony, the Kamajor commanders decided to put a spell on Patrick so that he would be allowed to physically touch the members of the Kamajor unit. According to their superstition, it was the worst of luck for a non-Kamajor to touch a Kamajor who's prepared to engage in battle.

They'd fought their way through the jungle to the outskirts of Koidu, where they positioned themselves along one flank of a three-pronged assault. They were the outer circle in a series of concentric forces: In the middle were the RUF, surrounding them was a battalion of Bangladeshis with UNAMSIL, and the Kamajors surrounded *them*. According to Patrick, the plan was to demolish anything within their circle to reclaim the diamond district, including UNAMSIL if they fought back. On the eve of battle, Patrick's unit dispatched a runner to flit through the forest and report to two other Kamajor units that they were in position and ready to attack.

Somewhere along the way, things went awry. Morning came and there was no signal to attack. The commanders sent scouts to probe the front lines, and before anyone knew what was happening, a fleet of UN helicopters had whirled in from overhead, foiling the attack at the last moment. The Kamajors took up defensive positions and the UN personnel who disembarked from the helicopters engaged in brisk negotiations with Patrick, who spoke on behalf of the Kamajors since he could communicate with them the best in his native French. What happened next depends on who's telling the story. According to Patrick, he was told by the on-scene UN commander that the RUF in Kono had agreed to disarm that very day and that according to the peace deal signed in May, the Kamajors were also required to lay down their rocket launchers and shotguns. The UN maintains that no one ever promised that the RUF in Kono would disarm that day, only that the agreement called for their eventual demobilization.

Either way, much to Patrick's professional disappointment—he'd invested a month living in the jungle only to have the bloody finale of his story torpedoed by the UN—the Kamajors agreed to hand over their weapons. One hundred and sixty-one Kamajors were disarmed, and eight RUF fighters turned over their weapons. Patrick was shipped to Freetown and kicked out of the Mammy Yoko as a pariah. As far as the UN was concerned, he had all but helped orchestrate the attack. He spent a week moping around Freetown without a visa or a press card, broke except for a gold nugget given as a gift from the Kamajor commander. Tyler and I did our best to cheer him up, but Freetown's only distractions are nightmarish beach bars filled with child prostitutes, drunken aid workers, deafening pop music, and marijuana-crippled former combatants. It was clear that we had to help him get to the DDR camp in Daru where the Kamajors were sent so he could salvage his story.

Which is how the three of us ended up at the camp, encircled by joyous Kamajors who were happy to see their friend again. Not even the Ghanaian camp adjutant whipping residents with a reed took the smiles off their faces.

"So how are things?" Patrick asked one of the fighters.

"No problem," the boy smiled back. "We get small-small rest, small-small food and when we leave we will be prepared to fight again."

That mentality illustrates one of the main problems with the peace process: The Kamajors, although loyal to the government, are controlled by no one. They operate according to their own rules and during years of combat have become as enamored with diamonds as the RUF. There is suspicion among some in the UN hierarchy that operational control over the Kamajors is indeed in the hands of the Sierra Leone military, which claims the group as allies when it's favorable to do so and distances itself from them when it's not.

"The SLA can turn the [Kamajors] on or off as it wishes," one UN official confided in me. "When they want them to run roughshod over the RUF, they claim they're beyond control. When the time is right to reel them in, they can do that too."

EVEN THOUGH THE KAMAJORS continued to stage such bold assaults against the RUF and the rebels continued to mine diamonds, both actions in violation of the peace agreement, the news wasn't all bad. In fact, despite the obstacles yet to be overcome, the peace process in the summer of 2001 was further along than any previous attempt to end the war in Sierra Leone. And I had many conversations with people in the DDR camps and elsewhere who were all too happy to retire from the RUF and try to make a legitimate living. Twenty-six-year-old RUF Lieutenant Mohammed Morrison was 19 when he left the ranks of the SLA and joined the rebellion. His reason for joining was the same as his reason for leaving for the DDR camp in Daru, and he sounded sincere when he said his goal all along had been to "make the country better for me and my friends."

In the early years of the war, the RUF dogma, outlined in a manifesto called "Footpaths to Democracy" penned by RUF leader Foday Sankoh, seemed to poor and illiterate blue-collar workers like Morrison to be a reasonable alternative to poverty, lack of economic opportunity, and governmental corruption. A jumbled mixture of patriotic and Maoist rhetoric, Sankoh's passage that comes closest to offering an excuse for the rebellion reads:

> No more shall the rural countryside be reduced to hewers of wood and drawers of water for urban Freetown. That pattern of exploitation, degradation and denial is gone forever. No RUF/SL [Sierra Leone] combatant or civilian will countenance the re-introduction of that pattern of raping the countryside to feed the greed and caprice of the Freetown elite and their masters abroad. In our simple and humble ways we say, "No more slave and no more master." It is these very exploitative measures instituted by so-called central

governments that create the conditions for resistance and civil uprising.[2]

Although the RUF's raison d'être proved to be little more than a cover for plundering the diamond fields for the sake of its commanders and their Liberian patrons, it's easy to see how uneducated youths with few prospects for the future could be lured into armed rebellion and brainwashed into thinking that they were fighting for a better future. Morrison spoke with pride about his command of fifty soldiers in the RUF's 5th Battalion, D Company, which fought near Yengema in Kono.

"Sometimes we'd go out on patrol and if we heard about government movements, we'd lay our ambushes and put the situation under complete control," he said, making a motion with his hands as if he were smoothing out bedsheets. The purpose of his unit was purely combat, providing forward and perimeter defenses for the diamond operations in Kono. The short, beefy commander had never even seen a diamond, he said, but he'd been a beneficiary of their revenues. His company was often resupplied with ammunition, food, and marijuana by the human mule-trains ferrying diamonds to the Liberian border. Most of their other supplies were stolen from SLA and ECOMOG units they ambushed. But after seven years in the rebellion without seeing any tangible political or social benefits, he had grown disillusioned with the cause. No one in command seemed interested in political dialogue, just diamond sales, he said. He thought about deserting, but had been in the RUF long enough to know what that meant if he were later caught.

So when he heard that a peace deal had been signed by Sessay and UNAMSIL in March 2001, he ordered his men that day to unload their weapons and travel with him to Daru. Out of the fifty under his command, only eight complied. Several of them I met in Daru were barely capable of articulating why they obeyed Morrison's order, their reasons for wanting peace being as mysterious and esoteric as their reasons for going to war. "Now they say it is time for us to come in from the bush," explained 19-year-old Mammy Massaquoi, a second lieutenant. Her face was covered in acne, accentuated with a shrapnel wound perforating her left cheek. "All is the work of Satan. That is why brother fought brother, but now the Lord has come and brought peace."

All of them fear reprisal for leaving the rebellion's ranks, a trait they shared with the Kamajors who lived side by side with them in the camp. On their own initiative, about 300 combatants and their families had received permission from the UN to construct a village next door to the camp, a sort of temporary home while they waited for their former villages and towns to be disarmed. Surprisingly, former RUF and Kamajor fighters seemed to live quite peacefully in the geometric grid of stick-and-mud homes.

While Patrick mingled with the Kamajor fighters from the unit he'd marched with, Tyler and I strolled through the town, dubbed Peace Village by the residents. We met retired combatants from both forces who seemed to have accepted the new reality of living side by side with those they'd been trying to kill only weeks before. Their conversion appeared so complete that it was difficult to believe. A Kamajor named Lahaji Bila hunted RUF in Kono; now he was the village's blacksmith. RUF Major Daniel Kallon defected from the Sierra Leone Army to the RUF after Kamajors killed his brothers in Yengema, but now he was building houses for his former enemies. I didn't understand how the members of the two forces could so easily forget, or at least overlook, the brutality of the war in which many of them had fought for years until I spoke to the camp adjutant. Ghanaian Lieutenant Charles Bendemba summed up his theory simply: "Hunger makes men see maybe war is not so good."

Could it be that simple? The prospect of regular meals for six weeks in the equivalent of a detention camp—even if it was simple rice and cassava leaves—could entice battle-hardened men and women to lay down arms and live in harmony? Bendemba wasn't being quite that simplistic, of course, but what he meant was clear enough. The RUF war was conducted not for any ideological dogma, noble cause, or even for retribution by a long-aggrieved people, but purely for the economics of diamond mining. Even the brainwashed could see that a choice between suffering in the jungle and risking death for the financial benefit of their commanders or taking the opportunity to try and live a normal life wasn't a difficult choice at all. In the end, many fighters were simply too tired to keep on battling one another. The civil war had reached the fatigue point for many. Morrison, for instance, had seen combat and death for almost eight years and was ready for a change. "It is not worth my life anymore," he said. "I am young. I am strong. This is my country and I want to make use of it now and make a better life."

But if all it takes is a hot bowl of rice to convince fighters to stop fighting, it probably wouldn't take that much to change their minds and decide to once again start carrying weapons. Bendemba was worried about the future waiting beyond the camp gates for his charges. Fifteen bucks didn't seem like much of a financial incentive to keep former fighters who had been protecting millions of dollars in diamonds on the straight and narrow. He equated fighting with the RUF with a drug addiction. If all your friends are addicts, you live in a crack neighborhood, and all you've known for years is getting high, it wouldn't take much to shove you over the edge once out of rehab.

"You go from here with an empty stomach and empty pockets," he said. "You must depend on your parents, your friends or maybe you have some precious stones for survival. Someone who is 18 and a general or a major in the bush thinks that he is a big man. He can have women, drugs, money, respect. Once you leave here, you're just like every other man."

When these men and women leave the DDR camp, the options are to head to their former homes, most of which in Daru's district were are still armed and dangerous, or to head to the capital to avoid retribution from those who kept their AK-47s.

"Me and my men are going straight to Freetown," said Morrison.

HE'S HARDLY ALONE. Freetown's population of former and current RUF combatants is rivaled only by the population of the RUF's victims. The RUF has formed a political party, the RUFP (the Revolutionary United Front Party), and although its headquarters is in Makeni, its campaigners are by necessity in Freetown. Freetown is now home to nearly a quarter of the country's population.

"The RUF has a lot of support," said a young man named Jonathan on the street near the Cockle Bay Guest House. "But they better not come to this place."

"This place" was the MSF Camp for Amputees and War Wounded, Freetown's repository for those with the most horrific of the war's tales. It was the only place for people like Jonathan, Ismael Dalramy, and other amputation victims to go, if they were lucky enough to find room. MSF volunteer doctors fitted camp residents with donated prostheses and treated them for illnesses, at least as much as funding permitted. There were some poorly attended workshops for people without arms to try to develop work skills with their prostheses, but what seemed to provide the only distraction from their suffering was soccer practice, held daily in the softening late-afternoon light. Every Saturday, there was a match between amputees and polio victims on the beach, and most of the camp's residents attended. Besides that, the only thing to do was recount their tales of horror to one another, their neighbors being the only people in the world capable of understanding what they went through.

Kabba Jalloh, for instance, lost his hands in Koinadugu, a haphazard collection of mud huts and zinc-roofed buildings in the mountainous jungle about 50 miles northwest of Koidu, but he feels lucky to have kept his life. Speaking in Temne through a translator—another man without hands—he stoically recounted how he was tortured by men who now wanted political legitimacy and his vote in upcoming elections.

He awoke one morning in the summer of 1996 in his field of cassava to find men in camouflage uniforms making their way through the bush on all sides of his small plot. He stood, confused. There was no telling who the men were, but they seemed to be moving easily and assuredly, seemingly uninterested in him. But there was a spark of fear in Jalloh. Men with weapons in Koinadugu couldn't mean anything good. It was time to leave.

As he gathered his children and two wives from the small thatched-roof hut in the center of his cassava farm, he didn't realize that the time to leave had passed him by in the night. Under the moon, hundreds of RUF soldiers had encircled Koinadugu. Thinking that he was escaping a trap instead of already being ensnared in one, Jalloh sheathed his cutlass used to harvest cassava and put his smallest daughter on his shoulders. They started walking toward the village center. They walked about ten feet before they were ordered to stop.

Several small boys armed with rifles approached from the bush. Don't worry, they said. We're with ECOMOG and we'll protect you. Come with us.

Jalloh couldn't read or write. He'd been a farmer his entire life. But he had enough common sense to suspect that ECOMOG didn't use children in its ranks. He began to sweat with fear.

Jalloh and his family did as they were told and eventually joined about fifty other residents, farmers and their families from nearby fields, at the local *barrie,* an open-walled concrete structure in the middle of the village used for community meetings and gatherings. They were outnumbered by soldiers, who surrounded them and separated the men and women.

Only seconds before the shooting started did one of the commanders finally laugh and admit that the villagers were going to be killed not by ECOMOG, but by the RUF. All of the men were machine-gunned to death, the women and children screaming in terror as their husbands and brothers and fathers vanished in a pink stew of pulp on the *barrie* floor.

Among the men, only Jalloh was spared, for reasons he can't explain. While his friends and relatives were being massacred, he was held off to the side, gaping wide-eyed, amazed that he'd awoken only thirty minutes before to a day he assumed would be as normal as all the rest stacked up behind it, filled with the typical hard labor of farming cassava. But nothing in his life would ever be the same and it was about to get worse.

When the last of the bodies stopped twitching, the RUF yelled at the women to run for their lives. Screaming and crying, they dragged their children into the bush, Jalloh's family among them. Soon he was alone with about 200 rebels.

"You will be the messenger," said the commander, ordering his men into action. Two men grabbed his left wrist and pulled his arm taut while a third grabbed him in a stranglehold from behind. A fourth grabbed the cutlass from Jalloh's waist and in one swift, savage blow, hacked off his arm just below the elbow. The blow was so clean that the men holding the hand fell to the ground, clutching the dismembered limb, provoking laughter from the watching rebels. The two fell into a bit of macabre comedy, dancing around the now screaming Jalloh, hoisting his arm into the air, jubilant.

His screams of pain and protest were ignored, and the other arm came off the same way.

Jalloh's arms were placed in a plastic bag and tucked into one of the soldier's backpacks. "We'll send those to your president," the commander told him.

After a short time, Jalloh was hoisted to his feet and a hand-lettered sign was placed around his neck. It read: "I am a victim of RUF. Leave now."

He was placed on the road to the next village and told to spread his message.

NOW THE RUF is trying to spread a different message, a political one. In spite of young Jonathan's opinion that it wouldn't be very effective for the RUF to campaign at the MSF camp, there are RUFP political posters glued to the cement walls of the camp's gates. To say that camp residents are bitter is a drastic understatement.

"But what can I do?" said Jonathan with a morbid laugh, holding up two arms that ended in stumps at his elbows. "Kick a grenade at someone?"

It's this blunt reality that the UN seems to actively avoid addressing, the fact that the brutality of the RUF war was so acute that it will take years before any semblance of normalcy can be expected in the lives of those who suffered under the RUF's guns and blades. Everyone I encountered was overjoyed that the shooting had finally stopped, but their moods were countered by a feeling of uncertain dread about the future, as if the current cease-fire were nothing more than a temporary respite from the horror they'd become accustomed to. They'd seen so many hopeful prospects die in a hail of renewed gunfire that very few seemed willing to be as optimistic as UNAMSIL that things would soon normalize.

To date, the UNAMSIL mission is the largest and costliest that the United Nations has ever fielded, comprising 17,500 soldiers and costing in excess of $612 million for 2001 alone. It's a massive test of the UN's ability to end conflict and, given the humiliations it suffered early on, "fixing" Sierra Leone seems to be as much a priority for the sake of saving face as it is for humanitarian and security reasons.

A good example of UNAMSIL's public relations efforts were the staged "child disarmament" ceremonies that disappointed every journalist who attended one. Through an agreement with UNICEF, it was decided that reporters wouldn't be allowed within 100 yards of any child with a weapon when UNAMSIL was present for fear that they might be photographed and thus—the theory was—further traumatized by having their images published in foreign newspapers and magazines. It was never properly explained how photographing child soldiers with weapons could possibly traumatize them any further than being kidnapped, drugged, and forced into combat, but those were the rules. So whenever UNAMSIL announced a disarmament event for children, it was guaranteed that the children had been disarmed well before the announcement.

We attended one of these events and that was mostly by mistake. Still eager to find quick transportation out to RUF diamond territory, we agreed to fly to Kailahun with UNAMSIL to cover one of the ceremonies. In truth, we intended to ditch the UN as soon as the choppers touched down and find a ride to Tongo Field with locals. By that point, UNAMSIL had handled us so thoroughly that we couldn't escape its clutches, constantly being hustled from one prepared encounter to another so that the only view we had of Sierra Leone was the one they wanted us to have. Although disarming children was a major facet of the peace agreement, we were eager to get out on our own because I was interested more in the reasons why children were fighting in the first place: the RUF's diamond economy. We brought a lot of money with us and were prepared to buy a car or truck on the spot in Kailahun and take our chances driving through RUF territory into their diamond regions if we could only escape from the UN.

The problem with our plan was that we'd never been to Kailahun before and didn't realize that a working vehicle was as rare there as hope and happiness. Kailahun was a withered, war-shattered corpse of a village that was only a few more rainy seasons away from being completely reclaimed by the sweating jungle that breathed its humidity in every direction; it had known nothing but the rebel war since 1991. Kailahun was the first major town to fall before the RUF when its hundred or so original members marched across the Liberian border five miles to the east. It had been under their control for ten years by the time we arrived there and it looked it. In peacetime, Kailahun could comfortably house about 500 people; at the tail end of the war, more than 10,000 refugees fleeing combat on all sides of the village crammed its streets and were slowly starving to death.

After we'd dropped from the sky and marched with Ghanaian soldiers and the UN entourage to the town center, we split from the group and started asking around about transportation. After an hour, in a town of at least 10,000 hot and desperate souls, we could only produce a motorcycle, not enough for me, Hondros, Tyler, and all of our gear.

We sat for awhile on the steps of a wrecked mosque across the square from the ceremony, listening to shells fired at us from Guinea falling a half mile away. Novicki, the UNAMSIL spokeswoman, kept craning her neck at us, no doubt wondering why the only international journalists on the mission were ignoring a ceremony being conducted purely for our sake. With nothing better to do, we wandered over to take an obligatory photo or two.

According to the script, the children being sent from the battlefield to a reprogramming center had already been identified, classified, and stripped of weapons and uniforms. An RUF commander shouted into a bullhorn and kids would come up to have their names checked off a manifest. Then there was a tribal dance and a bonfire of old uniforms that we were supposed to believe was an impromptu display of passion at being freed from the RUF's ranks, but it was clear to everyone that the entire display was devoid of anything impromptu. If any of those children had tried to be in any way spontaneous—especially by starting a fire—they would have been shot on the spot.

I stood in the shade, away from the dispersing crowds, settling into a profound funk about having to return to Freetown with the UN's dog-and-pony promoters when a hand settled on my shoulder. I turned to stare into a familiar face: Gabril Kallon.

"What are you doing here?" I asked.

He smiled broadly and pointed to his ID badge. I had forgotten. The killer had been hired by UNICEF.

7

THE WAY STATION:
Next Stop, Liberia

Kailahun, Sierra Leone

"**N**EVER IN MY LIFE have I seen a diamond. People say this war is fought for diamonds, but it's not true. If you show me a diamond, I will not know it."

The man who uttered those words, a wrinkled fighter named Eric Senesi, was a lieutenant colonel in the Revolutionary United Front. I was sitting next to him on a thin wooden bench, surrounded by RUF soldiers, and I could feel his silent, internal laughter convulsing his body as he tried to maintain a straight face. He was speaking to Ralph Swanson, a tall Sierra Leonean radio reporter who was holding a microphone in Senesi's face. When he claimed ignorance of diamonds, Senesi tented his fingers and held them to his chest in a "Who, me?" gesture of innocence, unconsciously drawing attention to his pale yellow T-shirt, which depicted the silhouette of an AK-47 assault rifle in a circle with a slash across it, under the words "RUF for Peace."

Like the shirt, his statement was a stab at improving public relations for the rebel group, which was trying to transform itself from a bloodthirsty band of murderers into a legitimate political movement. Unlike the T-shirt, the statement couldn't hold up under Swanson's unwavering gaze and, aware of how ludicrous the lie must have sounded not just to the reporters present but also to his assembled troops, Senesi couldn't stop a delirious smile from spreading across his face. It was either that or burst out laughing. It had a ripple effect; giggles vibrated through the crowd of RUF and even Swanson had to smile sardonically. It was a way of acknowledging the obvious without having to admit it on tape. Diamonds? No diamonds here. Nothing here but us peaceful rebels. . . .

By the time we spoke to Senesi, photojournalist Chris Hondros and I had spent four days in Kailahun District with GhanBatt-3, a contingent of Ghanaian soldiers serving UNAMSIL. We had been suffering under their institutional ineptness that was so thorough as to be almost poetic; we toiled around with them, lost in the jungle between four different warring factions, trying to save refugees and avoid getting stuck in the mud, eating cassava and frogs spawned from the rain. After being manipulated by the UN, we were determined to return to Kailahun to experience the contrast between a PR event and the real thing, and boy, did we ever.

Kailahun is the gateway to a place called the Parrot's Beak, a wedge of Sierra Leone that juts between Liberia and Guinea. Rebel groups of all three countries are effectively at war with one another and the Liberians and Guineans find it convenient to attack one another by skirting through Sierra Leone, dodging through RUF defenses before launching their attacks and running back across their borders. Such maneuvers obviously attract retaliatory attacks into Sierra Leone, since those being shot at generally don't know who's doing the shooting, only where it's coming from.

The fighting was spurred mostly by a Liberian rebel group called LURD, Liberians United for Reconciliation and Democracy, a ragtag assortment of various factions disenfranchised under Charles Taylor's government, but they seemed to spend most of their time fighting not the government in Monrovia, but other groups in Sierra Leone and Guinea, some of which may have aligned with LURD; no one seemed to know. Complicating matters further was the presence of an estimated 2,000 Kamajor fighters ringing Kailahun.

For anyone new to the Sierra Leone diamond war, it would have been easy to believe that Senesi had in fact never laid eyes on a diamond. Clearly, none of the wealth being stolen from the jungle was making its way to the estimated 10,000 people trapped and starving to death in Kailahun. The clues were in the small details: commanders wearing expensive boots that could have only come from Guinea or Liberia, an AK-47 so new it still smelled of the lubricant Cosmoline, a satellite telephone linking field commanders to RUF High Command in Freetown. Whether Senesi saw them or not, millions of dollars worth of diamonds had flowed through Kailahun since the early days of the war, en route to Monrovia, and eventually to Antwerp, London, and retail jewelers around the world. In the mid-1990s, helicopters flew from staging areas in Liberia to deliver weapons directly to Kailahun in exchange for the diamonds. They landed in a soccer field on the outskirts of town, the same one now used by the UN to evacuate the RUF's child soldiers.

The Ghanaians with UNAMSIL had tried to drive into this mess to visit Kailahun a few weeks before we joined them in June 2001, but had been repelled by Kamajor sniper fire and drunken RUF checkpoint commanders, little kids as young as 10 with heavy weapons and permission to kill anyone they pleased for whatever reason they wanted. The UN had been under mounting criticism for not yet fully deploying across a country that it was ostensibly demobilizing and rebuilding; therefore, establishing a permanent presence in Kailahun and other RUF strongholds was critical to the continuation of the disarmament process. When the Ghanaians were ready to try again, Hondros and I, along with six Sierra Leonean reporters, decided to travel with them, part of the first vanguard of the two-year-old UN mission to probe so far into the RUF hinterland.

By the time we arrived anyone there who could once have been called a civilian had long since been recategorized. Now they were called refugees, war victims, prisoners of war, and child combatants. Kailahun was a depressing human collage of teenage soldiers nearly blind from lifelong bouts with malaria smirking dementedly at graffiti-spoiled walls; naked toddlers abandoned to the whims of luck, fear, grief, and hunger; and the vacant stares of drooling amputees who were no more than a few hours from death's welcome embrace. All of this stumbling life took place, of course, at the point of a bayonet, the barrel of an assault rifle, and the stainless-steel explosive tips of thundering 120-mm artillery shells careening in from Liberia to blow holes in the jungle carpet. It was as stark an illustration of the impact of the diamond war on Sierra Leone's rural population as one could imagine. Nor could we have found a more appropriate microcosm of the UN's bumbling efforts in the war-whipped country, as our experience with the Ghanaian Army unit made us rethink the common characterization of the RUF as being disorganized. Compared to GhanBatt-3, the RUF could have been a crack team of U.S. Special Forces.

Somehow, despite the presumed leverage of the United Nations and the resources of UNAMSIL, once in Kailahun we seemed doomed to become refugees ourselves even though GhanBatt-3 had ostensibly come to this shattered, dangerous collection of roof-less buildings deep in the jungle to rescue people, people we quickly came to resemble: dirty, depressed, hungry, and losing hope by the minute.

The irony of our situation was ever present: We drove into the village with thirteen troop carriers, six armored personnel carriers, four Toyota 4Runners, four Nissan HiLux pickup trucks, two tankers of water and fuel, and 200 soldiers. We were a formidable procession, accompanied for a portion of our journey from the UN base in Daru by an Mi-24 helicopter gunship that flew in deafening patterns just over the palm trees at 150 miles per hour. When we rolled into Kailahun at noon on day one under 100-degree skies, we were given a hero's welcome, the bedraggled and war-beaten refugees from Liberia and Guinea assuming that we'd come to save them from starvation.

It turned out that we could barely feed ourselves.

Apparently not used to hosting journalists in their long-range patrols, the Ghanaians didn't go out of their way to make us comfortable, and that included making us fend for ourselves for food, which we didn't expect to do. Meals with the UN occurred once a day and each occasion was a stark reminder of the desperate situation in Kailahun. The Ghanaian cooks prepared nothing but "chicken stew"—although I'm not sure it was either chicken or stew; it was more like bones boiled in grease—and they didn't have the foresight to prepare it in a tent, beyond the view of those starving on Kailahun's streets. Every time they cooked it up in a large black cauldron, the smell of food attracted a crowd of silent, desperate spectators, who ringed the cooking area, mouths agape, eyes staring as ladlefuls of reddish goop were distributed to the troops. Having eaten nothing but grass and mangos for weeks, their hunger was palpable.

The locals—both refugees and fighters—turned on us the moment they realized that we carried no aid food or medicine. The UN's "authority" as administrators of the country's government and military security was quickly surrendered for the simple reason that there was no other choice. In terms of military assets, it was pretty much a draw. Even though the Ghanaians had the ability to order up air support in the event of a firefight with the local RUF squads, the Ghanaians were in no mood to fight. It would have gone against the entire purpose of the mission, which was to scout out the region, get a grip on how bad the refugee situation was, and prep the RUF for eventually handing in their weapons and ending the war. So we went from traveling with the world's premier peacekeeping force to being a traveling sideshow in about an hour.

Kailahun was no-man's-land, a place where fighting between RUF and the Kamajors was so fierce that farming was impossible and hunting was useless; there hasn't been game near Kailahun in ten years. The thousands of refugees clogging the town had stripped every banana, coconut, and mango tree in a three-mile radius. Going deeper into the jungle to search for food was suicidal since the Kamajor units were tightening around the area like a noose. Kailahun was off the radars of even the most daredevil aid organizations; driving a truck laden with food anywhere near the Parrot's Beak would have been like driving off a cliff, as it was likely to be hijacked within minutes of departing on its mission.

Hondros and I were contemplating our situation, sitting under a piece of balcony held onto a mortar-shattered building by a few strands of rusted rebar, the only refuge we could find from an explosion of rain that had apparently destroyed the Ghanaians' already thin grasp on control. When the rain hit, the mission descended into chaos, the force scattered throughout the town, everyone soaked and struggling with conflicting orders, darkness descending, pale eyes watching from empty windows.

A woman emerged from the gloom and motioned for us to follow her. Locals boiled frogs and rice for us, and in a darkened basement stinking of urine, we ate them by hand, a flickering candle offering barely enough light for them to see the gratitude on our faces.

KAILAHUN LOOKS BETTER at night without electricity in a teeming thunderstorm than it does during the day. Under the harsh light of the equatorial sun, it's hard to call the collection of caved-in, bullet-warped buildings a "village." It's more like a junkyard for houses caught in crossfire, a place where people can dump structures that have been destroyed by warfare, with only the barest evidence of its past as a peaceful place discernible through the destruction. In the middle of the main intersection, it takes hours of debate to agree that a slab of concrete and a rusty white pole were once part of a gas station. Decades-old paint valiantly struggles from beneath RUF graffiti to identify one building as a former municipal center. An eye clinic can only be identified by a lone piece of a long-since-shot-out sign hanging over the entrance, which nowadays is stuffed with sick and dying refugees and their doomed newborns.

People were everywhere: Slick RUF officers wearing Tommy Hilfiger clothing and Vuarnet sunglasses, an old Liberian man in tribal colors limping on a wounded foot swollen with gangrene, children of all ages wearing shirts and shorts composed more of holes than cloth, Kamajor infiltrators in burlap sacks and dread-locks, men with guns, women without feet, a young female secret society initiate adorned in black palm leaves and a black ceremonial mask depicting a screaming woman. Added to this motley mix were those of us with the UN mission: journalists, soldiers in Car-olina-blue body armor and helmets, Belgian relief workers, a Russ-ian "security consultant" to the United Nations, and men and women working for UNICEF who looked like they'd be more at home at a bridge game in West Palm Beach.

We spent the days driving through the jungle toward the very tip of the Parrot's Beak, our trucks crunching over boulders and through mud bogs until we reached the end of the line at Koindu, a frontline town a mile from the borders of both Guinea and Liberia, first stop for refugees who decided that war-torn Sierra Leone was better than either bordering country. Guarded by a bat-talion of weary RUF children, Koindu made Kailahun look mildly troubled in comparison. They were burned out from combat, fighting off Kamajors sneaking up from behind, Liberians on one side and Guineans on the other, both forces crossing regularly into Sierra Leone to attack the other from its borders. His head resting on the barrel of an AK-47, the 25-year-old commanding officer stared at his boots and told us that, on days when there was no shelling, at least 10 of the 30,000 or so refugees crammed into the village died every day from war wounds, starvation, or disease. How often is there no shelling? we asked.

"They shell every day," he said.

Security prevented us from spending more than half an hour in Koindu. One of the Ghanaian soldiers had thrown a package of crackers to a little boy on the side of the road from one of the large troop carriers and had sparked a brief riot among those clogging the roadside, who thought they were being fed. RUF brought the uproar under control with swift cracks of their rifle butts and several short bursts of gunfire overhead. The Ghanaians were nervous that we'd be taken hostage, held ransom for food and medical aid, so we left. Liberians shelled our convoy on the way back to Kailahun.

ON DAY FOUR, Hondros and I awoke in the back of one of the two-ton troop carriers surrounded by crates of rifle ammunition. We'd opted to spend the night on the wooden slats of the truck bed—where soldiers had slaughtered a captured goat the day before, bounty from the jungle that supplemented their daily rations—because a swarm of insects had infested our temporary quarters. In their attempt to provide us with a modicum of comfort, the Ghanaians had rigged an abandoned house with a portable generator, and by the time we returned from Koindu, a single high-wattage lightbulb had been burning all night, the only one in miles, providing a beacon for every flying insect in West Africa. There was no furniture in the house and no extra sleeping bags. So the options were to try to sleep on a writhing black carpet of flying ants, termites, wasps, and millipedes or retreat to the truck and take our chances with malarial mosquitoes.

Malaria won, hands down, and we forced ourselves into sleep to the bemusement of the Ghanaians charged with guarding the truck fleet.

Day four was a scorcher. We awoke to quickly ascending 85-plus-degree temperatures at 7 A.M. and a mob scene on the broad red-dirt road that pierced the town. Hysterical Liberians and Guineans were trying to get their names on a manifest for an evacuation helicopter that would, hopefully, arrive later in the day to fly them to safety, medical care, and—most importantly—food. Unbeknown to anyone at the time, the Guinean refugees were actually prisoners of the RUF, captured months before in a cross-border raid into Guéckédou, and most of them feared that the evacuation flight was their last hope for survival. But there was limited room and the RUF had only permitted UNHCR to take the most critically ill or injured. Christine Hambrouck, a Belgian with UNHCR, struggled to keep her head above the crowd, which seemed on the verge of pummeling her. Kids got trampled, and plastic bags filled with clothes and other possessions were ripped open, their contents spilled in the dirt. Everyone was yelling, trying to be heard over the din.

Surprisingly, the Ghanaians seemed fairly well organized that morning, apparently energized into competence by their unexpected success in convincing RUF High Command in Freetown to release some of Kailahun's prisoners and refugees. Those negotiations had been going on since our arrival, a maddening merry-go-round of false promises, patronization, vague threats, and appeals to morality. In Kailahun, no one could do anything without clearance from the on-site RUF commander. Everything the Ghanaians did—whether it was deciding to camp or occupy abandoned buildings, interview child combatants, or leave—required his approval.

But leaving with anyone who didn't arrive with us was up to the RUF's big chief, Brigadier General Issa Sessay, in Freetown, who could only be reached by secure satellite telephone.

Who the RUF allows to be evacuated is up to the RUF alone and the reasons are all theirs, a sweaty, bearded New Zealander with UNHCR told me as we slumped in the hot dirt watching the maelstrom surrounding Hambrouck. Shortly after sunrise, he'd received word that the RUF would allow UNHCR to take up to 200 refugees. Yet thousands more were to be left behind, some of whom died later that day from malnutrition, disease, or any of the hundreds of other things that were fatal about living in Kailahun. In fact, an infant girl died in the mob of refugees as we watched, helpless to do anything. She'd been registered to leave on the aid flight and succumbed to starvation within minutes of having her name added to the manifest. Hambrouck simply scratched out her name and that of her mother, who decided to stay and bury her child. A woman who had somehow survived a Cesarean-section delivery without anesthesia or medical instruments—her operation had probably been done with a machete—took her place.

Even the children-advocacy organizations were rewarded that day: RUF allowed fifty child soldiers to check their weapons with Save the Children and UNICEF and wait for an evac chopper. There are few things more terrifying than having a blank-eyed 12-year-old girl stick the barrel of a loaded AK-58 in your stomach, but there are also few things more satisfying than seeing her drop the weapon and squeal with long-lost childhood joy at the news that she'll soon be flying away from the frontline. But fifty kids are a drop in the bucket. For every preteen whose name was written on the manifest—in an even more chaotic shouting match between the child fighters and aid workers—there were twenty or thirty more who would be ordered into battle once we flew away with the lucky ones. Two of those kids almost certainly died within days of our eventual departure: 15-year-old lieutenants wounded in combat who lay slowly dying in a bleak and filthy RUF "field hospital" on the edge of town.

We discovered this place while resting in an overgrown soccer field where the Ghanaians first considered camping when we arrived in Kailahun. We lay out flat on the long grass where RUF resupply helicopters used to land to deliver ammunition and weapons from Liberia, smoking and evaluating our wisdom in throwing our well-being in with GhanBatt-3. Suddenly the rains fell, a slaking detonation of water in the air. I was drenched before I even got my eyes open. Hondros and I dashed for the trees and the minimal protection they offered. We spotted a low building with fire-blackened windows staring like dead eyes and darted between the birches and banana trees until we were somewhat protected by a low patio roof on the side of the building. Slumped in a corner, a young man wearing a Michael Jordan basketball jersey cradled an AK-47 and smiled at us through a haze of marijuana smoke.

We soon discovered that the boy was a security guard for the building, which was a makeshift hospital. Through the gloom created by the rain clouds, we could see shadowy figures limping through the hospital's halls; we cautiously pushed our way inside.

"Hey, sa," bellowed a voice from a room near the courtyard. "Hey, you got one stick a cig'rette, sa?"

We followed the voice into a small room, where a billowing patterned curtain provided minimal privacy. A bare-chested young man was sprawled on a filthy mattress, both of his feet heavily wrapped in gauze that had begun to turn brown. The concrete floor was covered in bloody footprints as if we'd walked into some sort of maniacal dance studio. Under the heavy thrum of the rain, the boy explained that he'd stepped on a crude land mine a few weeks before that blew off both of his heels. He could hobble around and felt that he was improving.

"I bedda dan all de mon here," he said with a strange laugh, as if he were truly amused by his comment.

Other rooms were not filled with the strange mirth of pending dementia, but were instead gravid with fear and grief. At 22 years old, the mine victim was the elder patient in the hospital, an echoing, fire-blackened maze of narrow graffiti-crazed corridors and garbage-littered chambers that were void of furniture, power, and running water. As we poked our heads into another curtain-covered doorway, a voice boomed from the darkness of the hallway.

"Hello! What you want here?"

A short boy in an orange Hawaiian shirt and matching shorts emerged from the shadows. A handgun was tucked into his waist. When we told him that we'd just ducked out of the rain and that we were journalists, he introduced himself as RUF Corporal James Morphison, local field medic.

"We have no medicine. No clean field dressings. We do what we can," he said, leading the way into the room we'd been about to enter. The room was dark and the walls had been painted gray long ago. Sprawled on the floor on rattan mats that had been placed on piles of wet rotting hay were two young boys. Both were near death, as much victims of the world's manufactured hunger for diamonds—and the RUF's willingness to feed that hunger—as victims of their enemy's weapons. The boy on the left, Jusu Lahia, lay on his back with his arms and legs bent into the air. He'd stiffened up like curing jerky thanks to a tetanus infection that was eventually going to kill him. About two months before, he was nearly cut in half by a Kamajor rocket that exploded next to him and peppered him with fragmentation wounds. One piece of exploding steel blew through his face just under the left eye, blinding it. Other pieces embedded in his shoulder, side, groin, and leg, all on the left side. A flower-patterned bowl filled with congealed blood sat on the floor and there were long, smeared bloodstains on the gray wall next to his hay-pile. A rusted wheelchair lay in the corner, looking like a fallen combatant itself.

Nearer the door lay Matthew Sween, propped against the wall wearing a hole-filled Mickey Mouse T-shirt. Sween was more animated, but only with dread and terror. During the same Kamajor attack that had ruined Lahia, a bullet punched through the small of his back, ricocheted off something inside him, and exited through the front of his right thigh. He sweated profusely and shivered with chills. Morphison and another medic had simply taped his wounds shut. There was no way they could operate on him.

"They will both die," Morphison said plainly, not bothering to lower his voice for the sake of his patients or Sween's young sister, who lay on the floor beside him, mopping his brow with a rain-wettened rag. No one in the room seemed surprised to hear the prognosis.

Sween stared with wide, unblinking eyes, obviously hoping that we'd come to help. The only thing we had, however, were four Cipro pills, a powerful antibiotic. We gave them to Morphison, although we knew they would be of little help to either of the wounded boys.

Soon, news spread that two white journalists were touring the hospital and dispensing pharmaceuticals. From the mounting gloom, crippled, emaciated patients oozing disease began plodding toward us like the undead. One was a 12-year-old civilian girl whose arm had been nearly shot off in crossfire. Another was shot in the knee, forced to lean on the wall with both hands in order to move closer to us. A retarded boy with severe polio simply sat in an ever darkening hallway corner, the whites of his staring eyes practically the only part of him that were visible.

The moans and creaks of the dim hospital soon proved too unnerving to endure much longer and we left. Morphison stood in the doorway watching us leave, the only person we'd met there who had clean clothing. "Come and visit again before you leave," he called after us.

WE DIDN'T.

Neither did the Save The Children reps or the UNICEF people, whose chopper swooped so fast out of the sky to avoid attracting gunfire that it seemed to simply materialize in front of us, a sudden tornado of rotor wash filling our eyes with dirt. It was explained to us that the RUF didn't allow wounded children to be evacuated because it conflicted with their earnest testimony that the rebel group didn't use children in combat. In Kailahun, such an assertion was demonstrably false, but denying the obvious was an RUF pastime. Again, the duty fell to Lieutenant Colonel Senesi to explain, in the presence of child soldiers, that the RUF had no child soldiers.

"All the children we have here will be under enemy pressure in the bush, so you have to train your children in case they are attacked or apprehended by the enemy in your absence," he said.

What about Sween and Lahia, who both admitted to being in combat on the front line?

"Well," Senesi said, "sometimes, if a child is especially brave, they will volunteer to go to the front and we allow them."

The UNICEF helicopter landed on the soccer field next to a UN Mi-26, a massive personnel helicopter that must have been three stories tall. There's no question that Sween, Lahia, and the other injured kids could hear the excited chattering of those chosen to leave as they endured a last minute photo-op for the sake of a National Geographic photographer who'd flown in from Freetown for the event. Hondros and I hunkered in the woods, out of the heat of the sun, looking like bearded, disheveled bums, too tired and uninterested in participating in a group shot of the now-former child combatants, many of whom had threatened and menaced us over the course of the past four days. Besides, we had more pressing things to deal with.

"I'm getting on that fucking helicopter," I announced. The look on Hondros's face said good luck trying. Although we were registered correspondents with respected U.S. media outlets, accredited through the United Nations and generally well-organized people, not a single excursion on a UN chopper, pickup truck, or troop carrier was without its share of mind-numbing complications that soon made us seriously contemplate buying our own vehicle and taking our chances in the bush, something we would have done in Kailahun if there had been any operable vehicles. Traveling on a helicopter was impossible without an MOP, a "movement of personnel" form that's meant to keep track of who's going where so that if one of the helicopters crashes or is shot out of the sky, the responsible UN person back at headquarters would know whose parents to call to claim the bodies, assuming they weren't eaten by hungry Kamajors. Needless to say, we didn't have MOPs.

But I was willing to risk a fistfight with the Ukrainian pilots to avoid being stranded with the Ghanaians a moment longer. So far, it had taken four days to accomplish a portion of the mission that had been estimated back in the comfort of the base at Daru to take 12 to 14 hours.

The desperate and determined look on my face when I approached the pilot was apparently an acceptable alternative to having an MOP. He let us both on the plane.

Rotor wash is hypnotizing, invisible waves of superspeed air that flattens long grass and makes palm trees move like disco dancers. It seemed that all of the refugees and RUF defenders were in the trees around the soccer field to watch some of their young colleagues fly off to a deprogramming center. Some waved, some stood still as statues until the blast of air became too powerful to face, and as we lifted off, quickly and into a turn before we were even fifteen feet off the ground, everyone had their heads buried in their elbows. The deafening roar of the chopper was welcome indeed and we craned our heads out the portholes to look down on Kailahun, the little roofless buildings fading rapidly into the jungle, challenging you to believe that some of the best gems sold throughout the world in the last seven or eight years had passed through this shelled and hopeless bush village.

I wondered what Sween and Lahia were thinking as they listened to us fly overhead.

8

"THE BASE":
Osama's War Chest

West Africa, Afghanistan, New York

IN JULY 2001—more than a year into the Kimberley Process—a Lebanese diamond broker named Aziz Nassour arrived in Monrovia, Liberia, for a crucial meeting. Although his name appeared on a watch list issued by the United Nations Security Council merely two months before, Nassour was received at Robertsfield Airport as if he were a government official, greeted by Liberian law enforcement and escorted past the obligatory customs and immigration checkpoints to ensure that he was quickly on his way through the streets of the crumbling, humid West African city.

Within an hour of his arrival from Antwerp, he was inside a drab four-bedroom safehouse, a place that, if it looked normal from the outside, revealed quite a bit about its residents on the inside. Plastered on the walls were posters celebrating the suicide bombings of

Hezbollah, the Lebanese terrorist group, and videotapes of Hezbollah attackers killing Israeli troops were scattered around the VCR.

The safehouse was run by Senegalese men and the meeting had been arranged by their boss and countryman, Ibrahim Bah, a diamond trafficker who lived in Burkina Faso, two countries to the northeast of Liberia. Bah was also a general in the RUF, the rebellion's senior logistics expert in the movement of weapons and diamonds between Burkina Faso, Liberia, and Sierra Leone. Several other high-ranking RUF officers were also in attendance.

The meeting occurred at a critical time. The two-year-old UNAMSIL had managed, after countless failures and broken deals, to kick-start a disarmament agreement between the RUF and the government of Sierra Leone that even the cynics agreed looked promising. By the time Nassour and the others sat down under the fanatical eyes of Hezbollah guerillas staring from the walls, the UN was claiming that half the country had been disarmed: More than 3,000 fighters had turned in their AK-47s and rocket-propelled grenade launchers and begun the process of reintegrating into daily life in Sierra Leone. If the schedule held fast, disarmament would be complete by the end of the year and, in theory, the war that had torn apart the small West African country over the course of the previous decade would be over.

This was good news for everyone but those who profited from Sierra Leone's diamond wealth, especially the men in the Liberian safehouse that day. In 1999, an estimated $75 million worth of gemstones had flowed from the RUF to the world market, a vast amount of capital for a bush army, moving completely undetected, untaxed, and unrecorded. In return, an army's worth of munitions, fuel, food, and medicine flowed back.

The United Nations banned Nassour and 130 others from traveling to or from Liberia in an effort to stem the tide of diamonds moving so easily from the RUF into the world market, and adopted Security Council Resolution 1343 on May 7, 2001, in an attempt to shut down one of the many branches of the illicit pipeline. Among other provisions, it banned countries from importing any diamonds from Liberia, regardless of whether they originated in Liberia or not; imposed military sanctions and travel sanctions on people like Nassour believed to be involved in the arms-for-gems scheme; and required the Liberian government to expel any RUF fighters seeking refuge in the country.

The list of those affected by the travel ban read like a "Who's Who" of the whole Sierra Leone melodrama. Besides Nassour, the list included Sam Bokarie, better known as Major General Mosquito, an RUF battle-group commander who fell out of favor with the RUF leadership in early 2001 and fled to Liberia. Mosquito was an instrumental middleman in moving diamonds out of Sierra Leone. Also named was Victor Bout, the former KGB agent who owns and operates the complicated network of private planes that ships munitions and weapons to the RUF from Eastern Europe. Wealthy Lebanese businessman Talal El-Ndine was named as well; he was the inner circle's paymaster. Ibrahim Bah was on the list, as was Nassour's cousin, Samiah Osailly, another Antwerp diamond broker.

But for smugglers and criminals, UN resolutions mean little. Nassour had business to conduct with the RUF. He told the rebels that he had buyers who needed to convert large sums of cash into easily convertible commodities, and diamonds fit the bill perfectly.

It's not known if Nassour told the RUF who the buyers were, but they probably could have guessed. On previous occasions, Nassour had done business with two Muslim men who referred to him as "Alpha Zulu" whenever they spoke to him on a satellite phone. The two 24-year-old men—Ahmed Khalfan Ghailani, from Tanzania, and Fazul Abdullah Mohammed of Kenya—were members of Saudi billionaire Osama bin Laden's Al Qaeda terrorist network. According to the FBI, they'd been buying diamonds from the RUF since 1998, the same year U.S. embassies were destroyed by Al Qaeda operatives in Dar-es-Salaam and Nairobi. Ghailani is accused by the FBI of helping buy the truck that destroyed the building in Dar-es-Salaam.

According to the FBI, it seems the first Al Qaeda contact was established between Mosquito and Abdullah Ahmed Abdullah, a top bin Laden aid. The two met through RUF General Bah in September 1998, and Abdullah discussed the possibility of buying RUF diamonds on a regular basis. As recently as January 2000—right under the nose of UNAMSIL—Ghailani and Mohammed had been in Sierra Leone's mother-lode district, Kono, with the RUF, overseeing diamond production on behalf of Al Qaeda.

Whether he mentioned his clients or not at the July meeting in the safehouse in Monrovia, Nassour's request of the RUF stood to benefit everyone involved: He asked the RUF to double their production at the diamond mines in exchange for a higher price for the rough. That way the RUF could pad their profits before having to hand over the diamond districts to the government as outlined in the disarmament agreement, Nassour would make out handsomely, and his clients could easily launder millions of dollars of cash. They could also turn a considerable profit: RUF diamonds usually sold to their first customers for about 10 percent of their uncut worth.

The timing of this agreement was critical. From the RUF's point of view, there was a finite amount of time, measured in months if not weeks, for the rebels to continue plundering the diamond fields before the government regained their control, with UN oversight. For Nassour's Al Qaeda clients, they had less than two months—until September 11, to be precise—to turn their cash into diamonds, which would then represent one of their few liquid assets.

Shortly after the meeting, news reports noted a frenzied pace of mining in Kono and other RUF-controlled diamond areas. "Sierra Leone's rebels are using the forced labor of children and young men to greatly expand their diamond mining here, despite an agreement as part of a fragile peace process to stop harvesting gems from one of the world's richest diamond fields," wrote *Washington Post* reporter Douglas Farah from Kono in August. "The rebels of the Revolutionary United Front are digging, in defiance of an accord with the government earlier this month, and the presence nearby of 800 UN peacekeepers. UN officials said their mandate was to enforce a cease-fire signed by the rebels and the government in November (2000) and did not include enforcing the mining ban."

It's impossible to say how much Al Qaeda money was converted to gems during this last-ditch megabuy, but it's likely that it served its overarching purpose very well.

On September 11, 2001, a group of Al Qaeda terrorists hijacked three commercial airplanes and crashed them into the World Trade Center's Twin Towers in New York and the Pentagon in Washington, D.C., in a catastrophic and well-organized attack on the United States. A fourth hijacked airliner presumed to be aimed for the Capitol building or the White House crashed in a forest in Pennsylvania after passengers fought with hijackers for control of the airplane. The Twin Towers collapsed, killing nearly 3,000 people, and 190 were killed at the Pentagon. The plume of smoke from the New York attacks could be seen by satellites in outer space. Intelligence experts put the blame squarely on Al Qaeda and its leader, Osama bin Laden.

As a first step in its retaliation, the United States launched a diplomatic mission to Europe and the Middle East in an effort to freeze the financial accounts of Osama bin Laden's terror network, tying up over $100 million in assets in the first three weeks. The aim was to cripple the Saudi exile's ability to fund future attacks and resupply its military assets in Afghanistan, Al Qaeda's base of operations.

But if bin Laden's currency-to-diamonds conversion scheme worked—and the indication is that it did, for Al Qaeda operatives seem to have begun three years before the attacks—the network kept up to several million dollars worth of assets in the form of milky white stones, the most compact form of wealth known to man.

"I now believe that to cut off Al Qaeda funds and laundering activities you have to cut off the diamond pipeline," said a European investigator quoted in the *Washington Post*. "We are talking about millions and maybe tens of millions of dollars in profits and laundering."[1]

"WHAT IS 'HEZBOLLAH?'"

It was an unexpected question for 44-year-old *Washington Post* reporter Doug Farah, especially under the circumstances. Although Sierra Leone was the proud home to thousands of Lebanese diamond merchants and their families—and the country's reputation as a fund-raising source for the infamous Iranian-backed terrorist group was practically common knowledge—the fact that he was being asked about Hezbollah by one of his RUF contacts seemed out of place. And that it was happening in the weeks following the September 11 terror attacks made it all the more intriguing.

He answered the question with one of his own: Why do you want to know?

That simple inquiry would lead, although he couldn't have known it at the time, to his eventual hasty departure from West Africa under threats to his life and those of his family by a powerful network of people. It was the tiny crack in a dam of information that would bring the Sierra Leone diamond story full circle and add a major piece of the puzzle to the world's biggest story that was breaking in places far removed from Sierra Leone: the U.S. war on terrorism that was, at that moment, building like a thunderhead over Afghanistan.

But the tale began undramatically, as many do, with a shrug and a plausible explanation. The RUF fighter told Farah that there was a safehouse in Monrovia used by General Bah that was occupied by Hezbollah members, but he wasn't sure what Hezbollah was. He told Farah that he'd been there and seen movies of men blowing up Israeli tanks and large posters of Osama bin Laden on the walls. The men who occupied the house claimed their membership with the Lebanese terrorist group.

Although he had no idea about the eventual significance of that piece of information at the time, Farah filed it away as a possible lead. A longtime correspondent in some of the world's most dangerous locations, Farah was a veteran reporter of the drug war in Latin America and was no stranger to conflicts that were run purely as economic endeavors. In the weeks and months following the September 11 attacks, he was pursuing the connections between foreign fund-raising in West Africa and its wars.[2]

Although he'd been to dangerous places in the past, Farah had never experienced a fighting force as unhinged as the RUF, a telling statement from a man who'd spent fifteen years prior to coming to

Africa covering wars in Central America, drug wars in the Andes, and the American occupation of Haiti.[3]

Since March 2000, Farah had been the *Washington Post*'s West African bureau chief, based in Abidjan, Ivory Coast, with his wife and infant child. He spent his time traveling throughout West Africa, but focused on Nigeria, the big brother of all West African countries. The continent's most populous country, Nigeria holds the most interest for Americans—one in six Africans is Nigerian—and it's the one that Western nations hope to be a stabilizing force in the war-torn region. Other countries of interest to Farah were those that don't have a map-location in the minds of most American news consumers: Equatorial Guinea, Guinea Bissau, Niger, Chad . . . and Sierra Leone. When Farah took on the job, Sierra Leone was reaching a watershed moment in its history—the breakdown of all authority with the deployment of UNAMSIL and the subsequent capture of over 500 of its soldiers.

Sierra Leone proved to be familiar soil for Farah. He felt he intuitively understood the conflict thanks to his background in Colombia, the big difference being that the end product of one war was illegal and that in the other was one of the world's most prized luxuries, a fact that made the Sierra Leone story all the more lurid. Diamonds and drugs can sometimes have a lot in common in regards to where they're harvested, what they fund, and how they're sold.

But the RUF defied most stereotypes about organized crime rebellions. The RUF's standards of conduct—and those of almost everyone else fighting in Sierra Leone—were nearly nonexistent, controlled mainly by drugs, booze, and savagery, making them wholly unpredictable and terrifying.

"Even the crazed death squad goons in El Salvador and the hit men in Colombia were not that far gone," he wrote in an e-mail message to me in late 2001. "And no group I was familiar with ever targeted children like the RUF and others did."

Farah filed a story about diamond mining in Kono, and how it had inexplicably reached a fever pitch in the summer of 2001 even though the RUF were to have stopped mining under the current peace agreement. One of the key points in his story was the obligatory washing-of-hands statement from UNAMSIL officials: The peacekeeping force was there to enforce the disarmament, not the mining ban. In other words, although it was a violation of the agreement, UNAMSIL was going to do nothing about it.

Farah returned home to Abidjan, where he turned the Hezbollah nugget over in his mind. There are an estimated 120,000 Lebanese living in West Africa, most of them in the import-export business. Although the number of extremist Shiite Muslims who would be inclined to actively fund Hezbollah is thought to be low, it's also thought that more moderate Lebanese contribute to the organization to keep from being shaken down. The fact that Bah may have ties to the group wasn't necessarily surprising. Intelligence agencies have long suspected Bah of coordinating diamond sales with them for as long as twenty years, during a time in which terrorists attacked American interests in Beirut with car bombs, hijacked airplanes, and kidnapped Americans. Bah has spent most of his life as a rebel, first in Senegal, then in Afghanistan, then in Lebanon. He is thought to have personally trained Charles Taylor and Foday Sankoh when they were in Libya in the early 1990s.[4]

Farah soon learned that a top Hezbollah member may have visited Abidjan recently. The man was named as one of the FBI's most wanted terrorists, a list that was released in the wake of the September 11 attacks and also published, with photos, in *Newsweek* magazine. Farah took the magazine with him when he again met with his RUF contacts a few weeks later.

The Al Qaeda story may have died there. None of the people he showed the picture to recognized the Hezbollah operative. But one of the RUF men picked up Farah's *Newsweek* and began idly flipping through the pages, looking at the pictures. At one point, Farah said the man gasped in surprise. He knew three of the others wanted by the FBI; two of them, he said, had been in Kono as recently as January 2001, working with a man known to them as Alpha Zulu, the code name of Aziz Nassour. All three of the wanted men were identified in the magazine as Al Qaeda members.

Farah was stunned. He'd gone to Sierra Leone with the hopes of connecting RUF diamond sales and Hezbollah, but it seemed that he had hit the jackpot, so long as the RUF man knew what he was talking about. Several other RUF soldiers came over and also recognized the three Al Qaeda operatives. He asked them to look at the pictures again. They said that they were sure; Bah also knew the wanted men, they said, because Bah had "fought in Afghanistan" and with Hezbollah. The Al Qaeda operatives were sent to Kono by "Alpha Zulu." He was the main man, they confirmed, and he's the one who rented the Hezbollah house in Monrovia.

The story gelled quickly in Farah's mind, like drops of mercury rolling toward one another to form one big pool. He'd heard the name Aziz Nassour in the past. Not only was the man a diamond merchant with a buying office in Bo, a diamond trading center in Sierra Leone, but he'd also heard rumors that Nassour was involved in running guns to the RUF and was close to both General Bah and Brigadier Sessay, the RUF leader. Farah knew Bah from previous meetings and an earlier *Washington Post* reporter had relied on Bah to make critical field contacts with commanders like General Mosquito. The outline quickly took shape: The RUF had sold diamonds to Al Qaeda through Nassour and his cousin,

Samiah Osailly. September 11 may have been the impetus for the RUF to ramp up their mining efforts in Kono.

That was the theory. To turn the theory into a news story, Farah would have to have a showdown in Freetown.

OMRIE GOLLEY'S SMALL SUITE at the Cape Sierra Hotel is guarded by a phalanx of RUF fighters and UN soldiers, most of whom lounge and sleep in the hallway outside his door, shortwave transistors providing a tinny backdrop to their continued presence. The suite is at the end of a series of narrow, unlit corridors, but because it's at the far end of the hotel complex, it also offers a commanding view of the ocean pounding black boulders at the nation's edge. The sound of the surf rolled across the unkempt lawns and into the room, where Farah and Golley sipped almost-cold beers and listened to it fill the long silences.

Omrie Golley is the RUF's civilian agent, spokesperson, and UN liaison as chairman of the RUF Political and Peace Council. He is a round-faced man with thick glasses, and lives in London. He's also one of the group's most level-headed and world-wise, which is why Farah went to him to arrange a meeting with other top RUF leaders about his Al Qaeda story. It wouldn't be wise to confront such unstable personalities with his charges without the presence of someone more sensible and literate like Golley.

But still, this was a frightening moment for Farah. He was simultaneously showing his hand and bluffing about an explosive connection between the world's most degenerate fighting force and the world's most evil enemy; he had to play his hand just right.

The plan was a simple and time-honored journalistic trick: Farah would tell them what he thought he knew and make them believe that he knew far more than he really did. Farah also wanted to scare the holy hell out of the RUF about how bad it would be for them—with elections less than six months away and the RUFP struggling for legitimacy—to be tied to Osama bin Laden.

So Golley arranged for a meeting between Farah and several RUF leaders, who Farah declined to name to preserve their confidentiality. The men sat around the room and listened to his allegations.

Then there was silence.

Farah sipped his beer nervously, amazed at how loud the surf sounded. He could see their wheels spinning, each person trying to decide what to lie about, what to admit, and what to say. Everyone was jittery.

At first, there was denial of everything. Eventually, one man spoke up. He may have heard of Aziz Nassour if he was the one called Alpha Zulu. Another chimed in with another piece of the story. Bit by bit, Farah's theory was confirmed. Finally, one of the RUF told Farah the whole plot, that he'd met with Nassour in Monrovia in July 2001 and they agreed that the RUF would increase its diamond production in exchange for a higher price. He confirmed that the men identified as Al Qaeda operatives were in Kono overseeing the operation, but were replaced when Bah complained to Nassour that the two were attracting attention by obviously not being of Sierra Leonean heritage. After hours of back and forth, the RUF had admitted what Farah had discovered: The rebels helped Osama bin Laden's group launder millions of dollars in cash. The RUF insisted that it didn't know that Nassour was a middleman for bin Laden; nevertheless, the terrorists now had an untold number of highly liquid diamonds they could use to fund further attacks against the United States and its interests abroad.

AFTER THE MEETING, Farah confirmed more details with American and European intelligence sources and returned to his room at the Mammy Yoko to write the article. He knew he'd landed on a big one, an "oh-shit" story in his words, and he was nervous about it. From his time in Colombia reporting on drug producers, he knew that warlords would ignore almost anything he wrote about them as long as it didn't affect their bottom line. There was little question that this article would have a huge impact on the diamond world, bigger by leaps than the Global Witness report in 1999.

He wrote and filed the story on November 1, 2001. It detailed the relationships between Bah, Nassour, and Osailly with the Al Qaeda operatives, a Tanzanian and a Kenyan who were implicated in the U.S. embassy bombings in those countries in 1998. The story focused on Liberia's role in the scheme, how Nassour skirted customs with official protection, how the Senegalese Hezbollah members were sheltered in their safehouse by the government, and how Bah flew to meetings with Al Qaeda intermediaries on a Liberian government helicopter. It ran on the front page of the *Washington Post* the next day.

Then the shit hit the fan.

AS THE *POST*'S West Africa bureau chief, Farah is used to drawing Liberian President Charles Taylor's ire. But he struck a particularly raw nerve with the Al Qaeda story. The Liberian government went out of its way to post Farah's picture, along with a scathing denial of the allegations and personal insults about him, on the home page of the country's official Web site. On a radio interview with the BBC, Liberian officials denied the story and threatened legal action against the newspaper. Bah—who refused Farah's request for an interview through mutual contacts—even weighed in with a rare interview with the Associated Press. He too denied Farah's story that RUF diamonds were being sold to Al Qaeda.

To Farah, the Web site was the most troubling; it seemed to insinuate that he was a target and he and his wife—who's normally unshakeable about such things—began to fear for their safety. Their home in Abidjan didn't provide a lot of psychic comfort; not only was it right next door to Liberia, it was also home to various and sundry Liberian dissidents, refugees, and rebels.[5]

The situation grew more dire when Farah returned home on a Saturday from a trip to Ghana to find an urgent message awaiting him from the regional security officer of the U.S. Embassy. He was asked to report to the embassy the following day, a Sunday, so Farah knew it was important. When he arrived, the man had him sit and then read a two-line cable from the U.S. Department of State: There was information of a threat on Farah's life.

Shaken and alarmed, he returned home and called his editors. He told them that he was going to lay low around the house for a few days and then see about going on a trip and making himself scarce around Abidjan for awhile. But before he could go any-where, his editors called back two days later and told him that they'd received word that Bah was looking for "retribution" against him. He was ordered to evacuate his family back to Washington immediately, no questions asked. In between bouts of frantic pack-ing, Farah managed to contact some of Bah's associates in an attempt to find out what Bah had in store for him.

Bah wasn't interested in killing him, Farah was told, just having him beaten to a bloody pulp and maybe arrested with planted drugs. That was hardly reassuring, so Farah called the embassy and requested diplomatic escort through the airport so that he could clear customs without having anything planted on him or being detained by a bribed official. Then he just had to sit and wait for the plane to leave. He and his family secured themselves in their home, a former embassy with steel covers that roll down over the windows at the end of a dead-end street. Farah employed three unarmed security guards and installed an alarm, complete with a panic button that would call armed guards from the security company to his house within five minutes if he needed them. Friends on the street kept an eye out for anyone suspicious. At night, the family locked themselves upstairs, behind a "mau-mau" door, a reinforced steel-plated vaultlike thing secured with heavy bolts.

On Thursday, November 13, Farah and his family fled Ivory Coast. U.S. embassy officials sat with them at the gate until they were safely on the plane and on their way to Amsterdam.

Two weeks after he broke the story that suddenly made the civil war in Sierra Leone front-page international news once and for all, Farah was back at a desk in D.C.

THE EFFECTS OF FARAH'S STORY rippled far and wide.

While the story about Al Qaeda purchasing RUF blood diamonds was breaking, the Kimberley Process was meeting again in Luanda, Angola. Most of the thirty-five nongovernmental organization, government, and industry representatives had finally agreed, after almost a year, to endorse a scheme of uniform cross-border documentation for imported and exported diamonds. A lynchpin of the plan was that participating countries could refuse to import diamonds that didn't adhere to the standards. This would encourage all exporting countries to take the process seriously. If their parcels couldn't be exported, they would lose out on valuable export taxes, giving diamond-producing countries an incentive to comply.

But the United States didn't like the idea. Approximately 80 percent of the world's diamonds are sold to U.S. consumers, but U.S. representatives with the Kimberley Process were worried that the scheme proposed could violate World Trade Organization policies. The WTO mediates trade disputes between countries that agree to allow the WTO to set trade rules that may be counter to laws within those countries. For example, an exporting country may argue to the WTO that an importing country's laws banning genetically modified corn constitute unfair trade. If the WTO sides with the exporting country, the importing country's law against the corn would be rendered null and void.

The United States was worried about the same problem with diamonds. The fear was that if a country was denied an import license on the grounds that it couldn't prove its diamonds were from clean sources, the exporting country could appeal to the WTO and have the Kimberley Process rules overturned. The U.S. therefore objected to the Kimberley Process's insistence that diamond-importing countries refuse entry to any goods that didn't come with a certified document trail.

But when Farah's story broke, the U.S. representatives suddenly saw the light. As the largest consumer of diamonds—some of which may have been used to launder money by terrorists who'd just leveled the worst attack on its soil in history—it took little coaxing. The Luanda meeting concluded with consensus on the details and participants set about drafting a resolution to be presented to the UN Security Council early in 2002.

The U.S. Congress wasn't far behind. The House of Representatives was stalled on a decision about Tony Hall's Clean Diamonds Act. The bill sought to write into U.S. law whatever system of rough and polished diamond controls was eventually adopted by the Kimberley Process, or institute its own based on the Kimberley recommendations; install a set of instant triggers that would impose sanctions on a country that didn't adhere to the controls on its diamond exports; and release $5 million in 2002 for countries that needed financial assistance to comply with export controls.

But like the Kimberley Process, the bill was stalled by legislators fidgety about instantly slapping sanctions on a country violating the rules. Those opposed wanted wiggle room to allow discretion on a case-by-case basis.

The day Farah's story was published, Hall released a statement that read, "Al Qaeda's workings may be news to most Americans, and the link between the money we spend on [diamonds] and terror certainly will shock consumers and the jewelers who employ many thousands of people in communities across our country. Conflict diamonds' exploitation by terrorists appears to have been well known to our intelligence agencies, and yet Congress still has not acted on any of the bills introduced over the course of two years." Twenty-six days after Farah's story hit the newsstands, the House overwhelmingly passed a compromise bill, 408 to 6.

The new bill doesn't feature automatic sanctions against violating countries, but gives the president the authority to level sanctions if he feels it's in the interest of national security. Also, the compromise bill addressed only rough goods, not polished, but again gave the president authority to confiscate rough and polished goods if there was convincing evidence that they were produced from conflict areas. Also, the bill allowed exemptions to seizure and sanctions in order to satisfy the WTO. But, still sensitive to the tragedy of September 11, the House kicked in an additional appropriation of $5 million for fiscal year 2003 and eliminated the original bill's six-month phase-in period. The new bill will take effect

200 + BLOOD DIAMONDS

immediately once adopted by the U.S. Senate and signed by President George W. Bush. As of March 18, 2002, the bill was read twice in the Senate and referred to the Committee on Finance, where it has remained as of this writing.

There were other effects from Farah's story. The diamond industry had a collective panic attack over the allegations, as expected. It was bad enough that its diamonds and policies of buying and selling had resulted in the death of some 3.7 million people in various African war zones and displaced another 6 million,[6] but now they were being tied directly to horrible scenes of destruction that had been burned into everyone's mind in the days following September 11. The attacks changed the political and social landscape in countries around the world. Overnight, it seemed that a new Cold War infrastructure had been created with terrorists and the countries that harbor and support them on one side and those pressed into a "war on terrorism" on the other. The collapse of the Twin Towers was only the first glimpse of this unbelievable new reality.

I watched United Airlines Flight 175 vaporize into the South Tower of the World Trade Center while at the Diamond Trading Company, standing next to Andy Bone, whose corporate cool evaporated as quickly as the U.S. sense of security. It was about a fifteen-minute walk back to my East London hotel, but I had no television in my room. I headed to a pub that I knew had several televisions. Out on the chilly streets of London, traffic flowed along as usual and pedestrians streamed by wearing headphones, oblivious to the attacks. Diamonds were the last things on my mind or anyone else's for a long time thereafter. I numbly watched the footage over and over: People falling a long way to their deaths from some of the tallest buildings on earth, the towers collapsing one after another like sand castles, the streets of a familiar city—

home to dozens of friends and family members—filling with ash and debris. Getting onto an airplane to Africa a few days later, I felt I was escaping into the farthest corner of the planet, leaving the chill and cucumber sandwiches for heat and crushing starvation, unaware that I was heading to one of the scenes of a global crime. I would learn later that many Lebanese in Kenema and Bo, the diamond trading centers, celebrated in joy at the news of the attacks.

In the following months, the United States began its counterattack on Afghanistan, bin Laden's base of operations where he found sympathetic shelter with the country's ruling Taliban regime. The U.S. methodically destroyed the Taliban and dealt a serious blow to Al Qaeda, which trained its terrorists there in windblown high mountain deserts, though bin Laden has so far evaded capture. But the one thing that's clear is that he and the people who lead his organization aren't as financially wounded as the United States would hope. Somewhere out there is a multimillion-dollar cache of goods from Kono. Whether the diamonds are in a Hamburg safe-deposit box or a cave in the Tora Bora mountains, they are now the terrorists' ace in the hole. As long as some cells of leadership can survive the American military assault, they will have the means to continue their war well into the future.

The diamond industry knows this. It hasn't been proven that Sierra Leone diamonds were specifically used to fund the hijackings, but it doesn't need to be. Uniformly, traders' and jewelers' organizations stampeded to condemn the connection.

Matthew Runci, president of Jewelers of America, and Eli Izhakoff, chairman of the World Diamond Council, released a joint statement that said: "It has been known for all too long that bandits masquerading as rebels have been using the proceeds from the sale of stolen diamonds to finance their criminal behavior in some

African countries. Nations involved in the diamond trade—as producers, processors and importers—must construct an effective monitoring system that protects the legitimate supply chain from the small percentage of illicit stones obtained by criminal elements.'"[7]

De Beers naturally weighed in as well: "[We] utterly condemn the way in which these [terrorist] organizations are preying on otherwise legitimate industries to further their criminal and murderous activities." The statement also reiterated that De Beers had ended purchasing on the open market and that the percentage of diamonds emanating from conflict zones was "small, but significant."[8]

The most important thing about this slew of legislation and condemnations is that it comes too late. Trafficking in conflict diamonds is a well-established business with millions of dollars on the line. The money props up not only rebel insurgencies and the bank accounts of their leaders, but it represents a substantial amount of revenue for the president of Liberia, who doesn't appear to be prepared to leave office any time soon; the trafficking also generates enormous profits for the gunrunning industry, as well as for thousands of middle-tier diamond brokers.

The truth is that conflict diamonds will be bought as long as they're available. They may not be purchased by Tom Shane's jewelry company, at least directly, but that's because they won't be offered to him. They'll enter the diamond pipeline long before they become jewelry, at jungle meeting places, village backrooms, and Freetown bars when no one is looking. They'll make their way into the legitimate exports of sellers who want to pad their parcels cheaply, safely sheltered by certificates issued by lax or bribed officials. The documents required by the Kimberley Process and the Clean Diamond Act will not stop the traffic.

They'll just make it harder to detect.

9

THE ROUGH ROAD AHEAD:
Mining for Peace

Freetown, Sierra Leone

IN JANUARY 2002, UNAMSIL officially announced that the war in Sierra Leone was over and that the Revolutionary United Front no longer existed as a rebel group. I was in Lagos, Nigeria, at the time and you could almost hear the collective sigh of relief wafting down the coast from the west. For a time, it seemed that the last and most crucial step of the peace plan—disarming the Kono region and taking its diamond mines from the RUF's control for good—might never be accomplished. The original deadline for disarmament for Kono, Kailahun, and Kenema Districts had been November 30, 2001, but that deadline passed with only a handful of soldiers turning in their weapons. Through December, rebels continued to mine diamonds and launder them through Liberia, with UNAMSIL taking little notice. Masimba Tafirenyika, the acting UNAMSIL spokesperson, was asked by a reporter two weeks after the deadline passed about the UN's response to the continued mining.

"This, including all other activities, are addressed by the government of Sierra Leone with the deployment of the Sierra Leone Police throughout the country," he said. "The Sierra Leone Police have been deployed in Kono and will be deployed in other areas."[1]

The deployment of the police—an organization historically as corrupt and inept as the SLA—did nothing to stop rival RUF miners from staging a riot in Koidu on December 18. Different mining factions threw stones at one another in the presence of police and UNAMSIL soldiers.

UNAMSIL stuck to its program of moderate diplomacy and employed the help of RUF Brigadier General Issa Sessay in appealing for peace and disarmament in the region, staging pep rallies and feel-good events in the contested areas. Until the end, Sessay used the continued occupation of the diamond regions as a trump card to try and negotiate the release of Foday Sankoh from his Bunce Island dungeon, claiming that only "Pa Sankoh" could get his children in the bush to give up their lives of rape and pillage for one of education and odd jobs, but neither UNAMSIL nor the government budged. One of the other reasons Sessay stalled for time, perhaps, was to allow his field commanders a little extra time to mine as many diamonds as possible before the inevitable end.

But eventually, the end did come, at least as far as UNAMSIL is concerned. In the last days of January 2002, the UN staged a bonfire event in which it burned more than 3,000 weapons confiscated from the rebels over the course of the last year and announced that peace had come once and for all to Sierra Leone.

Whether or not this is true, naturally, remains to be seen. The durability of the cease-fire in effect since March 2001, the fact that many areas of the country are now open to outsiders for the first time in more than ten years, and the mutation of the RUF into a recognized political movement shouldn't be confused with smooth sailing. When the war was declared over, many problems still existed and threatened a return to Sierra Leone's old patterns of violence. For example, the Security Council announced in January 2002 the formation of a special war crimes court for Sierra Leone. Representing a new chapter in international jurisprudence, the special court constitutes a blend of international and local laws and takes legal precedence over local Sierra Leonean courts. Whereas courts for war crimes committed in Yugoslavia and Rwanda were established directly by the Security Council, the tribunal for Sierra Leone was requested by the government in Freetown.

From the beginning the court's main targets were Major General Sam "Mosquito" Bokarie, RUF founder Foday Sankoh, and AFRC junta leader Johnny Paul Koroma. Sankoh, despite the RUF's earnest efforts to see him freed, remained in jail in Freetown; Koroma also returned to the capital, now a born-again Christian preaching reconciliation.

Immediately after the war, the special court represents a dangerous double-edged blade to peace prospects in Sierra Leone. Clearly, most of those living there demand accountability for war crimes committed by these men and others who would eventually be indicted. An important pillar of any peace process is justice, and seeing the men who dragged Sierra Leone through a decade of horror publicly accused and tried under international law is a critical component of the healing and rebuilding process.

But it's also something that the RUF has never been inclined to accept. Remember that the Lomé Accords gave the rebels everything they could have wanted—a government position for Sankoh, control of the diamond mines, and immunity from prosecution for war crimes—and it still failed miserably. UNAMSIL's bloody start can be attributed, at least in part, to the fact that with Secretary General Annan's public disagreement with Lomé's amnesty clause, RUF leaders preferred to fight the UN rather than risk being tried for war crimes. That the RUF's titular leader would be the first to stand before a UN-led tribunal when the RUF has tried everything from a prison break to diplomacy to see him freed seemed to provide a tailor-made excuse for them to abandon peace and renew the fight, especially for those RUF leaders who felt that they may eventually end up in the dock themselves. As Margaret Novicki of the UN mission once told me, a war crimes investigation would have to indict practically everyone. "Everyone's guilty," she said.

On another level, if the tribunal is successful and is conducted with little dissent from the RUF, the majority of RUF leaders— including the current one, Sessay—could end up in jail, gutting the fledgling party of anyone in a position to lead it. With elections scheduled for May 2002, and the RUFP on the ballot, this meant the indictment of elected officials was a real possibility. This course of events would be fine for most Sierra Leoneans, but it seemed unlikely that the RUF would be willing to risk its complete erasure from the political scene.

These are only the most obvious hurdles. Though the warfare and the amputations may have stopped, the RUF has left behind a shattered nation filled with ruined souls. Rebuilding homes and towns and restarting lives are only the first painful steps to recovery. People will have to revive businesses, find jobs, and figure out how to pay income taxes. It will be decades before farmers can feed the country again. Medical care and education will have to be modernized, democratized, and spread into the bush to avoid a replay of the disenfranchisement that allowed the RUF to grow in the first place. The military and police forces will have to be completely revamped and reeducated not only in standard law-enforcement techniques, but also in respect for human rights and international rules of law.

PARADOXICALLY, what destroyed Sierra Leone may be the only thing capable of saving it: diamonds.

For the first time in its turbulent history, Sierra Leone must manage its natural resources and mineral wealth. Diamond mining must be strictly controlled so that, for a change, the vast majority of the revenue will go to the people of the country, not to spoiled dictators and ruthless killers and their henchmen in Liberia and elsewhere. Important first steps in this regard are already being taken: Within a week of the UNAMSIL declaration of peace, Canadian mining company DiamondWorks announced that it would resume mining operations in Koidu, assured by President Kabbah that its permits and property titles acquired through Branch Energy (which acquired them thanks to the military efforts of Executive Outcomes) were valid. In a recent statement, Diamond-Works executives said, "This important step in the peace process has removed the remaining political obstacles to the re-establishment of the company's operations in Sierra Leone after an absence of nearly five years."[2] Through Branch, DiamondWorks owns a 60 percent stake in a kimberlite pipe in Koidu, and two exploration permits for part of the Sewa River totaling 6,800 hectares of land.

The quick reestablishment of legitimate mining operations should be seen as a positive development and it would be a welcome investment if the country continued to stabilize enough for De Beers to play a role once again. The company's partnership with the government of Botswana, which has the fastest-growing economy in the world, should be viewed as a shining example of what properly organized and regulated industry can do for the good of a country. Some critics will balk that a partnership between De Beers and Sierra Leone will add yet more decimal points to the company's wealth, but it's a far cry better than the utter anarchy that dominated the 1990s. If De Beers's greed for diamonds leads Sierra Leone's leaders to be greedy for the good of the nation, then who loses, other than those who may be paying too much for their jewelry downstream? In terms of free-market economics, they already pay too much. The only difference would be that they'd be paying it to legally employed miners, not men who cut off arms with machetes. In this case, greed can be good.

Stabilizing and controlling diamond exploration would have positive ripple effects that go beyond the end of one of the world's worst ongoing wars. There's no reason a country as beautiful as Sierra Leone shouldn't have tourism as one of its top five industries. Foreign and domestic exploration investment can create an economy of its own as mining companies will require far more than shovels and shake-shakes to delve fully into Sierra Leone's kimberlites; they'll require modern facilities, sorting and processing centers like those found in Namibia, South Africa, and Botswana. Running those facilities requires a skilled workforce and it's not unlikely that exploration companies would be willing to invest in the local education system for the sake of producing a labor pool from which to draw. De Beers has a good track record in this regard. The overwhelming majority of its employees are indigenous to the countries in which it operates.

The big risk to De Beers—and to Sierra Leone's diamond industry—is if Sierra Leone diamonds are tainted for good thanks to the RUF's war; but such a risk is minimal given the ability of De Beers, through its marketing and advertising clout, to create and maintain any reality it wants for diamonds. Two years' worth of publicity about conflict diamonds from Global Witness, Amnesty International, and other groups; numerous media reports on such high-profile television shows as *20/20* and *Nova*; and legislation by the U.S. Congress have not been enough by a long shot to overcome more than 100 years of marketing strategy. Most consumers still have never heard about "blood" diamonds and the African wars fought over them.

"The fact of the matter is that to the consumer it's a very low-interest issue," said Tom Shane, the American diamond importer. "Even with all the articles that have been written, we don't hear it in our stores being raised as an issue."

Shane's employees, like many other jewelry retailers across the country, are prepared to answer questions about conflict diamonds, but as tradition would dictate, the issue is never openly acknowledged unless a customer asks about it specifically.

"We don't raise it and flaunt the fact that it's not a conflict stone any more than I would say that it's not stolen," Shane said. "Why would it occur to them that it would be? It's not that we're ducking the issue in any way, shape, or form, but it's not something that's ever brought up, either by us or the customer."

Even if customers were interested in where their diamonds come from, there's little they can do except take the word of the jeweler as to their origin, in much the same way that the jeweler takes the word of the Antwerp polisher, who takes the word of the broker, and so on. Although experts may be able to determine the origin of rough goods if given enough of a sample to peruse, it's virtually impossible for anyone to tell where a polished piece came from.

"To control the conflict stones, you have to start at the source," Shane said. "The integrity of the system has to start at the source. You can't go backwards and verify. It's a one-way street, and that's just the honest fact of what we're dealing in."

CLEARLY, THE BIGGEST BENEFITS of peace will be to those who currently have no future at all and never will if the situation is allowed to stand. Children who grew up learning how to kill one another with smuggled Ukrainian machine guns can and should have the opportunity to become the generous, likeable, and well-humored people that many of their countrymen have proven they can be.

In spite of my disinclination, I often found myself liking many of the RUF members I met, a situation that can boggle the mind if you think too deeply about it. In Kailahun, I often found myself laughing at the jokes and antics of a fighter who called himself T-Ray, a shrapnel-scarred man who always carried a .45-caliber pistol in his left hand as if it were part of his body. In one sense, it was terrifying to be caught so off guard by feelings of natural friendship with a man who admitted killing "dozens" of people during his years with the RUF. Shouldn't I be hating this man with every ounce of my being? I'd think, in moments when I was suddenly crushed with shame at having laughed out loud at something he'd said, praying that no one had seen me.

But later I realized that the fact that we could find common ground at all is a source of immense hope. I fantasized about a time when Sierra Leone was at peace and I returned not to report on war or death, but for the sake of a vacation. The only helicopters would be the commercial ones flying back and forth between Aberdeen and Lungi Airport, and the children wandering Lumley

Beach Road would be burdened with schoolbooks instead of ammunition. The UN would be gone, along with most of the street crooks and hookers. Those who are today doomed cripples and hopeless amputees will have received proper support and medical care from the government in the hope that one day they'll be able to support themselves and their families. The forlorn and shell-shocked would be replaced with tourists, local families, businessmen, and the everyday worker-bees of a normal economy, the components of a successful and peaceful country.

Such visions would come only fleetingly, though. Invariably, they'd dissolve into the chaotic reality of Kailahun, where one of every twenty people I encountered were only days or weeks away from a painful death by starvation or disease and where no one went anywhere without their Kalashnikov. Other memories would flood my mind, defiant images that seemed to mock my fantasies of peace: Sween and Lahia were dead, I was sure. Dead of tetanus, and their images were never far from my mind's work: Lahia's eyes working against imminent paralysis to fix on me, saying most certainly "help me"; Lieutenant Sween's fear of death so palpable that you could smell it in that dank room, his chest rising and falling with short breaths of despair, knowing that he was doomed to die, painfully; Lieutenant Colonel Senesi laughing at his lie about never having seen diamonds before; Ismael Dalramy trying hard, and failing, to show me that he can dress himself without hands; the baby with no left foot, the one sacrificed to a Guinean mortar; the terrifying visage I literally bumped into in Kailahun, a clitoral-circumcision victim adorned in black-dyed palm grass and a too-small carved mask depicting a screaming woman; a truckload of children carrying AK-47s met on the four-wheel path to Koindu, eyes vacant enough to hypnotize; the St. Nicholas twinkle in the eyes of Jacob

Singer, eager to pay the RUF for their goods and get home to Australia; Andy Bone at the DTC, fretting over the impacts to his industry; the World Trade Center towers blooming like beautiful gray flowers of death.

The end of the war only provided a blip of hope, because in West Africa, something always seems to go wrong at the worst possible moment. Indeed, within weeks of peace being declared in Sierra Leone, LURD rebels in Liberia surrounded Monrovia and threatened to topple Charles Taylor's government. The situation promises to escalate and end badly, raising the question of how much pressure Taylor will put on his RUF compatriots to help quell the rebellion by again feeding him diamonds for cash.

When I dwelled on these thoughts, I realized that I would be a very old man if my vision of tranquility ever came true.

10

TRUTH AND RECONCILIATION:
Recovering from the Diamond War

Sierra Leone, Belgium

L IKE MANY OTHERS who were amputated by the RUF, in 1996 Ismael Dalramy pleaded with his captors to kill him when he saw the fate that awaited him. But his death would not have served the RUF's political purpose. They amputated his arms to deliver the message that people without hands couldn't vote for those who opposed the RUF.

On May 14, 2002, Dalramy and hundreds of other amputees waited for hours in a hot long line to prove them wrong. When it was his turn to vote, he marked the ballot with his toe, only one remarkable facet of one of the most remarkable days in Sierra Leone's history.[1]

When the United Nations finally succeeded in disarming the vast majority of those fighting in Sierra Leone's jungles, entire swaths of the country that had for the past decade been closed to anyone without a machine gun were once again open for travel, at least to UN monitors and humanitarian organizations. Only then was the destruction wrought by one of Africa's most brutal modern wars finally clear. Once thriving villages and towns had been erased from existence. Where there were formerly fields of cassava and simple farming habitations, there were now crude graves and weather-ravaged skeletons of homes and buildings. Human bones littered the roadsides. Tens of thousands of refugees clung to life all along the Sierra Leone border with Liberia and Guinea, starving, wounded, and diseased.

And still, diamonds brought weapons to the region. Less than two weeks after the election, 30 tons of rifles and ammunition were smuggled into Monrovia from Belgium through Nice, France. The consignment was paid for by Aziz Nassour, the Lebanese Al Qaeda go-between, and the arms were turned over to Sam "Mosquito" Bokarie, the former RUF field commander. Little more than a month later, another shipment of 15 tons arrived. Even though Al Qaeda's organized diamond deals were in disarray, RUF leaders, Qaeda operatives, and corrupt government leaders (including Charles Taylor's wife, Jewel Taylor) met in Burkina Faso in June 2002 to discuss how to continue their diamonds-for-guns schemes. The war may have been over, but it's clear that Sierra Leone's diamonds were still being smuggled away and used to buy weapons.[2] Exploitation of the mines by sundry smugglers and criminals continued to be a problem that wouldn't soon go away.

With the disarmament completed in Kailahun District, UNHCR kicked its relief efforts into high gear in early 2002 only to find that it didn't have enough trucks to move the refugees swiftly to repatriation camps. The effort was made more difficult when Liberian president Charles Taylor declared a state of emergency on February 8, 2002, in the wake of renewed fighting around Monrovia against rebel forces of Liberians United for Reconciliation and Democracy. Sierra Leoneans who'd fled to Liberia to escape the RUF now fled back across the border with thousands of Liberians. Between February 8 and February 12, 5,000 Sierra Leoneans and 6,000 Liberians seeking asylum straggled into the border towns. This was only a small portion of Sierra Leone refugees still stranded in neighboring countries, however. In all, UNHCR operated six camps in Liberia with approximately 35,000 refugees from Sierra Leone. Another 55,000 Sierra Leoneans were camped in Guinea and 8,000 more in The Gambia. The organization was only capable of moving about 1,200 people per week from the border of Liberia to temporary camps within Sierra Leone, and another 500 per week from Guinea.[3]

By March 2002, 47,000 fighters—both RUF and Kamajors—had been disarmed in Sierra Leone, 25,000 weapons had been destroyed, and UNAMSIL's mandate had been extended by the Security Council until September 2002.[4] But the number that carried the most significance was the 2.27 million people who'd registered to vote in the May 14 election, in itself an astonishing count considering what happened the last time Sierra Leoneans cast their votes. The question that hung over the city streets and village paths of Sierra Leone: What exactly would these people do? Would they vote with their hearts, as they'd done in 1996, the election that saw President Kabbah voted into office only to be run out on a wave of violence and amputation? Or would they succumb to voting for the reviled Revolutionary United Front Party in the hopes of avoiding another disaster, frightened into giving their vote to killers and thieves by the party's thinly veiled threat of a campaign slogan: "Only the RUFP can ensure peace."

Given the state of Sierra Leone by the time elections came up on May 14, it's hardly surprising that one of the UN monitors tasked with overseeing the vote told a reporter that "it's nothing short of miraculous" that the election was conducted without violence and in a manner that was consistently fair and trouble-free. This sentiment was hardly melodramatic; in fact, this characterization may have been understated. In the end, 80 percent of registered voters—constituting an estimated 40 percent of the population—showed up at the polls and 70 percent of them voted for Kabbah to be reelected to another five-year term. Considering what happened the last time elections were held, when hundreds of thousands of people were mutilated by the RUF, pictures of amputees struggling to cast their votes with smooth stumps were nothing less than a reaffirmation of the human spirit.

The contest itself was no less dramatic. The favored candidate was President Kabbah, representing the Sierra Leone People's Party. He was widely favored over the competition, although in truth there was little the man could point to in his past that qualified him to lead the nation. His previous presidency was interrupted after only a few months in office and it was during his tenure that the RUF overran Freetown not once, but twice. Kabbah proved himself a statesman by adhering to the world community's desire to face the RUF with ECOMOG rather than a force of mercenaries, thus winning Sierra Leone favor with the World Bank, IMF, the United Nations, and ECOWAS. Because of this—as well as the fact that the field of competitors running against him collectively had less to offer—the voters and the UN administrators who wanted to see him reelected were willing to overlook the man's other flaws, such as his approval of a series of extrajudicial executions of suspected AFRC coup-plotters once he was returned to office in 1998.

Facing Kabbah on the ballot was the AFRC's main coup-plotter himself, Johnny Paul Koroma, the junta's former leader who campaigned as "J.P.," a born-again Christian. The man who had been exiled to Liberia at gunpoint by RUF leaders Mosquito and Sessay, J.P. claims to have found God and been saved; his religious conversion compelled him to return to Sierra Leone to preach reconciliation and run for president. As *New York Times* reporter Nori Onitshi wrote in May 2002, Koroma was a notably different man, having fired his old security detail—led by a heavy man named Hiroshima Bomb, who wore skirts, a bowler, and jewelry made of machine-gun ammunition—in favor of suited men with black sunglasses.

Rounding out the bizarre roster of presidential hopefuls was the RUFP's last-minute, lame-duck candidate, a hitherto unknown RUF member named Pallo Bangura. Having failed to secure Sankoh's release, the RUF apparently had difficulty finding a replacement. Gabrill Massaqoui and Omrie Golley, the RUF's military and civilian spokesmen, respectively, both turned down the opportunity and grew more and more scarce around Freetown, perhaps realizing that the RUF was singing its swan song. Bangura was hustled onto the ballot at the last moment. His platform consisted of a single plank—his claim that he didn't know anything about the RUF's crimes against humanity.

On election day, the vote fell as most suspected it would: Kabbah received 70 percent. The next closest finisher was Ernest Koroma, a candidate of the All People's Congress, who rode the party's name recognition to finish with 22 percent of the vote.

J.P. Koroma—the bloodthirsty junta leader, diamond thief, dimestore warlord, and now man of God—came in a distant third with 6 percent of the vote.

As for the RUF, their hopes disintegrated in the face of endemic disorganization, failing to receive enough votes to even register beyond pollsters' margins of error. Their support, such that it was, collapsed everywhere. They even failed to earn a significant percentage of votes in Makeni, their northern heartland.

Overnight, the RUF and its political aspirations seemed to vanish like jungle vapors under the hot sun.

Things never improved for the rebel group. Less than a year after losing the election by a landslide, the Special Court for Sierra Leone began nailing the RUF's coffin lid shut, returning indictments against all of the top players in the war, including of course Foday Sankoh, who had remained in custody since May 2000, and Sam Bokarie, who was still on the loose in Liberia. In the opinion of many, Mosquito was working for Charles Taylor in his fight against LURD rebels. Also indicted were Brigadier Issa Sessay; J.P. Koroma, who vanished shortly after the elections and is reported to have been murdered; Sam Hinga Norman, the head of the country's civil defense forces and a former AFRC leader; Moinina Fofana, the Director of War Operations for the Kamajors; and Allieu Kondewa, the former Kamajor high priest.

Sankoh was indicted on seventeen criminal counts, including "extermination," murder, rape, pillage, sexual slavery, abductions, forced labor, use of child soldiers, and "outrages upon personal dignity," the charge that detailed the amputation and mutilation campaigns. At its heart, the indictment states that all of the atrocities that occurred in Sierra Leone since 1991 happened as a result of the criminal diamond-smuggling enterprise overseen by Sankoh and conducted with the full support and encouragement of Charles Taylor.

The RUF, including the accused, and the AFRC shared a common plan, purpose or design (joint criminal enterprise) which was to take any actions necessary to gain and exercise political power and control over the territory of Sierra Leone, in particular the diamond mining areas. The natural resources of Sierra Leone, in particular the diamonds, were to be provided to persons outside Sierra Leone in return for assistance in carrying out the joint criminal enterprise.

The joint criminal enterprise includes gaining and exercising control over the population of Sierra Leone in order to prevent or minimize resistance to their geographic control, and to use members of the population to provide support to the members of the joint criminal enterprise. The acts alleged in this Indictment, including but not limited to acts of terrorism, collective punishments, unlawful killings, abductions, forced labour, physical and sexual violence, use of child soldiers, looting and burning of civilian structures, were either actions within the joint criminal enterprise or were a reasonably foreseeable consequence of the joint criminal enterprise.

The court acted with vigor in its indictments, partly because its limited budget demanded that it move as quickly as possible to meet its mandated three-year term, but natural events intervened to rob Sierra Leoneans of the satisfaction of seeing those who'd destroyed the nation stand trial: Sankoh, increasingly demented and out-of-touch due to a stroke he suffered in jail, died in custody on July 29, 2003. It was an ungracious end. Sankoh's few court appearances prior to his death were dramatic only because it was clear that the RUF leader had gone insane. Confined to a wheelchair and in steel handcuffs, he mumbled spastically during his last court appearance in June 2003, his matted gray dreadlocks reaching almost to the floor. "I'm a god," he muttered in his last public statement. "I am an inner god. I am the leader of Sierra Leone."

The court had no better luck landing Mosquito in the dock. The battle-group commander's indictment was a carbon copy of Sankoh's and his prosecution was at least as anticipated. But the Liberian government announced in the summer of 2003 that the dreaded RUF commander had died in a battle with LURD rebels as they moved decisively on Monrovia. Almost unanimously, the Sierra

Leone media condemned the announcement as a fraud and David Crane, the court's lead prosecutor, demanded physical proof. It was long in coming, however, since Monrovia soon fell into chaos: LURD rebels advanced to within small-arms range of downtown, besieging the capital for three long and bloody weeks, making the legal show-down over Mosquito's remains take a back seat to the actual show-down between rebels, Charles Taylor, and the rest of the world.

Photojournalist Chris Hondros was there for it and, when he could, he reported back to me on scenes that rivaled Sierra Leone's nightmares. "It's another long day of horrors, one after another," he wrote in an e-mail to me in August 2003. The fighting in Monrovia was intense, pitting government "soldiers"—some as young as twelve years old—against rebels who fired light artillery indiscriminately into the city, killing scores of civilian men, women, and children. Typically, soldiers fought stoned and dressed in campy costumes, lending a surreal air to the street fighting. It was the sort of flash-fire human rights catastrophe that has for so long occurred in Africa with little notice from the United States. But the Special Court for Sierra Leone helped land the conflict on the front pages around the world. The flare-up was made more critical to the world community after the court unsealed a secret indictment against Charles Taylor for war crimes resulting from his support of the RUF's war.

The indictment was a bold and welcome move for the tribunal, and it was heralded as a decisive step in the effort to assign responsibility for a decade of horrors inflicted on Sierra Leoneans while helping to remove from power a ruthless dictator who, if his past record was any indication, would surely be responsible for more death and destruction in the future. Crane put out an international arrest warrant for Taylor through Interpol.

Yet Taylor was in Ghana when his indictment was made public, and despite pleas from the United Nations to execute the warrant,

Ghanaian authorities allowed Taylor not only to attend an ECOWAS meeting regarding the crisis in Monrovia, but to slip back into Liberia afterward, where he hunkered down to consider his moves.

There didn't seem to be much to consider. LURD rebels were all but shooting down his palace door—and killing hundreds of civilians in the process—and he was wanted throughout the world for war crimes. It seemed Taylor had nowhere to go.

Observers, myself included, began counting down the days until Taylor either attempted to flee to a friendly country like Libya or Burkina Faso or was captured and executed on the beach in the fashion of Samuel Doe, an outcome that would have disappointed few people. Even President Bush, who had been under mounting pressure to commit troops to end the conflict, called for Taylor's surrender to the Sierra Leone court.

But leave it to Nigeria to spoil the ending. Olusegun Obasanjo, the Nigerian president, offered Taylor exile in exchange for stepping down from power and allowing an ECOMOG force to deploy to Monrovia and restore order.

At the time of the offer, it was regarded as a pretty good idea. Monrovia was being obliterated in the fighting. Hour after hour, Hondros watched children die from flying shrapnel and errant gunfire. Hundreds were dying from war wounds and diseases; thousands more would soon die of starvation as food supplies dwindled and refugees became more and more desperate. Bush was being pressed to send U.S. Marines to end the fighting just as he and his military planners were sorting out their flimsy justifications for the invasion of Iraq. His critics wanted him to prove that their run at Saddam Hussein was more than just a personal vendetta. In other words, Bush's critics seemed to be saying that if invading Iraq was justifiable in a humanitarian sense, then clearly so too was invading Liberia to end the bloodshed. Not only were dozens of people dying daily—and their bodies were stacked outside the U.S. embassy in protest of the United States' inaction in the face of undeniable humanitarian need—but the leader of the country was indicted by a UN-backed tribunal for more than a decade's worth of war crimes. If ever there was a time to invade a country on behalf of its citizens to oust a bloodthirsty leader, this was it.

But Bush decided otherwise. The U.S.S. *Abraham Lincoln*—complete with Harrier aircraft, Blackhawk helicopters, and hundreds of U.S. Marines that could have ended the fighting in an estimated twelve hours if they had been deployed—staged in the Atlantic Ocean and did nothing. Bush preferred that ECOWAS handle the perilous situation, and the negotiations about the shape and content of a peacekeeping force plodded on and on. Taylor used the world's indecision to his advantage, announcing that he'd accept Nigeria's offer of exile, but only once a peacekeeping force was deployed. Bush and other world leaders said that they'd deploy a peacekeeping force—headed by Nigerian soldiers under ECOMOG command—but only after Taylor had accepted exile. While this ridiculous standoff was playing out, people in Monrovia continued to die in horrible explosions during daily shelling raids. Finally, after about three weeks of intense street-to-street fighting that had killed hundreds, a small vanguard of ECOMOG soldiers landed at Roberts International Airport in Monrovia in early September 2003. Taylor boarded his VIP jet and flew two hours to Nigeria, where he was greeted as a guest of the state by Obasanjo. Taylor is currently enjoying his exile in a private house in Calabar, a seaside city in Nigeria that has the convenience of being located on the border of Cameroon, should the need for another quick escape become necessary. Given his VIP status in Nigeria, it seems unlikely that Taylor will be testifying before the Special Court of Sierra Leone anytime soon.

In the wake of Taylor's departure, another small drama ensued: The purported body of Sam "Mosquito" Bokarie, badly decomposed, was finally delivered to the court in Freetown. As of this writing, in October 2003, the court is awaiting the results of DNA testing that will determine once and for all whether or not the dreaded rebel leader is dead.

Although Sierra Leoneans have so far been robbed of the chance to see their tormentors tried for the crimes that destroyed the country over the past eleven years, the deaths of Sankoh and Mosquito and the forced exile of Taylor mark the end of their "joint criminal enterprise." Peace has indeed taken hold in the country, the first time in its 40-plus-year history since independence. The question now is: How long will it last and how will the government deal with new threats to its stability?

The question is not an idle one. UNAMSIL's mandate has been extended again and again by the Security Council, but the latest phase-out date of December 2004 seems to be the one that is embraced by most international observers as the true end of international involvement in the troubled country. Many question whether Sierra Leone will be ready by that time to govern itself or if it will simply be ripe for another insurgency.

Particularly troublesome is the fact that since the elections, Kabbah's government has done precious little to implement promised reforms. The police force is nowhere near capable of providing local security, especially in the diamond-mining regions, and the military has yet to show that it can independently provide adequate border security.[5] Of particular concern is the fact that the DDR program—which sought to provide job skills to demobilizing combatants—is largely considered a failure; even in the situations where former fighters successfully completed their training, they've been released into a job market in which unemployment is the only growth category. There are precious few jobs in Sierra Leone, creating yet again a population of semiskilled youths who are disenfranchised and alienated with the government of Freetown. Adding to this tension are the Kamajors, who have steadfastly refused to demobilize and stand ready to fight again at a moment's notice.[6]

Lastly, and most significantly, even though organized rebel exploitation of the diamond mines has ended, Sierra Leone has had little to no success in ending smuggling. Even though the Kimberley Process has since been adopted by seventy countries that ostensibly monitor diamond exports, Sierra Leone's diamond regions are poorly watched. According to a September 2003 report by the International Crisis Group: "The diamond mines, now often considered a curse rather than a blessing by the population, remain poorly monitored and managed, and illegal alluvial mining costs the government tens of millions of U.S. dollars in revenue each year."

On April 22, 2002, what would be the second largest diamond ever found was rumored to have been pulled from the ground in eastern Sierra Leone. Supposedly weighing in at a whopping 1,000 carats, the stone promptly disappeared, leading the government to put border guards on high alert, assuming that the massive find was bound for the old smuggling routes. A cryptic report by Reuters News Agency quoted Foday Yukella, deputy minister of natural resources, as saying that no one knew where the stone was, where it was discovered, or if, in fact, it actually existed. But the government wasn't taking any chances.

"As a government we are undertaking a massive search for the whereabouts of such a diamond," he told the news agency. "The ministry has been informed some top diamond magnates in West Africa have entered Sierra Leone with the aim of getting the alleged diamond out. . . . Border security forces together with the immigration authorities have also been put on alert."[7]

When I read the news item, I couldn't help but think of Jango, Jacob Singer, and his Polish sponsor, Valdy. I wondered what they were doing at the time of the find. As far as I know, no blood diamonds entered circulation due to their efforts, at least not in late 2001. Shortly before I left Sierra Leone for the last time on October 4, 2001, their half-million-dollar deal to land Kono diamonds was on shaky ground. It seemed that Jango couldn't convince any of his Kono District sources to travel to Freetown with such a valuable cache of goods with the end of the war near at hand and UNAM-SIL more actively deployed through the country than at any other time in its two-year history. As was his peculiar mode of operation, Singer refused to leave Freetown and Valdy wasn't about to make a trip to Conakry for $500,000 in $100 bills to give to Jango to travel to Kono himself and retrieve the diamonds. He offered him $300 to travel to Koidu and bring back a sample of the goods the RUF proposed to sell. Jango refused.

"There's no way," he told me emphatically. I didn't need to ask why. Getting diamonds on credit from the RUF was to take your life in your hands. If anything were to happen to a single stone between Koidu and Freetown and back, Jango would be dead before week's end.

When I finally boarded a helicopter to take me to Lungi Airport and my flight to Ghana and eventually home, the trio of smugglers had reached an impasse. Valdy sulked under the banana trees near the Solar's outdoor bar, talking to no one and angrily smoking one cigarette after another. Singer was seen more frequently in the company of hookers than smugglers, and Jango only came around to hang out with me and other journalists rather than those he supposedly worked for.

In spite of the fact that it seemed they'd failed to smuggle diamonds out of Sierra Leone, I was under no illusion that smuggling had been eradicated, or even made appreciably more difficult with the coming of peace and the adoption of new import/export protocols. When I read about the rumored 1,000-carat find, I knew that if someone was determined enough to smuggle it away, it would be done, even though the logistics would be more difficult; after all, the thing would be the size of a softball if it existed. Something that big would be hard to pass around the diamond centers without drawing a great deal of attention . . . until it was cut into smaller stones, that is. Then, like all the blood diamonds that had been smuggled out of Sierra Leone before it, they would be anonymous and untraceable, as elusive as Osama bin Laden and impossible to identify.

Stones stolen from Sierra Leone at the tip of a machete and the barrel of an AK-47 could literally be anywhere, from safehouses in Monrovia to safe deposit boxes in Belgium to the display cases of jewelry stores in the neighborhood mall. Until international export controls such as those suggested by the Clean Diamond Act and the Kimberley Process are implemented and enforced to screen legitimate diamonds from those tainted by warfare and brutality— and until peace comes and takes hold in impoverished, desperate countries where diamonds are found—there will be no way to tell whether or not a cherished diamond ring was once washed in the blood of innocent Africans.

If nothing else, the story of Sierra Leone's diamond war has proven unequivocally that the world ignores Africa and her problems at its peril. Just like global commerce and the widening reach of terrorism, events far from home often have very tangible impacts. Sierra Leone has shown the world that there is no longer any such thing as an "isolated, regional conflict."

Perhaps there never was.

CODA

Koidu, Sierra Leone

JULY 2011

I

"YOU WANT TO SEE STONES? Here, I will show them to you."

He was a heavy man, sweating and squinting in the sun. He reached into his pocket and pulled out a small paper parcel, carefully shaking into his palm three tiny diamonds that, considering the wide, clear-cut moonscape of the mine on whose banks we stood, looked rather paltry. Bare-chested men with shovels and shake-shakes were visible for hundreds of yards in every direction, splashing in muddy water and moving piles of dirt, dwarfed below a veritable mountain of mine tailings nearly 100 feet high. This was the Number 11 mine on the outskirts of Koidu, and it was considered tapped out as far back as the 1960s by the state-run National Diamond Mining Company, which chopped down the trees, dredged the soil, and left the pile of tailings to be reclaimed long ago by a carpet of grass and saplings. Although this dump pile was officially abandoned, the government donated it to the men who worked it, almost all of them former RUF soldiers and feared killers. The object was to keep them off the streets of Koidu and prevent them from terrorizing the citizens.

"All these guys are fighting for their survival," said Mohammed Komba, the Kono District youth coordinator who'd smoothed the way for my visit and knew that this was the only job available for most of them. "It keeps them away from crime and armed robbery."

Just barely, it seemed. As veterans of the civil war, most of the men toiling in the mine were in their thirties and early forties, and many bore the scars of their time fighting in the bush. They weren't pleased at the sight of visiting white journalists, and my colleague Mike Seamans and I braved a few angry flare-ups resulting from our aimed cameras. Like people elsewhere in Sierra Leone, they were sensitive to the fact that somewhere along the line, we were paid to be there and that made our lot in life a far sight better than theirs. For these men, who once commanded field units and enjoyed the comparatively lavish lifestyles blood diamonds bestowed on them, survival now depended on finding shards of diamonds overlooked fifty years ago. Knowing that they can turn—and have turned in the recent past—to strong-arm tactics when diamonds weren't being found put us on edge. In fact, the pit boss who proudly displayed his measly diamond chips quickly stuffed them back in his pocket and retreated to a nearby shack when I tried to photograph them. He'd assumed I was a buyer and wasn't happy to learn I was a reporter. Komba nervously watched our backs for signs that the men's indignation might turn to outright anger, and when things became tense, he negotiated a series of hasty payoffs to placate the former fighters.

These men were something of a concern in Koidu. Sierra Leone's civil war had been over for nearly ten years when I could finally return and visit the Kono District, its wealthiest diamond area, which had been impossible to travel to in 2001. Kono was also home to the country's largest concentration of former combatants, the majority of them unemployed and restless, and while most bands of RUF soldiers had long ago broken up and blended back into daily life, these men—all from the same unit and still loyal to their local commander—had not.

It was risky to visit the mine. Despite Koidu's reputation as Sierra Leone's crown jewel for diamond extraction, poverty there was at a dangerous, desperate level. Although the country has agreed to international standards for controlling diamond mining to avoid smuggling and theft, in some areas of the Kono region mining still occurred off the books and even government monitors dared not go there.[1] Some wise soul in Freetown saw the utility in simply giving this gang an old mine to plumb for leftovers—technically in exchange for guarding the tailings dump from unauthorized freelance diggers, but as everyone acknowledged, more to keep them occupied. Everyone knew it was only a temporary fix. This mine, like most other surface mines in the area, was all but depleted of treasure. The men would eventually dig through the whole mountain of tailings and wonder what's next. But for now, the scheme seemed to work.

"You can work here for years and get nothing," Komba said, summing up artisanal diamond-prospecting in a nutshell. "Then you can go tomorrow and find something. If they didn't find them, they wouldn't be here."

Just as in the past, the men toiling in these mines can sometimes hear distant echoes of explosions rippling through the jungle from the direction of the city. This time, however, the explosions are from commerce, not warfare. With surface mines largely tapped out by the RUF a decade ago, almost all of the wealth in Koidu is held by a pair of international companies that own kimberlite complexes and guard their holdings behind razor wire and with heavily armed private security forces: South Africa–based Koidu Holdings runs the largest operation, Koidu Kimberlite Project, and a conglomerate of international investors runs a smaller site called the Thunderball Mine. Rumor has it that the best restaurant in the provinces is inside the Koidu Holdings compound, as is a state-of-the-art medical clinic and a well-stocked company store. We don't know for sure, however; like almost everyone else in Koidu, we weren't allowed inside. Outside the compound, poverty, unemployment, disease, and crime were the order of the day.

Companies like Koidu Holdings look for diamonds differently than the ragged-looking men at the Number 11 mine. They blast with dynamite down into the earth, following the paths of two kimberlite pipes, and use bulldozers and earthmovers to extract rocks and pulverize kimberlitic boulders. No one uses a shake-shake at Koidu Holdings, whose compound is near the outskirts of town and is visible from the downtown market. Dynamite shakes the rafters for miles in all directions.

The Number 11 mine isn't completely without mining machinery; there's a working Caterpillar backhoe parked in the middle of the dirt field, but it's not being used. The cost to rent it and fuel it is $1,500 per day, we're told, and no one in sight even remotely has so much money. So they use shovels and dig in its shadow.

We left once everyone was mollified with the equivalent of about $30. If the former RUF crowd that had gravitated around us divided it up evenly—which I doubted given that it all went into the pocket of the pit boss with the diamonds—they would each end up with about 50 cents. Everyone seemed to think that was a reasonable fee for the pictures we took, and we were gone before anyone had the chance to change his mind.

Anyone who doubts that the gap between diamonds' marketing mythos as symbols of love and the realities of their origins was as wide as ever in 2011—even without warfare to exacerbate the difference—need only spend a few days in Koidu, a run-down collection of cinderblock buildings, mosques, and market kiosks still teetering in the wake of war, held together with bush sticks and clotheslines. Throughout the RUF war, Koidu got the worst of it and has yet to recover. Overrun and occupied by rebels practically throughout the 1990s, the town remained too dangerous to visit the last time I was here in 2001, even as peace was being negotiated. Rebels plundered the diamond mines and even dismantled houses to dig through the foundations in search of stones. More than anywhere in Sierra Leone, Koidu has proved worth kicking over the dirt at one's feet; diamonds can be found everywhere, which might explain why the roads have never been paved.

The point was made early in my visit. In getting from my guesthouse on the edge of town to a Lebanese money changer in the center, I'd tried to outrun a gathering rainstorm but got caught in the downpour on the back of a hired motorcycle only about halfway there. Drenched, I waited out the deluge under a blue tarp strung over an alley with a knot of locals trying to keep their cigarettes dry. Two boys occupied themselves with a broom, pushing accumulated water out of the tarp overhead every few minutes, while the rest of us watched the hand-dug sewer paralleling the road fill with a muddy torrent of runoff. I was amazed at the volume of water that, like a flash flood in a desert arroyo, filled and soon overflowed the knee-deep trench. The sight captivated the others for a different reason.

"You see," said a man at my elbow, "the rain will loosen the precious stones. Many people will follow the stream and look for diamonds."

Considering the flotilla of garbage being borne on the tide, it seemed an unlikely source of the kind of gemstones one would see at Tiffany's, but the man assured me it was true.

"You know the creek?" he said, referring to a stagnant cesspool a bit farther up the road. I referred to it as the Urinal based on how I'd seen the locals use it every time I drove past. He claimed it was the source of more than 700 carats of diamonds gifted to England when Sierra Leone gained its independence fifty years before.

At the moment, that was especially hard to believe. Just as during my last trip, I was staggered by the degree of poverty and desperation possible in a place that produced millions of dollars' worth of precious gems from its very ground. But at least last time, there was an excuse—ten years of otherworldly warfare and inhumane butchery provided an easy means of explaining the misery.

Not anymore. The RUF was long gone, at least from the surface. Its leaders were either dead or convicted of war crimes by the UN-backed Special Court for Sierra Leone. Charles Taylor, captured in 2006 after an attempt to escape from his home in exile in Nigeria, was awaiting a verdict at The Hague. Rank-and-file soldiers had drifted back into society. From what I could tell, the men at the Number 11 mine were the exception in that they were still loosely affiliated with one another, but whether that was for some vague future revolutionary purpose or just due to enduring kinship was impossible to say.

Yet there was clearly a tense frustration in the air around Koidu, a vague feeling of trouble brewing that took some time to identify as a deep-seated sense of injustice. In a place like Sierra Leone it's sometimes too easy to take such a thing for granted. But gradually it sank in for me that I wasn't alone in struggling to understand why—with regular TNT explosions rumbling the ground, announcing that Koidu Holdings was unearthing more of the country's wealth within sight of where I stood shivering in the alley—there was still no electricity, no jobs, and no adequate health care for most people in a place teeming with riches.

These disparities, and these conditions, are identical to what led to the RUF war in the first place.

I LIT OUT FOR KOIDU soon after arriving in Freetown, my first trip to West Africa since I left in 2001. After ten years, I thought, this was the perfect time to return and answer a question that had pestered me since I left, one that I pondered earlier in these pages. What would a peaceful Sierra Leone do with itself? Could it rise to the potential—in its people, in its resources, in its natural beauty—that so impressed me a decade before? Could it take control of its future, having learned the harrowing lessons of its past?

From afar, it was tempting to get the impression that all was fine. No instances of large-scale violence had occurred since the 2002 election that marked the end of the war. Taylor is the last of the main actors to be dealt with, and though a verdict has yet to be announced in his long-running war crimes trial, few are worried that he'll be given any second chances to prove himself as a statesman. The Sierra Leone Army had been so modernized and professionalized that the country sent soldiers on peacekeeping missions to Darfur, Sudan, and Somalia, setting milestones in the country's military history. While politics sometimes resulted in headlines about riots and isolated unrest, the government appeared stable and business was booming. Diamond mining and other mineral extraction began again soon after the war, and—until the global financial crisis hit in 2008, dealing a blow to luxuries markets everywhere—diamond exports had been growing steadily, from $42 million in 2002 to $142 million in 2007. (They are again on the rebound as the recession fades, with $109 million exported in 2010, a 28 percent leap from the previous year—the latest figures available at this writing.) Competing with diamonds as a source of revenue are gold, iron ore, bauxite, and rutile, all of which have lured their own unique extractive industries. Sierra Leone's total exports have climbed from $65 million in 2000 to $341.2 million in 2010, an impressive 48 percent increase over 2009. Oil was recently discovered offshore, adding to the country's already impressive portfolio of riches.[2]

Other indicators seemed equally heartening. In 2010, Sierra Leone moved up twelve positions on the UN Human Development Index.[3] Having been in last place for so long, the country had nowhere to go but up. Roads were rebuilt (or were in the process of being rebuilt) between major cities, including many in the provincial hinterlands, with funding from European Union nations and the World Bank.

Perhaps most critically, the issue that brought Sierra Leone to the attention of the world in the first place—the illicit sale of conflict diamonds by rebels into mainstream trading channels—appears by many measures to have ended. By definition, no conflict diamonds can be produced where there is no conflict. The Kimberley Process, the 2003 international agreement that bans blood diamonds from circulation, is assumed by most of the world to be appropriately policing the trade.

But I knew better than to accept impressions imparted by headlines and press releases, especially regarding the Kimberley Process, which I had been skeptical of from the beginning. I wanted to see for myself just how far Sierra Leone has come and where it continues to fall short. In a nation of contradictions, it shouldn't have surprised me to find successes and failures in equal measure. The difference is that the successes pale in comparison to the failures—and as Sierra Leone itself has demonstrated so tragically, the price of failure can literally be a matter of life and death.

THERE WERE THUNDERSTORMS when Mike and I landed at Lungi International Airport at 3:30 A.M. in July 2011, on the cusp of the rainy season. My instinct that reality would differ from the cheerful impression given by bureaucratic reports and export statistics was reinforced with every step I took into the country, beginning with the airport. Lungi didn't appear to have had so much as a fresh coat of paint since I was last there. Security officers barely glanced at my passport before stamping it and clearing the way to the baggage claim, which was lorded over by aggressive gangs of con artists stampeding to fill seats on boats, ferries, hovercraft, and taxicabs bound for the mainland.

The airport's location across the wide Sierra Leone River from downtown Freetown could be called a joke if the river weren't so arduous to cross, a task made all the more trying thanks to most airlines' perplexing habit of scheduling arrivals and departures in the middle of the night. One's choices for reaching Freetown include expensive taxis that take up to three hours to circle north through Port Loko or a fleet of rickety vessels that sink with alarming regularity. I had been hoping for the speed and relative convenience of a commercial helicopter, but they had been grounded after one too many crashes into the bay.

Seas were rough in the wake of the storm, and the water taxis' floating wharf rolled in the surf like a funhouse ride. But the porters carried our luggage on their heads with no fear of slipping and sending the bags into the drink, their work lit crazily by the boat's bobbing floodlight, which cut a golden prism through the downpour and helped, at least somewhat, to light the way for us less sure-footed passengers.

Across the river, Freetown loomed in the mist like the remnants of a dream that refuses to be forgotten. Dim lights sketched the rough outline of the coast and the mountains beyond the city. It took me a moment to figure out what was so familiar and yet so wrong about the city's silhouette. The lights were clustered in one dense spot in the downtown area, giving the impression that Freetown was much smaller than I knew it to be. No lights in the outlying neighborhoods meant no power there: after a decade of reconstruction and international investment in Sierra Leone's mineral industry, the government still couldn't provide electricity outside the downtown district. In fact, only 8.5 percent of its households countrywide have electricity.[4]

Wandering Aberdeen in the daylight, I marveled that it was as choked as ever with garbage and misery. It smelled the same, a combination of fish and burning refuse. It was shockingly clear that whatever benefits Sierra Leone was deriving from its peacetime industries were not filtering down to where they were needed most. There were businessmen and schoolchildren walking the streets, as I had envisioned a decade before, but just as many drifters and beggars clogged the beaches and the roadsides, victims of double digits in both inflation and unemployment. I even recognized some of them; one of the first people I saw was Osman, the one-time wedding singer and former RUF prisoner who had been forced to mule-train weapons between RUF positions and the Liberian border during the war. He'd gone mad before I met him the first time, and he clearly hadn't improved. He was half-naked, raving at ghosts and gesturing at unseen demons. I didn't say hello.

Of course, some things had changed. UNAMSIL was long gone and the Mammy Yoko Hotel was closed for renovations. Paddy's, the sweaty pit of a tavern that inspired the beach bar scenes in Leonardo DiCaprio's 2006 movie *Blood Diamond* (scenes that wholly fail to capture the reeking milieu of base human motivations on display at the real thing), had been run out of business. The MSF Camp for Amputees and War Wounded, once home to more than four hundred war victims and their families, had been closed, with some of its residents having been relocated to another facility on the other side of town, but most having simply drifted off to make their way elsewhere in the world. One difference— surely meant as an improvement but that instead had an Orwellian effect—was a proliferation of advertising buzzwords for a mobile phone company that were plastered on everything: "growth," "prosperity," "health," "progress." That these were antonyms for everything in sight and served only to amplify the unavoidable wretchedness was clearly lost on the company.

In other words, Sierra Leone was just as forlorn as I'd left it, complete with a gang of shady Russian diamond dealers talking in whispers at the Solar Hotel's breakfast table, and a cast of assorted ne'er-do-wells peering from the banana trees waiting for their opportunity to be my "friend." I recalled quite clearly from my earlier visit that friendship between locals and foreigners doesn't always mean what you think and, if you're not careful, you could find yourself entwined in dealings you want no part of. At a minimum, you'll end up with an entourage of beggarly hangers-on who all expect to be fed, supplied with beers, and provided with myriad and often unusual gifts. Some are more persistent than others. A young barber named Mohammed, who went by the nickname Fifty Cent, cornered Mike and me just outside the Solar's entrance and, before I could fend him off, had asked me to buy him a Honda generator. When I politely told him I couldn't afford it, he said he would settle for an electric razor.

I'd been in Sierra Leone for less than twelve hours and was already feeling antsy to leave Freetown. I wanted to get to Koidu, the epicenter of diamond production both then and now. But without the UN to act as my personal helicopter chauffeur, I had to find a vehicle. That wasn't proving easy; strangers hanging out at the hotel demanded rip-off prices to hire an SUV. I decided to see if I could find an old source of help, a person who I knew could pull strings and help smooth the way. But I didn't know if he was alive, much less whether he was still in the area. I turned to Fifty Cent and cut off his pleading with a raised hand.

"Do you know a man named Jango?" I asked. "Take me to him."

JANGO, AS IT TURNED OUT, was just as much the leader of Aberdeen's area boys as before, commanding the same degree of respect and deference as I remembered. We fell quickly back into stride, another instance when it seemed I'd entered a time warp. Catching up with me over beers, he looked as if he'd not aged a day. Although we hadn't corresponded even once since we'd parted ways at the Diamond Airlines helipad a decade before, it was as if I'd only been gone for a few weeks. Even his means of employment was the same, though he brokered deals for diamonds less often than in the past. Cheap stones from conflict zones were still to be had, but required traveling closer to Côte d'Ivoire, where Forces Nouvelles rebels controlled the mines in the north and used proceeds to rearm for a conflict dating back to 2002. Jango had been dispatched to Ghana, one of the many way stations for Ivoirian diamonds on their way into legitimate channels, in attempts to broker deals for his old boss Jacob Singer, who still made frequent trips to Sierra Leone to shop for cheap goods that continue to circulate on the black market.

Technically, that shouldn't be the case. When it was adopted in 2003, the Kimberley Process promised to end the trade in conflict diamonds, in large part by demanding that its participants rigorously monitor where the diamonds they export come from. When diamond parcels are issued their official KP certificates upon export, their guarantee depends on the assumption that local customs officials and diamond inspectors have done their jobs and accounted for the source of each gem being sent to market.

In reality, the process doesn't work out nearly as well as hoped. "Although three of the five countries neighboring Côte d'Ivoire, namely Ghana, Guinea and Liberia, are Kimberley Process participants, those States continue to struggle with the implementation of the Scheme, and loopholes in their systems of internal controls continue to allow the circulation of Ivorian rough diamonds," according to an April 2011 report by the UN Security Council, which has banned the import of Ivorian diamonds since 2005 due to their use in the conflict. "Information obtained by the Group indicates that local diamond dealers, in addition to a number of foreign nationals from neighbouring States, continue to purchase diamonds in Séguéla [Côte d'Ivoire], which are then transported to Bamako [Mali], Conakry, Dakar and Monrovia, from where they are exported to other international markets."[5]

Due to weak internal controls in the surrounding transit countries, Ivorian conflict diamonds can easily be mixed with those that have been mined legitimately and then exported under the cover of a KP certificate. After that point, they're never questioned again as to their true origin. The nongovernmental organization Partnership Africa Canada (PAC) reported in 2009 that half of the diamonds exported by the Democratic Republic of Congo couldn't be traced; they were completely unaccounted for until they arrived in the capital for valuation prior to export. "For all intents and purposes, the DRC might as well label these diamonds 'origin unknown,'" according to the PAC report, "Diamonds and Human Security." The Kimberley Process has inarguably created an easier way of smuggling conflict diamonds than in the past, when claims of a diamond's origin relied on an unofficial "don't ask, don't tell" policy between people buying and selling. Now, they're slipped into the mainstream with the Kimberley Process's official seal of approval.

What's worse, the Kimberley Process has almost no mechanism for dealing with this problem. Site visits to review how participants are following the agreement's dictates and principles are infrequent, and follow-up visits to ensure those falling short are tightening the screws can take years. Rogue participants can flaunt the system for years with no real worry that they'll be sanctioned. There seems little will among Kimberley Process leadership to use its only punishment tools, suspension or expulsion from the club. And since the scheme's chair changes year to year, it's easy to dither long enough to pass off a problem state to the next leader.

"A lot of governments have been happy to use the Kimberley Process as a fig leaf of respectability, so they can say, 'OK, look we're doing something,'" Elly Harrowell of the NGO Global Witness, one of KP's primary architects, told me when I began looking into this problem in 2009. "A lot of people, especially in the public, seem to think it's case closed."[6]

What had spurred my questions was the case of Zimbabwe, a stark illustration of how toothless the Kimberley Process has proved to be since it was adopted with much fanfare as the cure for blood diamonds. A KP participant, Zimbabwe had for years been ruthlessly using its state security units to force civilians to dig for diamonds at the Marange field near the border with Mozambique, a diamond area discovered in 2006. Armed forces of President Robert Mugabe's Zimbabwe African National Union–Patriotic Front party (ZANU-PF) violently took over the mines from local diggers after agreeing to a power-sharing arrangement with the opposition party Movement for Democratic Change. The diamond fields served as a sort of payment to Mugabe's soldiers to ensure their loyalty; different brigades rotated to the area in order to spread the wealth. Unauthorized diggers were beaten and killed, with the death toll in the hundreds. Civilians, including children, mined the diamonds at gunpoint. Women reported being sexually assaulted. Many of the diamonds were smuggled out to Mozambique and then onward into the $72 billion diamond jewelry market.[7]

To most people who monitor the trade in conflict diamonds, this seemed an open-and-shut case of a KP participant blatantly violating its commitment to the program. Human Rights Watch and other NGOs decried the abuse and called on the Kimberley Process to level sanctions on Zimbabwean diamonds.

But the Kimberley Process, unbelievably, questioned whether the country's actions violated the agreement. KP representatives argued that the diamonds from Zimbabwe weren't conflict diamonds, in that rebels weren't using them to wage war against the government. That the government was effectively waging war against its own citizens, and selling the bounty of that war into the multibillion-dollar international diamond market as perfectly clean stones approved by the Kimberley Process, seemed not to matter. The Kimberley Process operates by consensus, and the consensus was to cop out on a technicality—its official definition of conflict diamonds doesn't include clear examples of gross human rights violations perpetrated on a country's citizens by its own government. The Kimberley Process gave Zimbabwe a grace period to end the abuses rather than punishing it economically.

Not everyone agreed with this approach, including De Beers, still the most powerful name in diamonds. Bruised by allegations that it had been complicit in conflict-diamond trafficking during the 1990s, particularly by association with its fictional doppelganger in the DiCaprio movie, the company was as determined as ever to support strong measures to wipe out the illicit commerce, if only for the sake of public perception.

"Providing confidence about where these special symbols that mark moments in our lives come from is integral to their enduring value," wrote De Beers chairman Nicky Oppenheimer in a Bloomberg op-ed in 2009, adding that he would have preferred the Kimberley Process take more "decisive action" against Zimbabwe.[8]

Bowing to international pressure, the KP temporarily banned diamonds from Marange, but allowed the government to continue mining and stockpiling them until a KP monitoring team could determine whether it had ended abuses and complied with other demands. The ban was lifted in 2010 after Mugabe's government agreed to partner with private investors who promised mining would be done with respect for human rights, paving the way for Zimbabwe to sell a cache of more than a million carats. But the KP seems to have been the only organization to believe this promise. The New York–based RapNet, one of the world's largest private diamond trading networks, run by Martin Rapaport, an outspoken Orthodox Jew who railed against the KP's gutless response to the situation, called for a boycott against Marange diamonds even if they have Kimberley Process certificates. He threatened to expel from his trade network anyone caught dealing in them.

Despite this public, intra-industry vote of no confidence in the Kimberley Process, its chair unilaterally lifted all remaining restrictions on Zimbabwean diamonds in June 2011. Two months later, Human Rights Watch issued another report of rampant violence and abuses against unlicensed miners in Marange, this time at the hands of both the government's and its private partners' armed security forces.

"Zimbabwe police and private security guards employed by mining companies in the Marange diamond fields are shooting, beating and unleashing attack dogs on poor, local unlicensed miners," the report reads. "Some members of the international diamond monitoring body, known as the Kimberley Process, have tried to argue that conditions in the areas controlled by joint ventures are not abusive, and that those diamonds should be certified and allowed onto international markets. But Human Rights Watch has found, on the contrary, evidence of serious abuse by private security guards patrolling the joint venture territory."[9]

The report also quoted Tiseke Kasambala, Human Rights Watch's senior Africa researcher, as saying, "The ongoing abuses at Marange underscore the need for the Kimberley Process to address human rights instead of capitulating to abusive governments and irresponsible companies. . . . The Kimberley Process appears to have lost touch with its mission to ensure that blood diamonds don't make their way to consumers."[10]

Two of the KP's main architects even abandoned the program. Ian Smillie, one of the founders of Partnership Africa Canada, resigned in 2009 over what he called the scheme's "pretence that failure is success." In his 2010 book, *Blood on the Stone: Greed, Corruption, and War in the Global Diamond Trade,* Smillie expanded on the concerns that he shares with many people:

> Can this trade in stolen and blood diamonds be stopped? The Kimberley Process Certification Scheme has helped to put a hold on the worst of it, but in the few cases where it has been tested—Côte d'Ivoire, Venezuela, Zimbabwe—it has stumbled. If a diamond-fuelled conflagration were to erupt in the Eastern DRC or anywhere else, there is little evidence that the Kimberley Process would be able to cope. It looks too much like the nearsighted Mr. Magoo, walking around in a fog, barely missing collisions with swinging girders and falling anvils through pure blind luck.
>
> The Kimberley Process is failing, and it will fail outright if it does not come to grips with its dysfunctional decision-making and its unwillingness to deal quickly and decisively with non-compliance. African governments need to tighten their controls, and trading countries need to make sure there are no loopholes in theirs. The industry itself needs to be much more forthright in demanding protection and enforcement from the governments that have passed Kimberley Process laws aimed at doing precisely that. The campaigning NGOs are unlikely to go away, and sooner or later, consumers will get the message. If things don't improve, the reputation of diamonds will fall, along with their attractiveness for engagement rings and other expressions of love.[11]

And in December 2011, Global Witness—which was the first organization to bring the issue of conflict diamonds to light in 1998—followed Smillie's lead, calling the Kimberley Process a lie and a failure in how it has reacted to Zimbabwe. The group quit the KP over fears that the Mugabe government would use its diamond revenue to fund a crackdown on political opponents in the months and weeks leading to 2012's elections: "We don't want to lend our credibility to, or be associated with, a scheme that could very well end up having blood on its hands if all this cash that KP has endorsed is used to fuel violence," said Annie Dunneback, the organization's senior campaigner. "We don't want to be a part of that."[12]

Rather than the watchdog the KP insists that it is, it's actually proven to be a handy cover for dictators, insurgent groups, and smugglers moving goods from their origins as blood diamonds to the corner jewelry store, where its certificates assure even concerned consumers that they are buying legitimate diamonds for their loved ones.

It's the same in Sierra Leone, Jango told me.

"I will show you," he said. "When do we want to go to Koidu?"

I WANTED TO LEAVE immediately, but Jango turned out to be no better at finding cheap private transportation than I had. Inflation had grown from 12 percent to more than 16 percent between 2009 and 2010, and the leone was only half as valuable against the dollar as it had been during my previous visit.[13] The weaker currency combined with higher prices for everything from gas to food to lodging makes Sierra Leone more expensive than in the past.

So, opting for a local approach to travel, very early one morning we made our way to a motor park to be shoehorned into a decrepit bus for the seven-hour drive to Koidu. Designed for twenty-five passengers, the bus wouldn't budge until at least fifty were packed aboard, with children counting as half. It's what made it cheap, at the equivalent of about seven dollars. Luggage was wedged under the seats and piled in the aisles, along with spare parts for the bus, livestock, and sacks of grain. As we waited in a humid downpour to see if the springs would crack or the rivets pop with each new suitcase jammed into place, the bus's leaden, sweaty air felt like a disease incubator. I quickly learned that the only way to endure the ride was to pick one position you hoped wouldn't constrict your circulation too badly for the next quarter of a day and meditate yourself into some happy place in a far-off land. You could move only once in that period, during the halfway stop for lunch, water, and fresh air. It took at least ten minutes for the passengers to untwist themselves from their neighbors and disembark.

Apart from the discomfort, the trip was uneventful until the second half of the journey, when the only road to Koidu degraded and became full of potholes. With every lurch, passengers cracked heads. Combined with the limb-numbing fetal position I was forced to sit in and the claustrophobia of being sealed in by windows closed due to the rain, the roller-coaster jerking began to make me stir-crazy. The feeling was shared by others, and I soon became aware, over the din of eight children sharing the seat behind me, of people arguing somewhere toward the front of the bus. I caught only snatches of the conversation, but it was clear that two men were shouting in frustration about the condition of the road. I clearly heard someone yell, "You have all the diamonds coming from Kono, but look at the schools, look at the hospital, look at this road! There is no power, there is no transportation. Where is the money going?"

Getting off the bus in Koidu was like arriving in a frontier town in an Old West movie, where the strangers stand on the train platform and eye the dusty streets and wonder what sort of trouble lies ahead. The longtime RUF stronghold was still filled with former RUF fighters, including many desperate for work. In the course of our stay, Jango recognized dozens of rebel veterans, including some he took pains to avoid encountering. I found myself doing mental math on everyone I interacted with: Men apparently within five years of my age I presumed to have been officer-grade RUF; odds were good that those in their late teens and early twenties had been child soldiers. It was strange to be deep in the Sierra Leone provinces again and have nothing to fear from kids up to age 17— they were too young to have fought in the war.

Koidu is loosely arranged like a wagon wheel, with the hub being a massive cotton tree known in the dark days as the "chopping tree" because its gnarly knee-high roots proved perfect for performing amputations. The city had been thoroughly pillaged as if by wild animals, but only partly put back together. It was easy to get the impression that the war had ended just the week before.

Our first task once we got settled was to find a Lebanese diamond merchant to help us get the lay of the land. We cold-called on a few, but none were willing to speak with journalists; we would learn later that the Lebanese did not get along as well with the Sierra Leoneans in Koidu as they had in Kenema ten years before. With unemployment and poverty so high, the Lebanese were regarded as foreign vultures who were exploiting Koidu's diamond wealth, stealing it from those to whom it rightly belonged. The Lebanese, of course, had been a mainstay of Sierra Leonean diamond trading for decades; nevertheless a strong scent of distrust hung in the air that we would come to understand more fully in the coming days but that at the moment lent an uneasy vibe to our door-to-door wandering. Finally, one merchant told us to find Kassim Basma, their elder statesman and chair of the local Lebanese community.

We found his office hidden in a maze of dirty alleyways jammed with engine parts from a neighboring auto repair shop, and random, half-empty rooms furnished only with cracked and forgotten furniture. In the anteroom where we waited for a Russian flunky to announce our presence, one of a set of rusted handcuffs was locked to the iron grate covering the window. The other cuff dangled below, leading one to morbid speculation about what might have been done here during the war, before this became an elderly man's office. With Basma, I was hoping to repeat my success in talking to Fawaz S. Fawaz in Kenema during my last visit to the country. Though he'd been cagey about showing off any diamonds, Fawaz had helped us get our bearings in a strange place.

"Ah, but Fawaz is dead," Basma said when I dropped the only name I knew in the West African Lebanese diamond community. "If it's the same man I'm thinking about, he died of a heart attack not too long ago. S. Fawaz, yes? From Kenema? Too bad. He was a young man."

I didn't remember him as particularly young, but I did vividly recall Fawaz's towering pile of Marlboro butts and how quickly he added to them; I figured we must have been talking about the same person. If so, his demise didn't surprise me, but I didn't say so. Basma was also chain-smoking. The largest thing on his desk was a joke lighter the size of a pocket dictionary.

Basma was friendly, but wary of our questions. Like his late colleague, he insisted that business was slow and that there were no diamonds to display. As Mike and I continued to chat with him, doing our best to be disarming, he seemed to warm up. Like others who had described Kono's mines to us, he complained that many of the old surface mines were washed up and competition was fierce among the Lebanese to trade with those who were still producing stones. The big exploration companies working the Koidu Kimberlite Project and the Thunderball Mine didn't bother with men like Basma; they took care of their own exports and didn't need him. He dealt more with small-scale diggers like those we would later see at the Number 11 mine, men hired by miners licensed by the government to explore a certain area for diamonds. When the transactions were made, he provided the seller with a receipt from a big notebook he kept, the cornerstone of what the Kimberley Process called "internal controls" on diamonds' origins. The Government Gold and Diamond Office issues Basma the Kimberley Process certificates when he travels to Freetown to export the goods and pay his taxes; should a monitor show up to question him about the details of his parcels, as he said happened from time to time, he referred them to the notebook.

"The Kimberley Process works properly," he said. "It decreased smuggling and increased exports."

After a quick glance at his Russian friend, who sat silently in a chair next to the desk, he added, "It's not bad, actually, as long as you're a law-abiding citizen."

I thought this an odd statement and took the chance to press him. "Isn't it true, though, that there are still people selling diamonds who can't prove where they've come from? Or who aren't licensed to mine? Or who may have smuggled diamonds from, say, Côte d'Ivoire?"

He didn't balk as I'd expected.

"Yes, yes, it's true," he said. "But I have not seen any Ivoirian diamonds lately. Stones like that come in from Guinea."

"What do you when you're offered stones like those?"

Basma smiled and held up his palms in a half-shrug as if to say, Let's not fool each other here.

"Look, if you have illicit people coming here, you can't refuse, because then they will smuggle it," he said. "But if *you* buy it, as an official exporter, you can legalize it. *Some*body will buy it if not me."

This was an unexpected admission, so I asked him to explain. Basma argued that buying stones of unknown origin and mixing them with legitimate diamonds for export was a means of cleaning up the black market, a unique argument that I'd never heard anyone try before. He seemed trying to convince me that the purpose of the Kimberley Process was to put all diamonds under an umbrella of legitimacy no matter where they came from. But before we could continue, his friend, who looked alarmed at the turn our conversation had taken, abruptly left the room. Basma sat back as if that signaled the end of our conversation. Thanking him for his time, we showed ourselves out.

The moment we stepped onto the street, a cop who was marching our way stopped us. It was nothing serious, a low-grade hassling that involved us explaining our presence in town, but the officer was humorless and stern and the angry interrogation had me wondering if we had crossed some invisible local line. I was pretty sure it wasn't a random stop, considering that white-skinned people were fairly common in Koidu and we hadn't turned many other heads. Maybe we were being paranoid, but we assumed from that point on that certain people were keeping their eyes on us.

II

Before I left for Sierra Leone, I knew that I would find myself in situations that, if less dire than before, would still be strange and trying. The story had changed in ten years, and it was no longer about the RUF's greed-fueled program of murder for control of diamonds; it was now about the government's almost total inaction, in the RUF's absence, in closing the yawning gulf between the value of Sierra Leone's natural resources and the crushing poverty that continues to cripple the country. Moreover, it's about the danger that situation poses. The country has been here before, and the outcome was cataclysmic. It is no mystery what led to one of the worst wars of the past fifty years. The government's own Truth and Reconciliation Commission investigated the causes and came to an unambiguous conclusion: "The Commission finds that the central cause of the war was endemic greed, corruption and nepotism that deprived the nation of its dignity and reduced most people to a state of poverty."[14]

While I expected to confront that poverty up close in an attempt to understand why the lesson hadn't been learned, I did not expect to find myself clad in OR scrubs observing an operation in a hospital that has no power, no running water, and no modern equipment—an experience I had at the suggestion of a local doctor so that I could see just how great the divide was between Koidu's poverty and the wealth being stripped out of its land just outside the city limits.

Dr. Bailor Barrie is a 2004 graduate of Sierra Leone's only medical school and the founder, along with American Dr. Dan Kelly, of Wellbody, an organization that runs a free clinic for treating wartime amputees and their families. I met Barrie not at the clinic, but at Koidu's main hospital, where we'd come for personal reasons rather than professional ones: It seemed that the bus ride from Freetown had felled one of our small band. Jango had been fine when he got on the bus, but seven hours later, his eyeballs were crusted over like Scotch eggs and he was shivering from chills and throwing up bright green bile the consistency of paint. He had malaria.

The day before our arrival in Koidu, the *New York Times* ran a promising article speculating that infant mortality rates would soon improve in Sierra Leone, thanks to a new, free health care program for pregnant women and children that had begun in 2010 and was being temporarily bankrolled by foreign donors. There is no such thing as socialized medicine or education in Sierra Leone. Aside from a handful of free clinics run by charities or foreign donors like Wellbody, even so much as scheduling an appointment with a doctor costs money, as Jango discovered when he was told he'd have to pay in advance just to get in line. And since health care is one of the many things Sierra Leoneans cannot afford, most women never see a doctor throughout their pregnancies and give birth at home. The *Times* piece was a cheerful story that expressed hope for a brighter, healthier future for newborns and mothers with high-risk pregnancies.

Our experience, however, was less cheerful than the article had led us to expect. For one thing, although the new program waived *official* fees charged by the hospital, it did nothing to address a long list of unofficial payments for everything from clean sheets to blood transfusions. As Alicia Lay, one of several American medical students who worked at the hospital as part of their study of tropical medicine, explained, the money goes not to the hospital, but to whoever collects the "fee." It's one of the most common forms of corruption and graft encountered in Sierra Leone—the random shakedown. It happens everywhere from the airport to the Freetown ATM, where the armed security guard expects a few bills for watching your back while you conduct your transaction. And heavily funded new medical program or no, it happens in the hospitals as well. In fact, we passed a sign taped to the wall outside one of the wards reading: "Notice! All deliveries are free. All Caesarean sections are free. Available drugs at the maternity are free. Therefore, patients are advice [*sic*] not to buy drugs from the nurses. By Management."

When Lay and her colleagues introduced us to Barrie, I immediately recognized his voice. He had been one of the passengers on the bus arguing about the injustice of Koidu's sad state considering the millions earned in diamond export taxes. Eager to pick up the conversation anew, he equated the situation to low-grade everyday graft, except on a much larger scale. The reason people go without medical care is the same reason entire communities are left without electricity—somewhere up the chain, someone is making off with what's owed to those on the ground floor.

"My own personal view is that the government is corrupt," he said. "The money [from diamond revenues meant for communities] goes into their pockets or their bank accounts. Kono is the wealthiest district in the country, but we don't even have a college."

The hospital was a fitting place for this conversation. The one-story government facility of concrete wards was a "hospital" only in that doctors and sick people frequented it. There were no X-ray, MRI, or CAT-scan machines, because those require electricity and the hospital has none. A collection of battery-powered ultrasound devices—which could have been recharged at any of the local kiosks in town that rent plug-in time for cell phones—sat on a shelf unused because no one knew how to operate them. Instruments were sanitized in an industrial pressure cooker heated on a propane burner; and because the plumbing didn't work, the water came from a hand pump in the courtyard via bucket brigade, as did the water for flushing toilets and washing surgeons' hands. It's too risky to give surgery patients general anesthesia, Lay said, because they can't intubate patients who stop breathing. The hospital has no pulse oximeters to ensure the blood is receiving sufficient oxygen.

The excuse for all this deficiency is that the government has no money to pay for improvements and modern equipment, an argument that's hard to buy with round-the-clock diamond production happening fewer than five miles away.

The following day, we accepted an invitation to watch a hysterectomy performed on a young woman who had a large fibrous mass around her uterus. As in the Wild West, a doctor had made the diagnosis by feeling her bloated abdomen and making an informed guess.

"Are you nervous?" I asked the surgeon, Dr. Bardu Abdulai.

"Of course not."

"But isn't this sort of a high-risk surgery?"

"I do them all the time."

With that, we entered the OR. The patient, a 23-year-old woman, lay welded with dread to the operating table as if she was about to be executed by lethal injection. "The Macarena" was playing on a transistor radio. Lay was assisting Abdulai with the operation, along with three or four nurses and assorted helpers playing the roles of anesthesiologist, orderlies, and whatever else ORs generally require. Some of them wore flip-flops, but the doctor at least wore white Crocs sandals, which kept the blood off his feet when it started dripping off the operating table. Mike and I, our faces largely obscured behind surgical masks, were wide-eyed. In our time as journalists, we'd each run the long, ultimately fruitless gauntlet of U.S. hospital bureaucrats, HIPPA regulations, and insurance companies in attempts to observe surgeries for various stories over the years and had never even dented the iron wall of privacy surrounding patients' rights, even when the patients wanted us to be there. Here, we weren't even asked to wash our hands before we began creeping between the doctors for a better shot with our cameras.

The patient was given sedatives and a local anesthetic, and just before the first incision was made, we were asked not to stand between the patient and the window—the doctors needed the sunlight to see what they were doing.

IT WOULD BE ONE THING if Sierra Leone had to make do in this way because the country was truly hopeless, if there was nothing available except direct charity to pay for the nation's most basic needs. But regularly timed explosions serve as a constant reminder that Sierra Leone has more than enough resources to afford a more comfortable and dignified life for its people. Those resources, however, are sealed off from those living in Koidu by physical barriers and armed guards.

The Koidu Holdings project is a massive undertaking to excavate two kimberlite pipes known as K1 and K2. I'd never seen an industrial mine before and was awed by the scale of the operation. I got no closer than the locals, however; I was turned away at the gatehouse because I hadn't made an appointment in advance. Despite several phone calls made during my week's stay in Koidu to the company's media relations department—itself an odd concept in the heart of the West African jungle—no one was available to accommodate a reporter showing up unannounced. Company representatives vetted my professional credentials in the process. They asked me to give details about what I'd written about Koidu Holdings in the past, which included only one short article in *The Economist* about diamonds in general, in which I mentioned the company's scaled-down production (as well as that of many other diamond companies, including De Beers) during the global economic crisis. I went through the same process with representatives of the Thunderball Mine, who asked for references to my past work. After I pointed them to my professional website (which includes links and material related to this book), they initially gave me clearance to visit. But when our small fleet of hired motorcycles arrived outside the barbed-wire fence surrounding the pit, the foreman and an armed security guard turned us away. Someone in the company had called from Freetown and nixed our appointment at the last moment.

While we waited for permission to visit Koidu Holdings, we were hassled again by the police, who followed us as we walked past the police station and peppered us with questions on our way to inquire at the mine. It was disconcerting enough that we decided to hire motorcycles to whisk us past that short section of road on our return. I chalked it up to underpaid civil servants trying to intimidate foreigners into paying a bribe, but Jango, more in tune with local subtleties, wasn't so sure. I had trouble buying the idea that police and PR stooges alike were actively discouraging our inquiries, but I had equal trouble understanding how over the course of a week no one could spare an hour to chat face-to-face. Even when I offered to return to Koidu later in the month, I got nowhere.

In any event, I didn't need to get into the mine to gauge its magnitude. Every time I traveled from our room at Uncle Ben's Guest House on the outskirts of town to the city center, it dominated the view to the south. Giant earthmovers crawled across a steep mesa of waste tailings and dirt. I often mistook the scheduled blasting for thunder. And the mine's plans to expand its operations were on everyone's lips.

The Koidu Kimberlite Project processes fifty tons of kimberlitic rock an hour and produces about 120,000 carats of diamonds a year; by 2015, the K1 mine will reach more than 1,000 feet into the ground and the K2 mine will be 800 feet deep. The South Africa–based company employs nearly eight hundred workers, 90 percent of them Sierra Leoneans.[15] But it hasn't exactly been welcome in Koidu. For one thing, the diamond mines were located at the edge of existing villages on the outskirts of the city—and getting to the diamonds involved getting rid of those who lived in the villages. With the blessing of the government and the local chief, the company "relocated" 284 households, which affected 2,380 people.[16] The plan was to build an entirely new village for these residents beginning in 2005 and to move them during a series of so-called "rolling resettlements." But the company began blasting apart the kimberlite before everyone safely moved, leading to massive protests against the company. On December 13, 2007, police faced off with hundreds of unarmed demonstrators assembled outside the gates leading to the mine to protest the detonations, yet Koidu Holdings proceeded with blasting as scheduled that day. When the protesters went wild at what they considered a provocation, police opened fire in a manner later described by government investigators as "indiscriminate, disproportionate and reckless." Two people were killed and ten were wounded. The same commission reported that had Koidu Holdings "shown a little bit of restraint and sensitivity towards the demonstrators . . . by not proceeding with the blasting," the outcome might have been different.[17]

Tensions have eased in the intervening years, but they're likely to flare anew. Koidu Holdings has proposed a $150 million expansion that will allow it to tunnel below its current mines and find more diamonds. Improvements in the operation will allow it to ramp up processing in order to churn through 180 tons of rock per hour and produce more than half a million carats of diamonds a year.[18]

However, the plans require the company to expand its "blast envelope"—a mining euphemism for widening its borders—and as a result, residents of another 660 Koidu households will be displaced and moved to a new resettlement camp. As before, the company will build them new homes far from where they now live and compensate them for lost crops. Sierra Leonean newspapers often refer to the affected residents as "victims."

Koidu's relationship with its largest employer is complicated. On one hand, a palpable resentment toward the South African firm is not hard to detect: Living by the light of cell phones and flashlights after the sun goes down simply feels unfair while electricity courses round the clock through the Koidu Holdings compound as it mines diamonds worth hundreds of millions of dollars. Knowing that there is a fully staffed modern medical clinic inside the razor wire breeds contempt when local doctors have to boil their scalpels in pots of well water. On the other hand, everyone wants a job with Koidu Holdings and is envious of anyone who has one.

"You're dealing with a country where there is a 10 to 15 percent literacy rate and very high expectations," said Paul Ngaba Saquee, the paramount chief of Tankoro Chiefdom, where Koidu Holdings mines are located. "They want everything done by Koidu Holdings and that's not possible.

"Every time they hear a blast, they say, 'My God, they're taking all of our diamonds,'" he continued with a laugh. "I admit, Koidu Holdings is not good at marketing themselves. The one year they were shut down [while the 2007 shootings were being investigated], the crime rate went up, prostitution went up, divorce rates went up [due to unemployment]. We need to increase economic opportunities. The fact of the matter is, this outfit is good, and I'm speaking not in absolute terms, but in relative terms. We have to create an enabling environment for their business."

These opinions are not widely held in Koidu, and they've done little for the chief's popularity. A few months earlier, Saquee was mobbed by a group of students organized to protest at a community meeting where the company's latest expansion plans were being discussed. Saquee stood in support of company representatives, and as he attempted to leave, angry students surrounded his car and began banging on the hood and doors. Saquee's driver panicked and tried to flee in reverse, colliding with a car belonging to the secretary of the Ministry of Labour and Social Security, badly damaging both vehicles.

Although Saquee was born and raised in Koidu, prior to his election as chief, he worked in the United States as a supervisor for a long-haul trucking company. He returned to Sierra Leone and campaigned for the top job in the chiefdom after his predecessor, his father, died. Being chief is difficult to begin with, but it's much more so when one is such a vocal supporter of the city's most controversial company. Saquee has been called a sellout and worse. He chalks it up as shortsightedness among his people, who have lost everything in the war and prefer immediate returns over long-range vision.

"We've been taken for a ride for a long time," said Saquee's lieutenant, Dr. Tamba Kpetewama, who summarizes critics' attitudes as "we deserve something in return."

"We're not saying everything is great," Kpetewama said, "but certainly it would have been worse without Koidu Holdings. This place was destroyed because of the war, but Koidu Holdings was the first company to come back in. They fixed roads, they fixed bridges, but when you're talking about Koidu Holdings, most people are not very objective. Koidu Holdings is a much better situation. This is one of the best things to ever happen to our country."

Like other diamond exporters, Koidu Holdings pays a 3 percent federal tax on the value of its diamonds, which in its case amounts to $3 million of governmental revenue. Its mining lease agreement requires it to set aside 0.25 percent of its gross revenue from exports for use exclusively for community development, another 0.1 percent of gross revenue for agricultural development, and $100,000 annually for scholarships and skills training. It has a local profit-sharing arrangement (though, as of this writing, the company has yet to be profitable) in which 5 percent of annual profits will go to the Tankoro Chiefdom, 3 percent to the Kono District Council, and 2 percent to the Koidu City Council. The company also pays annual surface rent to landowners and local councils.[19]

"The impact of this project on the local community and economy is huge," Koidu Holdings CEO Jan Joubert claimed in a company press release. "We are currently one of the largest contributors to government revenues in terms of taxes, royalties and contributions to development programs."[20]

Those living in the company's shadow clearly haven't gotten their share of this avowed largesse. That this disparity echoes 1991, when the RUF leveraged simmering resentment into early support for its rebellion, seems to be dangerously absent from most conversations. Dr. Barrie is one of the few people I met who expressed concern about it.

"Honestly, to me it's the same as before the war," he said. "There's a lot of things, a lot of unemployment, a lot of suffering, while these stones are taken from right here. These are all things that were here before the war. It's all the same."

Critically, it's no illusion that the game is stacked to benefit industry and its enablers in the government. It's clear to most which people among them benefit most handsomely from the diamonds being mined around them. For those in the Tankoro Chiefdom, they need look no further than their own chief.

When I met Saquee, we spoke in a courtyard inside his walled residential compound, which included two buildings, a concrete gazebo, and a carport for his Land Rover. Although it's part of the resettlement village, his is the nicest home in the neighborhood—all of it (including the car and driver) provided by the mining company. Moreover, Saquee personally receives a sizable chunk of the surface rent the company pays, $4,350 per year. In a country where the average annual income is $150 to $200, that's a fortune. When the company expands, the payment will double. To many in Saquee's community, it's no mystery why he's such a fan of Koidu Holdings.

"The truth is," Barrie said earlier, speaking about the government in general, "it's all about corruption."

FRAUD, BRIBERY, NEPOTISM, graft, and outright theft are so rampant among governmental institutions and elected leaders in Sierra Leone that it's dangerously easy to assume they're as intractable in the local culture as palm wine and kola nuts. A confidential report commissioned by President Ernest Bai Koroma shortly after his election in 2007 called corruption in government "the greatest impediment to the country's development."[21] Here's a small sampling: The country's former ombudsman, Francis Gabbidon, was convicted and jailed in 2009 on 168 counts of misappropriation of public funds.[22] A WikiLeaks cable hinted that senior members of the military spent a $1.9 million aid grant on flat-screen TVs and hunting rifles.[23] The former agriculture minister was convicted of stealing $1.5 million of World Bank development funds; the judge who sentenced him by imposing a mere fine of $250 was convicted in turn for being bribed into giving him a light sentence.[24]

As former chief justice Desmond Luke has said, "If you have been here for some time, you will know that anybody and everybody is stealing everything."[25]

In many countries, corruption in government is often considered a punch line, but in Sierra Leone, it's no laughing matter. In fact, the Truth and Reconciliation Commission, set up in the late 1990s to create a historical record of the causes of the civil war, identified corruption as the number-one factor. Everything else— the influence of Muammar Qaddafi on the RUF's leaders, Charles Taylor's disruptive hand in regional destabilization, weak controls on the diamond industry—was secondary:

> The Commission came to the conclusion that it was years of bad governance, endemic corruption and the denial of basic human rights that created the deplorable conditions that made conflict inevitable. Successive regimes became increasingly impervious to the wishes and needs of the majority. Instead of implementing positive and progressive policies, each regime perpetuated the ills and self-serving machinations left behind by its predecessor. By the start of the conflict, the nation had been stripped of its dignity. Institutional collapse reduced the vast majority of people into a state of deprivation. Government accountability was non-existent. Political expression and dissent had been crushed. Democracy and the rule of law were dead.[26]

The Anti-Corruption Commission, established in Freetown in 2000, was deemed so ineffective that Britain, Sierra Leone's largest foreign donor, ended direct budgetary aid to the country in 2007. In spite of a string of recent investigations that snared some big-name grifters, Sierra Leone still ranks 134th out of 178 countries listed on Transparency International's Corruption Perception Index.[27]

"When you talk about corruption, I don't know where to begin," said Sahr F. S. Kaimachiande, the Kono District parliamentary chief. "You call it corruption. I call it petty thievery."

In one example he gave, he'd arranged for the delivery of seventeen truckloads of mosquito netting to be donated to the hospital from an aid organization. They never made it to the hospital.

"Do you know where I found them?" he asked. "In the market being sold."

For nearly an hour, while we sat on a second story balcony of a spacious stone house filled with people waiting for an audience with him, Kaimachiande ran through a litany of such examples. As the parliamentary chief, he represented the Kono District in the government in Freetown, much like a member of the United States Congress, and he had many people lobbying for his time and attention. A question I asked spurred his complaints. Someone had mentioned that Kono is the most corrupt of all the country's districts, and I wanted to know his view.

The problem, he said, is that elected leaders in Sierra Leone are more interested in retaining power and accumulating wealth than fighting for change. "It's more perpetual politics than governance," he said. Representatives are too scared to stand up to the president and speak their minds. Sierra Leoneans have a deep-seated instinct for self-preservation that makes them myopic. Those who lived through so much death and suffering during the war and who still struggle to survive from day to day tend to think only in terms of their immediate needs. Planning for the future doesn't often enter the equation.

Kaimachiande gestured toward the road below us, indicating along its shoulder a long earthen berm from which ragged trenches had been dug. We'd seen many roads in the same condition throughout Koidu, as well as piles of construction material for sidewalks and seemingly abandoned Bobcat bulldozers parked on street corners. Pedestrians trying to get to many businesses had to cross these trenches over planks and navigate around rusted spikes of rebar left lying about and threatening to impale someone. But we hadn't seen any actual work taking place. That, Kaimachiande explained, was because the project was between contractors. The first three or four had simply collected money and done nothing but tear up the road and leave town. That coup may have solved their immediate needs for money, but they would never be trusted with a road project in Koidu again, something they either didn't consider or didn't care about.

"What am I going to do? Should I drive the bulldozer?" Kaimachiande joked.

I thought it was a good question.

"What *are* you going to do?" I asked. "I mean you're a member of Parliament. Can't you fight for change?"

He looked at me as if I hadn't been listening. Politicians don't agitate, because they don't want to risk losing their jobs. That included him.

"Do you know what they call me in the newspapers in Freetown? The Honorable Chief Rubber Stamp."

III

BY THE TIME I got back to Freetown, I was in need of some good news. Ten years had been a long enough time for me to forget just how mentally taxing Sierra Leone could be. After visiting Koidu, I'd drawn a dark scenario for its future. When I was here last, the big question had been whether or not the war was really over. Back then, you could practically still smell the gun smoke in the air, and the injuries—both physical and mental—were still freshly written on everyone I passed. I hoped that the war would truly end, if only so that Sierra Leoneans could have some breathing room and an opportunity to resume their prewar lives. With enough distance from the horrors of the 1990s, I felt, they would finally have a chance to get on a track leading them away from such nightmares forever. The potential for such a future was obvious to everyone.

Instead, I returned to find that opportunity being squandered. The record needle has skipped all the way back to the late 1980s, and the same tunes are lined up to be played again. Perhaps most frustrating, no one seemed to know how to stop this reversal, or even agreed that it should be stopped. In one ear, a friend of President Koroma's was telling me that the government has made great strides and that increasing investment in Sierra Leone by businesses as varied as diamond companies and international hotels proves the future is promising. And in the other ear, a candidate for the Sierra Leone People's Party who'd fled to Norway during the war said the country is actually worse than it was in 2002, when the country was little more than a rubble pile filled with bones and spent ammunition.

More than ever, the time-warp sensation was overpowering. Only, instead of feeling as though I'd been transported back to when I was here last, at the end of the war, I felt as if I'd gone even further and was visiting the country at the *beginning* of the war. Sierra Leone of 1991 must have been a lot like Sierra Leone of 2011. It has all the ingredients: a weak central government riven with corruption, greed-blinded chiefs in the provinces selling out their own people for cash, resource industries run with no transparency or accountability, and a citizenry yet again disenfranchised and starting to feel its resentment rise. The country I visited in 2011 seems exactly like the country described by the Truth and Reconciliation Commission: "Endemic greed, corruption and nepotism . . . deprived the nation of its dignity and reduced most people to a state of poverty." All that's lacking is a warlord to spark the flames, and West Africa has never been short of those.

I felt the need to measure my impression against a knowledgeable third party, afraid that having been away for so long was giving me a jaundiced view of things. Was I expecting too much in too little time? I called Michael Owen, the U.S. ambassador to Sierra Leone, who assured me that I was seeing things accurately. In fact, he had trouble settling on which of Sierra Leone's problems poses the most significant threat to its future. He was particularly concerned about youth unemployment in combination with the conditions in Kono and Kailahaun Districts. In fact, Kailahaun is arguably worse than Kono; Owen said there are no doctors in the district, none of the roads have been paved since the end of the war, and the economy is "moribund."

"The conditions there are indeed terrible," he said. "They have not improved much since the end of the war. The infrastructure is bad, the schools are bad, health care is bad, doctors are not there, doctors don't show up, teachers don't show up, they have a lot of unemployed youth. . . . The situation in both districts is really very, very bad, and I don't see frankly much sign of improvement in the near term."

Owen believed that President Koroma, while motivated and committed to change, was hampered by a lack of "human capital." A large Sierra Leonean diaspora occurred during the war, when many educated people fled the country, particularly to the United States. While some are returning and bringing home their experiences in America in business and government, "there's really very little [that government institutions] have in terms of people who can actually carry out programs," Owen said. "The capacity constraints in all the ministries are really quite severe."

As an example, he points to Sierra Leone's attempt to join the Extractive Industries Transparency Initiative (EITI), a global effort to improve governance over mining industries in resource-rich countries by instituting standards that all signatory countries must adhere to. Sierra Leone has fallen woefully behind schedule.

"They're having enormous difficulty pulling everything together to adhere to the requirements of the EITI, and they've been put on notice that time is running out," he said. "That goes back to that lack of capacity. They just don't have the sort of midlevel management in their government to put in the system they need to meet the requirements of EITI."

This deficit manifests itself in tangible ways, particularly in how the government manages, or fails to manage, extractive industries mining diamonds, gold, iron ore, and other valuable minerals—in other words, the lifeblood of Sierra Leone's future. The government, according to Owen, has yet to control so much as one of its most important industries—diamonds—much less figure out how to maximize revenue from it.

"From all I hear, there are still large segments of the diamond sector that are entirely unregulated and unpoliced," he said. "There are areas in the Kono District that are off limits to everybody, and I'm not entirely clear what's going on there. In spite of the fact that they've signed on to the Kimberley Process and made all these pledges, enforcement is still a major issue."

Owen ticked off a checklist of deficiencies as if reading the ingredients from a recipe for revolt, one that's been followed before. Dire poverty, endemic corruption, paramount chiefs on the take from foreign investors (not just in diamonds but agribusiness as well), untreated post-traumatic stress disorder in former child soldiers, a pending health-care crisis if the government can't find revenue to take over the free medical program once donor funding dries up.

I tried to find something that we could agree was a positive sign. I asked Owen about forgiveness and reconciliation. Before my arrival, I'd expected to find hostility between former rebel soldiers and their victims. But it hardly ever came up. Jango was adamant that internecine violence was over. "We took care of that a long time ago," he said. "It's no problem now."

In the words of one man: "We may not ever be able to forget what happened, but we can forgive."

This was an amazing sentiment, repeated often. I wanted to believe that no matter how bad things got, there wouldn't be a return to the sort of deadly violence that had brought me here in the first place. Owen, however, couldn't offer any reassurance.

"This unemployed youth thing, that's a major problem, nation-wide and here in Freetown particularly," he said. "You have a lot of former child soldiers who've never really recovered from the trauma of war. Many of them never went to school and have very limited skills. They're probably suffering from PTSD, and I think the presence of a large number of these young men is really a risk factor for the future.

"I still do worry," he continued after giving it some thought. "There's a lot of anger underneath the surface in a lot of people. Under the wrong set of circumstances, that could come out again. Things seem calm on the surface, but I'm just a little concerned that there's still some definite anger underneath."

I DID FIND MY glimmer of hope, but where I least expected it: on the side of a steep hill east of Freetown, surrounded by the poorest and most desperate people I'd met yet. They are child miners who crush rocks in order to afford enough food to go on living. They aren't looking for diamonds—they are simply *crushing rocks*, big ones into little ones and then the little ones into gravel, with the hope of selling piles of them to construction companies for use in making concrete. There is an entire colony of these child laborers and their families, living as squatters on hills offering a clear view of Freetown's white sand beaches and another road construction project that politicians showcase as evidence of progress.

I found these hill dwellers completely by accident, after allowing myself to be hailed on the street outside the Solar Hotel by a passerby. "Are you a journalist?" he asked, in the same manner one would ask a person with a stethoscope if he is a doctor. He was pointing to the camera slung on my shoulder.

He told an amazing story. He worked at a school near Lakka Beach that offered free education to children so poor that their only hope for survival was through backbreaking labor in ad hoc gravel quarries. He described little kids, some of them orphans, swinging hammers as if on a chain gang, perfectly hopeless until discovered by the headmaster, who searched the hills continuously for new pupils, like Jesus looking for lost lambs. Would I like to meet him and visit the school? Naturally, I said yes, even though I suspected he'd exaggerated the story to make me more interested.

But I was wrong. The founder and headmaster is a man named Foday Mansaray, a fit man in his early forties. He was all business when he showed up at the Solar Hotel the next morning to meet Mike and me for breakfast. He brought along enough supporting material to apply for a World Bank loan—receipts, report cards, photos, even an audio file of a radio show that had been done on the children that aired in Holland.

Throughout his presentation I kept expecting an appeal for funds, but it never came.

"I just want you to tell the story," he said. We piled into a taxi and headed toward the hills with Mansaray explaining that these rock quarry colonies were a result of the war, when rural families fled the provinces to the perceived safety of Freetown, usually with no skills, no education, and nothing more than what they could carry. But without the means to return home when the war was over, they were forced to innovate. They'd been crushing rocks for more than a decade, eking out the barest of existences. From the road, we could see tumbledown shanties and lean-tos built with zinc siding and bush sticks teetering on the hillsides. As we began our climb, the tinny sound of hammers on rocks pinged down to meet us.

The life of a rock breaker is as hard as it sounds. There are no jackhammers or bulldozers; everything is done by hand. Men with shovels start by removing soil to expose large granite boulders, some the size of small cars. They burn wood or tires to heat the boulders and make them easier to split into chunks with chisels and sledgehammers. Once the rubble is small enough to lug downhill, the women and children take over. Older kids use mallets and small sledges to crush the rock into pebbles, while very small children use ball-peen hammers. On our way up the hill, we passed a three-year-old girl who used a rusty old hammerhead on a stick to smash rocks held in place by her tiny foot, which was clad only in a flip-flop. Mansaray had never seen her before.

"You see," he said, "I always find more children. Every time I find more."

Speaking gently to the toddler, he learned her name and those of her parents. She pointed in the direction of her home, and Mansaray told me he would come back tomorrow to speak with the parents, hoping they would agree to send the girl to his school and get her out of the quarry. Usually such conversations were straightforward. The parents may be uneducated and illiterate, but they were smart enough to know that there was no future for their children in what they were doing. But others were harder to convince because every swinging hammer meant more gravel they could sell. On a few occasions during our visit, Mansaray spotted students crushing rocks who should have been in school. Some tried to hide, knowing they were in for a scolding, but Mansaray had eyes like a hawk.

Not only is gravel mining a hopeless existence with no prospects for improvement, but it's also dangerous. Children often miss the rocks and hammer their toes and shins, and most miners have had gravel shards hit their eyes and cut their faces. Most of the schoolchildren have injuries. Mariatu Sesay, an eight-year-old girl, fell and broke her arm at the elbow a year ago. Although set by a doctor, the bone healed at an odd angle and is permanently deformed.

As the rocks get smashed smaller and smaller, they're moved closer to the road along a chain of crushing stations, until eventually the pea-sized gravel is piled in knee-high cones that can be spotted by passing construction trucks in need of material for concrete. When buyers come, as often as twice a week or as infrequently as twice a month, the gravel is measured into a pan the size of a large skillet and sold for 1,300 leones per panful. That's about 30 U.S. cents, to be split by everyone along the chain. An industrious rock crusher can fill about ten pans per week, but whether anyone buys that much is out of his control. All along the road from Freetown, we saw many piles of gravel for sale.

We also saw many new homes being constructed, some along the very paths the rock breakers used to bring the stones down the mountain. To Mansaray, they were monstrosities. He'd tried to convince some of the future homeowners—most of whom were wealthy businessmen, he said—to donate money to his school so that tiny children didn't have to produce the raw material for their homes through the sort of hard labor usually reserved for prisoners, but he'd never had much success.

Of course, Sierra Leone has laws prohibiting child labor, and the country's Family Services Unit, which is charged with enforcing it, has an office less than two miles from the quarry. But it didn't surprise me to learn from Mansaray that officers would investigate his complaints only if he paid a "fee" for their transportation to look into it. He quickly gave up on help from the government and decided simply to rescue the children himself.[28] He keeps a copy of the child labor law in his pocket to read to skeptical parents.

The school itself, situated across the road from the hills where the children live, is easy to overlook if you aren't paying attention. It's nothing more than two small tentlike structures made of tarpaulins stretched around a frame of tree limbs with a zinc panel on top. The floors are dirt.

About 250 children are enrolled in the Borbor Pain Charity School of Hope, "Borbor Pain" meaning "suffering children." On the day we visited, school was already out for the older children, and it was the last day of instruction for the seventy or so smaller kids who greeted us with rehearsed songs reserved for special visitors. Mansaray said the school takes a break from classes during the month of August, which is the rainiest month of the rainy season and usually proves too miserable for either teaching or learning. Mansaray needed the break himself so he could work full-time to solve an immediate funding crisis—two of his four teachers were threatening to quit because of overdue wages.

While the children took turns reciting the alphabet, Mansaray recited a long list of needs. Not only was there no money to pay his teachers, who were owed the equivalent of about $150, but there was none for notebooks, pencils, report cards, or chalk. The school needed new desks and chairs; as it was, the children sat on drift-wood benches and wrote at crudely constructed tables, and there weren't enough of either for all the students. Eventually, he wanted to offer them lunch, but with all of the school's more pressing needs, it just wasn't in the cards yet. When he wasn't looking for new children to bring down from the mountain in hope for a bet-ter future, he was in Freetown chasing money by dropping in on businesses, emailing practically everyone he'd ever met who could send $50 through Western Union, or not infrequently, simply appealing to strangers. In such a corrupt country, he tried to encourage trust by promising to share receipts with donors down to the penny, so that they would know where their money was spent. That meant extra time at painfully slow computers at Inter-net cafés, scanning documents and emailing them around the world, but he was determined to prove that there were still people in Sierra Leone who could be trusted to put donated money to the uses for which they were meant.

In spite of the school's needs, he emphasized repeatedly that the one group he wouldn't harass for money in his effort to keep the school running were the students' parents.

"Everything is free for the children," he said. "Everything."

Before the war, Mansaray lived in Freetown and held a variety of odd jobs, from ditch digger to cell phone salesman. When fighting began, he joined the cyclonic movement of refugees who fled from place to place hoping to find a safe haven from the RUF's guns and blades. He survived a brief capture by RUF soldiers in Kono and eventually made his way back to Freetown. He was in the city during Operation No Living Thing, an attack so brutal that he decided it was time to flee the country. He spent years living in refugee camps in Guinea.

Mansaray and his school form but one example of people in this small community who have stopped waiting for the government to improve their lives. Alfred George, who worked for 12 years with the Environmental Foundation for Africa but who is now unemployed, uses his experience with ecological issues to try to end the gravel mining. It may be hard to imagine community members caring about environmental degradation from clear-cutting trees when there's no telling where the next meal will come from, but there are tangible reasons to address it. Digging boulders out of the hillsides has resulted in an infestation of snails on the flatlands; with their natural ecosystem disturbed, the snails' eggs wash downhill during the rainy season. Snails destroy crops. In addition, to help prevent large-scale deforestation, George promotes what he calls an eco-stove; made of clay, it requires fewer pieces of coal or firewood to heat water than a typical campfire.

And a woman named Abbey Kamara who lives next to the school does her part as well. She and her husband, Ibrahim, adopted a two-month-old baby boy when his mother, who was single and had no other known relatives, died of a throat infection while breaking stones across the road. His twin sister fell ill and died soon after. The couple already has three small children, but Ibrahim told me that there had never been any question that they would adopt the baby. Like Mansaray, he said God told him it was the right thing to do.

After my visit to the school, I saw Mansaray frequently in Freetown, meeting him occasionally for coffee or lunch, but just as often by happenstance, as he was hustling to or from funding meetings or school suppliers. I saw him on my last day in town, as he was coming out of a copy center with a fresh batch of report cards for the new semester. He'd just finished studiously blacking out the line on the front where other headmasters would fill in the fee for attending school. As he did every time we met, Mansaray reminded me that Borbor Pain was free, and so its report cards didn't need that line.

Mansaray provided me with the thread of hope I had been looking for. In a country rich in precious stones, it's inexcusable that children have to mine common ones in order to survive, but here was someone who had learned the lessons of the past and was trying hard not to repeat them, at least in the lives of some.

"All this hardship that I went through with the war prompted me, and the word of God prompted me, to establish this kind of thing because I don't want children to go in pain," he said. "I think education is the key because the children are the future of Sierra Leone.

"If you let these children go down astray, then the country is going down astray."

ACKNOWLEDGMENTS

IN LATE SEPTEMBER of 2001, I was stranded in Kabala, in northern Sierra Leone, one of those inevitabilities that come with the territory when the UN is your chauffeur. To this day, I don't know what the delay was, but for several hours I dozed fitfully in the ovenlike cargo bay of an Mi-8 helicopter, Flight 096, with three Ukrainian pilots and a Nepalese UN administrator. The Ukrainians stripped to their plaid boxers to battle the heat, which came in through the open passenger door and the open cargo doors under the tail boom with each hot breath of wind. The spectacle of three very pale, very flabby men wandering around a helicopter nearly naked was apparently the social and entertainment event of the year in Kabala, for there was soon a perimeter of gawkers ringing the sports field where we were parked. SLA soldiers kept them far from the chopper, though, and we killed time by giving one another vocabulary lessons in our native tongues.

One of the copilots, a man named Sergei, only knew one set of English phrases, a memorized mantra that he recited haltingly and painfully before each flight: "Ladies and gentlemen, welcome aboard flight UN zero-nine-six flying from the Mammy Yoko to Mile 91, Magburaka and Kabala. Flight time to Mile 91, approximately 40 minutes. This Mi-8 aircraft is equipped with emergency exits here, here, and here and this is a nonsmoking flight. We hope you enjoy your flight."

We mostly taught one another crude terms and profanity and boasted about our home countries' military might and the comparative beauty of each country's female citizens, but it was an effective way to kill time. By coincidence, these men had flown me around Sierra Leone more often than any others and it's not a stretch to say that we finally became friends while sitting there in Kabala that day, sweating nonstop and waiting for passengers who were apparently important enough to delay the flight. I wrote down their names when I left the chopper back at the Mammy Yoko Hotel and promised to send a postcard from Colorado.

On November 7, 2001, an Mi-8, Flight 103, crashed within a minute of takeoff from the Mammy Yoko. It was bound for nearby Lungi Airport, but plunged into the Atlantic Ocean near the lighthouse marking the western edge of Man of War Bay. All seven people on board died, including all three of my Ukrainian friends. The other victims included another Ukrainian copilot, two Zambian soldiers, and a civilian from Bulgaria working with UNAMSIL.

Therefore, I'd like to thank Lieutenant Colonel Vladimir Savchuk, Captain Sergei Filippovich, and Captain Sergei Ayushev for their companionship, optimistic demeanor, low flybys, and rudimentary lessons in Russian. I'm sorry I never sent that postcard.

Otherwise topping my list of people to thank are my editor, Jill Rothenberg, not only for her hard work, organizational acumen, and excellent suggestions but also for the range of her vision and the depth of her passion about this work; Holly Hodder of Westview Press for her encouragement and confidence; John Thomas, without whose unsurpassed editing skill and critical eye this would have been a much lesser work; and Doug Farah of the *Washington*

Post for paving the way. I would like to thank Meg Campbell and my parents, Howard and Mary Campbell, for their support and help while I traveled and researched this book.

In no particular order, a potpourri of thanks go out to the following: Christine Hambrouck, Jonathan Andrews, Maya Ameratunga, Veton Orana, Margaret Atieno, and Saleh Tembo of the United Nations High Commissioner for Refugees for their insight and companionship in Kailahun; Walter Pinn, Major (Nigeria) Mohammed Yerima, and Margaret Novicki of the United Nations Mission in Sierra Leone; Aya Schneerson of the World Food Program; Chris Robertson of Save the Children; Lieutenant Colonel T-Ray and Major Gabril Kallon of the Revolutionary United Front; Jango Kamara for more reasons than I can list; the staff of the Solar Hotel for the constant use of their telephone and the staff of Jay's Guest House for their taste in music and tolerance of reporters with a taste for Johnny Walker at 2 A.M.; journalist Sophie Barrie for the companionship and the reading material; Tamara Connor, formerly of Boulder Travel, for the grace and flair with which she was able to get me into places like Sierra Leone, according to a jangled schedule and on budget, no less; Teresa Castle of the *San Francisco Chronicle*; Margaret Henry of the *Christian Science Monitor*; photographers Tyler Hicks and Patrick Robert, for their inspiration; Tim Weekes and Andy Bone of the Diamond Trading Company; Tom Shane of The Shane Company; Betsy Cullen, R.N., of Boulder Community Hospital, for on-the-road medical advice; Hassan Saad of the Sierra Leone Police; Fawaz S. Fawaz in Kenema; Saffa Moriba of the BBC; David Lemon and Jonathan Vandy of the Sierra Leone Government Information Service's Eastern Region office; Mamei Jaya and Elizabeth Gbomoba of the Sierra Leone Broadcasting Service; Ralph Swanson of Freetown's KISS-FM; Major (Ghana) M'Bawine Atintande and Major (Ghana) Moses

Aryee of GhanBatt-3; Iggy Pop and David Bowie for "Lust for Life," the soundtrack to my African travels; Eric Frankowski and Greg Avery for listening to me gripe from faraway lands; Holly and Gary Nelson for use of the writer's hideaway deep in the Rocky Mountains; and to those in Kailahun who fed us when the United Nations wouldn't.

Special thanks are extended to photographer Chris Hondros for his enduring friendship, without which most of my journeys would have been intolerable; and my good friend Joel Dyer, who was always willing to help me decompress with far too few rounds of golf.

To Rebecca Marks I owe more than just thanks: you are the love of my life, my inspiration and my destiny. My heart and soul are yours forever.

Finally, this book could not have been written without the help of countless people in Sierra Leone—taxi drivers, fixers, smugglers, and hotel clerks—who provided intuitive leads and invaluable logistical assistance. Standing out among these people is Robert, whose last name I never thought to ask, for being a perfect combination of chauffeur, editorial assistant, and bodyguard.

But those most deserving of thanks are the victims of the RUF's diamond war. Without their willingness to recount, often in excruciating detail, the worst chapters of their lives, this book would not exist. I hope that it offers a small amount of justice to the horrors that they've suffered.

Steamboat Springs, Colorado,
December 13, 2001

NOTES

Prologue

1. *Human Development Report* (New York: United Nations Development Programme, 2001).

2. *CIA World Factbook* (Washington, D.C.: Brassey's, 2001).

3. Report of the Panel of Experts Appointed Pursuant to Security Council Resolution 1306 (2000), Paragraph 19, in Relation to Sierra Leone, S/2000/1195, presented to the UN Security Council at the Global Policy Forum, New York, December 20, 2000.

4. U.S. Rep. Tony Hall (D-Ohio), "Congressional Leaders Urge Action on Conflict Diamonds," press release, Washington, D.C., July 3, 2001.

5. United Nations Mission in Sierra Leone, www.un.org/Depts/dpko/unamsil/body_unamsil.htm.

Chapter 1

1. Jacques Legrand, *Diamonds: Myth, Magic, and Reality,* edited by Ronne Peltsman and Neil Grant (New York: Crown Publishers, 1980), p. 7.

2. Kevin Krajick, *Barren Lands: An Epic Search for Diamonds in the North American Arctic* (New York: Times Books, 2001), p. 29.

3. Ibid.

4. Douglas Farah, "Al-Qaeda Cash Tied to Diamond Trade." *Washington Post,* November 2, 2001, p. A1.

5. Legrand, p. 72.

6. Legrand, p. 78.

Chapter 2

1. Mary Fitzgerald, *West Africa* (Footscray, Australia: Lonely Planet, 1998), p. 837.

2. See the Web site www.crimesofwar.org.

3. Matthew Hart, *Diamond: A Journey to the Heart of an Obsession* (Marble Falls, Texas: Walker Publishing Co., 2001).

4. Hart, p. 163.

5. Report of the Panel of Experts Appointed Pursuant to Security Council Resolution 1306 (2000), Paragraph 19, in Relation to Sierra Leone, S/2000/1195, presented to the UN Security Council at the Global Policy Forum, New York, December 20, 2000.

6. *The Heart of the Matter* (Ottawa, Canada: Partnership Africa Canada, 2000).

7. Douglas Farah, "Al-Qaeda Cash Tied to Diamond Trade." *Washington Post,* November 2, 2001, p. A1.

8. Report of the Panel of Experts Appointed Pursuant to Security Council Resolution 1306 (2000), Paragraph 19, in Relation to Sierra Leone, S/2000/1195, presented to the UN Security Council at the Global Policy Forum, New York, December 20, 2000.

9. Ibid.

10. Ibid.

Chapter 3

1. Member-states of ECOWAS are: Benin, Burkina Faso, Cape Verde, The Gambia, Ghana, Guinea, Guinea Bissau, Ivory Coast, Liberia, Mali, Niger, Nigeria, Senegal, Sierra Leone, and Togo.

2. Report of the Panel of Experts Appointed Pursuant to Security Council Resolution 1306 (2000), Paragraph 19, in Relation to Sierra Leone,

S/2000/1195, presented to the UN Security Council at the Global Policy Forum, New York, December 20, 2000.

3. Ibid.

4. Ibid.

5. Ibid.

6. Ibid.

7. Ibid.

8. *The Heart of the Matter* (Ottawa, Canada: Partnership Africa Canada, 2000).

9. Ibrahim Abdullah and Patrick Muana, "The Revolutionary United Front of Sierra Leone: A Revolt of the Lumpenproletariat," in Christopher Clapham (ed.), *African Guerillas* (Indianapolis: Indiana University Press, 1998).

10. Kevin A. O'Brien, "Military-Advisory Groups and African Security: Privatised Peacekeeping?" *Royal United Services Institute Journal*, August 1998. Undoubtedly, Executive Outcomes's work in Angola must have been very impressive to Strasser. Similar to the Sierra Leone government, the Angolan government was under siege by UNITA, a rebel force that had total control of the country's oil fields and diamond mines. EO was hired to take back the town of Soyo, the location of a major oil field, in 1993. A small force succeeded in doing so, but Soyo was later recaptured once the South Africans left. The government returned to the company requesting a larger force and offering oil concessions as payment. To facilitate this arrangement, a Canadian oil company called Ranger (which has close associations with top EO officials) put up $30 million for the operation. UNITA was thoroughly routed by 500 mercenaries, some of whom had fought on the rebels' behalf in the 1980s. The company also retrained the Angolan Army, which began inflicting heavy casualties on the rebels, and helped them retake the diamond fields of Saurimo and Cafunfo in Luanda Norte Province. The operation led to the signing of the Lusaka Protocols, which effectively ended the civil war, at least for a time. EO, through its subsidiaries and its gray network of affiliate companies, was paid with lucrative oil and diamond concessions.

11. "Mercenaries Grab Gems." *Weekly Mail & Guardian* (Johannesburg), May 9, 1997.

12. J. A. McGregor, *Due Diligence Report on Branch Energy Diamond Proper-ties, Sierra Leone and Angola, 1997* (Toronto, Canada: Watts, Griffis & McOuat Consulting Geologists and Engineers, 1997).

Chapter 4

1. Andrew Rawnsley, *Servants of the People* (London: Hamish Hamilton, 2000), pp. 176–184.

2. Ibid. Ominously, the solicitor's fax said that Sandline was innocent of sanctions-busting because it was pursuing the deal with Peter Penfold's encour-agement. An arms scandal would be a death blow for Cook. He wasn't aware that at the time he learned of the brewing tempest, customs had already raided the Foreign Office in a search for evidence. The *Sunday Times* printed his worst nightmare on May 3, 1998, with the headline: "Cook Snared in Arms for Coup Inquiry."

3. Bill Berkeley, *The Graves Are Not Yet Full: Race, Tribe and Power in the Heart of Africa* (New York: Basic Books, 2001), p. 55. One ECOMOG faction stationed in Liberia dealt with an armed band of men loyal to the country's former despot, Samuel Doe, by partnering in an ore-mining deal near the Sierra Leone border. But when the ECOMOG command replaced the offi-cers involved in the dealings, the new leaders didn't want to participate in the profit-sharing arrangement and attempted to disarm the insurgents. The rebels duly attacked, killing sixty ECOMOG soldiers. The fight over the mines spiraled and, over the course of a few months, eventually led to another round of slaughter in Monrovia.

4. Report of the Panel of Experts Appointed Pursuant to Security Coun-cil Resolution 1306 (2000), Paragraph 19, in Relation to Sierra Leone, S/2000/1195, presented to the UN Security Council at the Global Policy Forum, New York, December 20, 2000.

5. According to the article "UN Monitors Accuse Sierra Leone Peace-keepers of Killings," *New York Times*, Feb. 12, 1999, p. A10, "A United Nations human rights mission has charged that regional peacekeepers in Sierra Leone have summarily executed dozens of civilians. Numerous reports of rebel violence against civilians in Sierra Leone have circulated, but in a report the mission describes systematic rights violations by both insurgents and peacekeepers. . . . the report accuses the monitoring group established by

the Economic Community of West African States, or ECOMOG, of executing groups including children and some 20 patients at Connaught Hospital on Jan. 20. The report says that ECOMOG forces bombed civilian targets, shot at 'human shields' formed by the rebels and mistreated the staffs of the Red Cross and similar groups."

6. John Bolton, testimony before the International Relations Committee, U.S. House of Representatives, Washington, D.C., Oct. 11, 2001.

7. Ibid.

8. Ibid.

9. Sebastian Junger, *Fire* (New York: W.W. Norton & Company, 2001), pp. 192–193.

10. Ibid.

11. Matthew Hart, *Diamond: A Journey to the Heart of an Obsession* (Marble Falls, Texas: Walker Publishing Co., 2001).

12. Global Witness, "Conflict Diamonds: Possibilities for the Identification, Certification and Control of Diamonds," June 2000, London.

Chapter 5

1. Timothy Green, *The World of Diamonds: The Inside Story of the Miners, Cutters, Smugglers, Lovers and Investors* (New York: William Morrow & Co., 1984), p. 23.

2. Kevin Krajick, *Barren Lands: An Epic Search for Diamonds in the North American Arctic* (New York: Times Books, 2001), p. 104.

3. Matthew Hart, *Diamond: A Journey to the Heart of an Obsession* (Marble Falls, Texas: Walker Publishing Co., 2001).

4. Green, p. 27.

5. De Beers Group, Annual Report 1996, Johannesburg, South Africa.

6. Hart, p. 223.

7. Ibid., pp. 125–127.

8. Ibid., p. 135.

9. Interview with Tom Shane, December 19, 2001, Denver, Colorado.

10. Report of the Panel of Experts Appointed Pursuant to Security Council Resolution 1306 (2000), Paragraph 19, in Relation to Sierra Leone, S/2000/1195, presented to the UN Security Council at the Global Policy Forum, New York, December 20, 2000.

11. De Beers Group, written testimony before the U.S. Congress, House Committee on International Relations Subcommittee on Africa, Washington, D.C., May 9, 2000.

12. Hart, p. 136.

13. Ibid., p. 199.

14. Ibid., pp. 120–121.

15. De Beers Group, Annual Report 2000, Johannesburg, South Africa.

16. Hart, p. 137.

Chapter 6

1. Interview with Margaret Novicki, UNAMSIL spokeswoman, June 2001, Freetown, Sierra Leone.

2. Foday Sankoh, "Footpaths to Democracy," 1994, Kailahun, Sierra Leone.

Chapter 8

1. This account is recreated from a *Washington Post* article, "Al Qaeda Cash Tied to Diamond Trade," Nov. 2, 2001, and interviews with the author, *Washington Post* West Africa Bureau Chief Doug Farah, in December 2001.

2. Interview with Doug Farah, via e-mail, December 2001.

3. In 1985, Doug Farah was a correspondent for UPI in El Salvador and Honduras at the height of the Contra revolution and then became a stringer in the region for the *Washington Post,* the *Boston Globe,* and *U.S. News and World Report* once UPI sank in 1987. In 1990, he started covering the drug war in Colombia and became a staff reporter with the *Post* in 1992. He kept his beat in Latin America until 1997, when he was promoted to international investigative correspondent, specializing in drugs, overlords, organized crime, and money laundering. He was invited to apply for the West Africa bureau position when it came open and moved to Abidjan, Ivory Coast, in March 2000 with his wife and 8-month-old son.

4. Report of the Panel of Experts Appointed Pursuant to Security Council Resolution 1306 (2000), Paragraph 19, in Relation to Sierra Leone, S/2000/1195, presented to the UN Security Council at the Global Policy Forum, New York, December 20, 2000.

5. In fact, Taylor's NPFL invaded Liberia from Ivory Coast on Christmas Eve in 1989. Like many cities in West Africa, Abidjan is a dense, decaying

slum of violent crime, disease, and poverty. Many media organizations base their West African bureaus there simply because it's roughly in the middle of the region to be covered, not because of any perceived degree of relative safety. Most upper-class homes feature armed private security forces and "rape cages" in the bedrooms. A rape cage is an iron security device in which female residents lock themselves in case of a criminal siege on their home. The presence of such things also speaks to the quality of the security forces.

6. U.S. Rep. Tony Hall (D-Ohio), "Congressional Leaders Urge Action on Conflict Diamonds," press release, Washington, D.C., July 3, 2001.

7. Matthew Weissenberger, "Industry Responds to Diamond–Terrorist Link," Nov. 8, 2001, www.NationalJeweler.com.

8. Ibid.

Chapter 9

1. UNAMSIL Press Briefing, Mammy Yoko Hotel, Freetown, Sierra Leone, December 14, 2001.

2. "Canadian Firm Resumes Diamond Mining in Sierra Leone." *Daily Trust* (Lagos, Nigeria), Jan. 23, 2002, p. 16.

Chapter 10

1. Alexandra Zavis, "As Peace Returns to Sierra Leone, Many Live with Legacy of the Brutal Past." Associated Press, May 28 2002.

2. Alex Yearsley, "For a Few Dollar$ More: How Al Qaeda Moved into the Diamond Trade." April 17, 2003, at www.globalwitness.org. Global Witness, London.

3. United Nations Mission in Sierra Leone, UNHCR spokesperson Maya Ameratunga, press briefing, February 15, 2002, Freetown.

4. United Nations Mission in Sierra Leone, UNAMSIL spokesperson Margaret Novicki, press briefing, March 22, 2002, Freetown.

5. International Crisis Group, "Sierra Leone: The State of Security and Governance." September 2, 2003, at www.intl-crisis-group.org. ICG, Brussels.

6. Ibid.

7. Christo Johnson, "A Very Large Stone from Sierra Leone." Freetown, Reuters News Agency, April 26, 2002.1. Interview with Michael Owen, U.S. ambassador to Sierra Leone, August 15, 2011, via telephone.

Coda

1. Interview with Michael Owen, U.S. Ambassador to Sierra Leone, Aug. 15, 2011.

2. International Monetary Fund Country Report No. 11/195, "Sierra Leone: Poverty Reduction Strategy Paper—Progress Report, 2008–10," Washington, D.C.

3. Ibid.

4. Ibid.

5. Chair of the Security Council Committee established pursuant to resolution 1572 (2004), concerning Côte d'Ivoire, to the President of the Security Council, April 20, 2011, S/2011/272, items 289–290.

6. Greg Campbell, "Blood Diamonds Are Back: Why the U.N.-Sanctioned System That's Supposed to Ensure That Gemstones Aren't Mined at Gunpoint Is Backfiring," *Foreign Policy*, Dec. 24, 2009.

7. Human Rights Watch, "Zimbabwe: Rampant Abuses in Marange Diamond Fields; Police, Private Security Guards Attacking Miners" (New York, Aug. 30, 2011). See also http://www.hrw.org/africa/Zimbabwe.

8. Quoted in Campbell, "Blood Diamonds Are Back."

9. Human Rights Watch, "Zimbabwe."

10. Ibid.

11. Ian Smillie, *Blood on the Stone: Greed, Corruption, and War in the Global Diamond Trade* (London: Anthem Press, 2010).

12. Interview with Annie Dunneback, from her office in London, Dec. 6, 2011, via telephone.

13. IMF, "Sierra Leone: Poverty Reduction Strategy Paper—Progress Report, 2008–10."

14. "Witness to Truth: Report of the Sierra Leone Truth and Reconciliation Commission, Vol. 2," Oct. 2004, Freetown.

15. Koidu Holdings press release, "Koidu Kimberlite Expansion Project Gains Momentum," June 17, 2011, via email to the author.

16. National Advocacy Coalition on Extractives, "Sierra Leone at the Crossroads: Seizing the Chance to Benefit from Mining," March 2009, Freetown.

17. Report of the Jenkins-Johnston Commission of Enquiry, March 2008, Freetown, pp. 85–89.

18. "Koidu Kimberlite Expansion Project Gains Momentum."

19. Koidu Holdings untitled press release, March 24, 2011, http://www.sierraexpressmedia.com/archives/21309 (accessed Dec. 7, 2011).

20. "Koidu Kimberlite Expansion Project Gains Momentum."

21. Mark Doyle, "Sierra Leone 'Riddled with Corruption,'" BBC News, Freetown, Nov. 14, 2007.

22. Sierra Leone Anti-Corruption Commission, Annual Report, 2009, Freetown.

23. "Corruption in Sierra Leone: Rich Pickings; Bad Apples Are Still in the Barrel," *The Economist,* March 17, 2011.

24. David Tam-Baryoh, "Corruption in Sierra Leone: Who Will Guard the Guards?" Worldpress.org, Jan. 15, 2002, http://www.worldpress.org/Africa/352.cfm (accessed Dec. 7, 2011).

25. "Corruption in Sierra Leone."

26. "Witness to Truth: Report of the Sierra Leone Truth and Reconciliation Commission, Vol. 1." 2004. Freetown.

27. "Sierra Leone's Corruption Problem, a Mortal Enemy: The government is having some rare success in trying to eradicate an old sore," *The Economist,* Nov. 19, 2009.

28. I paid this office a visit on my way back to Freetown, asking what the FSU was doing about the child laborers I'd witnessed just up the road. The administrator I spoke to said she had no knowledge of children breaking rocks in the quarries, but said she would investigate.

INDEX